Productive and Unproductive Depression

Productive and Unproductive Depression

Success or Failure of a Vital Process

EMMY GUT

Basic Books, Inc., Publishers   New York

Library of Congress Cataloging-in-Publication Data

Gut, Emmy.
    Productive and unproductive depression : success or failure of
vital process / Emmy Gut.
        p.   cm.
    Bibliography: p.
    Includes index.
    ISBN 0–465–06395–0 : $24.95
    1. Depression, Mental.   I. Title.
    [DNLM: 1. Depression.   2. Depressive Disorder.   WM 171 G983p]
RC537.G88   1989
616.85'27—dc20
DNLM/DLC
for Library of Congress   89–42798
                                                                CIP

First published in Great Britain by Routledge
11 New Fetter Lane, London EC4P 4EE
1989
First published in the U.S.A. by Basic Books, Inc.
Copyright © 1989 by Emmy Gut
Printed in the United States of America
89 90 91 92 RRD 9 8 7 6 5 4 3 2 1

This book is dedicated to those
without whom it would not have been written:
to the memory of my mother and my husband Henry,
to John Bowlby, and to my patients.

Contents

Contents

Case illustrations

Foreword

The approach Emmy Gut brings to the problem of becoming depressed is both hopeful and helpful. Her thesis is that becoming depressed should be looked on as a signal that there is an important problem in our life that is not receiving the attention it requires. She argues that we would be wise to give time to it, first to identify it, then to examine its many aspects, disagreeable and painful though they may be, and thereafter search for the best available solution. This means, instead of merely deploring a depressed mood as a useless burden we cannot escape, we should respect it as a potentially useful part of human nature to be attended to and heeded.

There are many situations in life that cause us distress and perplexity, often combined with shame or guilt about the part we may have played in causing them. Perhaps a working role is lost or a valued personal relationship broken. Then the life we have known is no more and we have to construct a new one. How do we proceed? Can the old role be recovered or the old relationship be reinstated, or have we to seek anew, and, if so, how and where? Or perhaps a favourite plan to reach some cherished goal, to which much time and energy have been devoted, runs into difficulties. Do we persist with the plan, believing that a little more effort will achieve our end, or do we modify it, or abandon it and seek to reach our goal by some other means? Do we abandon the goal altogether as beyond our reach, and, should we decide to abandon it, what next? Solving such problems needs time and attention, and often a great deal of courage, especially when we believe, rightly or wrongly, that we bear some responsibility for what has happened.

Success or failure in weathering these adversities turns on many factors. An obvious one is the value to us of the relationship or situation lost. Another, less obvious but more weighty, is the degree of responsibility we believe, or strongly suspect, is ours. Yet another, often overlooked, is whether we have available kind friends who can understand and sympathize with our predicament or whether, by contrast, we are surrounded by people unwilling to share our pain and perplexity, eager only to dismiss our problem as trivial or as one we should be able quickly to solve on our own, or even tell us we have only ourselves to blame for the trouble we are in.

But these external factors, important though they be, are only one side of the problem. The other side turns on what sort of person we are. For example, how as a rule do we set about tackling a situation that we find frightening or painful and about which we may also feel some measure of shame or guilt? Do we, once recovered from the initial shock, do so realistically, acknowledging the true gravity of the blow and such responsibility as we may bear, and then mobilize our resources to deal with it? Or do we, wittingly or unwittingly, voluntarily or involuntarily, seek to evade the issues and divert our attention systematically to less painful matters? Do we seek help with confidence and make good use of what we receive? Do we reject what is offered or else expecting only blame or rebuff, make no attempt to find it?

These are the poles between which individuals vary in every possible degree, from those who grapple with personal problems with confidence and success to those who turn away from them so completely that they lose sight altogether of what is troubling them. Many of us lie somewhere in the middle, grappling effectively with some problems, evading others, at times seeking help, and at others too frightened or unhopeful to do so. All too often when a problem is evaded, the depressed mood that results is alleged to have come out of the blue. That is a dead end.

In her book Emmy Gut examines why people grow up unable to cope with painful problems and instead become locked in some fruitless strategy of avoidance which, however successful it may be in the short term, leads them in the longer term to become prone to depressive moods with no useful outcome. In throwing light on these issues she adopts a developmental approach and draws on the detailed knowledge now becoming available of how experiences with parents or parent substitutes, starting in the first year of life and continuing throughout the years of immaturity, influence personality development in either a favourable or an unfavourable direction. This perspective she integrates skilfully with her extensive clinical experience of helping people prone to unproductive depressions to make use of their depressive moods in more productive ways. Her book is thus a contribution to the still scanty therapeutic literature that is guided by an up-to-date knowledge of developmental psychology and the role of adverse life events in the genesis of depressive conditions, as well as by an understanding of psychodynamic processes based on traditional psychoanalytic sources.

In her writing she combines her knowledge of the literature dealing with the origin and treatment of depressive conditions with a style commendably free of jargon. Since her book is illustrated with many examples of human beings who, with or without professional help, have found ways to adopt more effective means for coping with their personal problems, it will appeal to the intelligent layman as well as to those professional psychotherapists who are seeking more effective ways of helping their patients.

John Bowlby

Preface

Many people are incapacitated by periods of depression, sometimes prolonged, sometimes frequent but intermittent. Their plight has long been studied by members of the mental health professions, and in recent years attention has been drawn also to the hardship their condition may create for their children and for others who are in close contact with them.

In psychiatric studies of depression, typical clusters of symptoms that may appear together with the depressed mood have been examined and described, and it has become established practice to differentiate them into diagnostic entities to which different treatments can be applied. Since the early decades of this century, classical psychoanalysis has studied intrapsychic dynamics causing chronic or recurrent states of depression and also developmental factors making a person depression-prone. In recent decades, attention to the role played by interpersonal relations and personality development in pathological mourning as well as in chronic or recurrent states of depression has led to new developments in psychoanalytic theory of depression.

In addition, a great deal of recent research in developmental, cognitive, behavioral, and social psychology, as well as in sociology, social anthropology, neurophysiology, and biochemistry, has led to new approaches in the exploration of depression, to new conclusions, new theories, and new terminologies. In these circumstances, can a new book based largely on the experience of psychoanalytic psychotherapy contribute anything fresh to the enormous literature on the subject and be meaningful to members of all mental health professions seeking answers? I hope so. Studies in depth based on long-term, intimate acquaintance in one-to-one relationships are not in competition with or opposition to objective research with broad populations: they complement each other.

It has been an accident of fate that has caused me, in the search for further explanations, to free myself to some extent from a number of professional and cultural influences that I shall mention in Chapter 1 as tending to maintain prevalent views of depression. I experienced the grief of deep mourning when, in late middle age, I lost my husband in relative social isolation in a foreign country. On the basis of the then prevalent cultural and professional misconceptions about the normal time and nature of readjustment after such a loss, I had unrealistic expectations of myself in this matter, so that my efforts finally culminated in a period of disquieting depression. I was amazed by the pronounced difference in the subjective experience of grieving a loss in such circumstances and of being depressed, and became interested in exploring whether this was only my personal experience or could apply generally. After having found in Bowlby's and Parkes's work explanations of the processes of grieving that matched my own experience, and after ample opportunity to discuss these issues with them, I was ready to find my own explanations for the difference between grieving and being depressed and to compare these with the literature on the subject. The interest accorded my approach and my papers (1982, 1985) by students and authors in the field has encouraged me to develop my views and present them in book form.

The views that emerged are rooted in my long personal life experience and in my work first as a psychiatric case worker and then as a psychoanalytically trained psychotherapist and teacher of psychotherapy. They have evolved from observation of others in long-term intensive therapy and in close personal relationships, as well as from introspection; from the study of case descriptions in professional literature, and from the study of some characters in great fiction. Yet, I recognize that, however persuaded I may be of my conclusions on this basis, they have to be seen as hypothetical until their validity has been borne out by the results of objective research including in its samples creative, successfully functioning members of our society.

Even though still hypothetical, my model of adaptive depression – of the cause, work, and process of depression – offers two advantages which are major motives for my writing this book. First, it may encourage members of the helping professions to look with more sympathy and tolerance at their own episodes of depression. Second, increased tolerance would enable them to observe with greater understanding and empathy what goes on in their friends when they are depressed, as well as in their patients, clients, or subjects of research, and to help them let their depression become productive. Unless we have a model for what is adaptive in getting or staying depressed, it is difficult to differentiate between adaptive and maladaptive reactions in a severely depressed person.

In closing this preface, I want to thank Edward T. Hall for having urged me to proceed with a book, rather than first writing further papers on my subject; and for helpful orientation to the world of editing and publishing. Such orientation I also owe to Robert S. Wallerstein.

During the years of actually writing this book I have received indispensable help in many ways. John Bowlby and Jules Bemporad read the entire manuscript, and some chapters twice, encouraging me with their constructive criticism. Robert Langs, who read Part III, provided useful comments. Several Swedish colleagues read either parts of or the entire manuscript and offered valuable suggestions, particularly Kurt Gordan, Berit Lagerheim, Kerstin Laurén, Ulla Löfgren, and Lisbet Palmgren.

Molly Townsend has, mostly by correspondence, given me untiring editorial help and companionship, reading and rereading many versions of my chapters, improving on their formulation and organization, and constructing the index. Gill Davies of Routledge has been a most congenial editor, by providing support without intruding on my personal way of producing a manuscript, and by her choice of a professional reader. Many thanks also to Jo Ann Miller of Basic Books for her interest and encouragement. The comments provided by the readers of my publishers, their questions, objections, and suggestions of pertinent literature were stimulating and improved my awareness of my prospective audience.

I am indebted to the authors whose cases I have used as illustrations: Dorothy Bloch, Michael F. Basch, Emanuel Peterfreund, and, posthumously, Silvano Arieti. Special help for which I am very grateful I owe to Chaim Potok for the publication of his novel *My Name Is Asher Lev* and to Margaret McRae and Norman Endler for their autobiographical descriptions of severe depression. The opportunity to analyze these vivid accounts made it unnecessary for me to expose detailed life histories of my patients to make my points. My thanks also to those friends and patients who have given me permission to use their experience; also to the *International Review of Psycho-Analysis* and the *British Journal of Psychotherapy* for permission to use sections of my papers (1982 and 1985, respectively). My appreciation of the enabling contribution of my patients is expressed elsewhere in the book.

Last but not least, warm thanks to John Rehn for teaching me the indispensable use of a computer and word-processing program.

Introduction

There is an alternative model ... the "adaptation" model. The signs and symptoms composing depression represent attempts at adaptation to the immediate circumstances, and reflect adaptive processes that are part of the organism's ordinary repertoire.

Davis (1970:110)

The core of my presentation

Characteristic of my approach to behavior deserving the attribute "depressed" are the following points:

1 I present a model for the normal affect of depression as a potentially adaptive response: whenever we perceive, largely unconsciously, that a significant physical or psychological effort of ours is failing in its purpose or coming to a halt, and when we cannot grasp what is amiss, we react with an affective response that I call "the basic depressed response." Like all affective responses it is accompanied by a set of typical physiological symptoms. Its adaptive function is to facilitate and protect concentration on intensified conscious and unconscious scanning, exploration, and integration of relevant experience in ways that can lead to a resolution of the internal deadlock, or to the recognition that the situation cannot be changed, so that a fruitless effort to do so can be abandoned. I see it as normal for this response to remain activated until the inner deadlock is resolved. Even unconscious perception of significant physiological dysfunction appears to arouse the depressed response, but in this book only the response to psychological dysfunction will be explored.

2 I take the position that feeling and/or behaving depressed because of a disquieting perception of an internal dysfunction is a universal response and that the specific cause and the specific adaptive function of the depressed response are distinct and separate from the causes and adaptive functions of other unpleasant affective and emotional responses, such as grief, anxiety, guilt,

shame, or anger, although for various reasons any of these latter responses may appear in combination with the depressed response.

3 I see a "normal depressive mood" (Jacobson 1971:66) and a "major depressive episode" or "major depression" (DSM-III 1981: 205) as two ends of a continuum. The person who reacts with "normal depression" differs in life experience, personality, life circumstances, or physiological condition from the person who reacts with "major depression". 1 The basic depressed response as such is the same in both; that is, it arises from a perplexing inner deadlock. But while in the former the depressed response succeeds in facilitating the application of inner and outer resources to the internal deadlock so that the provoking problem is resolved, it fails in the latter to provide for such a productive outcome.

4 I take up those factors I see as causing depression-proneness, and explore how this develops during the formative years, and how interpersonal relations and cultural pressures contribute to the unfavorable development.

5 For therapy this means that, aside from other helping measures, the potentially adaptive work of some of the depressed symptoms in a given person deserves attention. When being depressed does not facilitate a process leading to successful coping, one needs to identify what impedes this intrapsychic task and to assist the patient in overcoming the obstacles. This is why it is useful to study a person's feeling depressed and behaving depressed not only with the traditional interest in the nature and intrapsychic dynamics of the overt symptoms of this state, but also to establish how the patient's capacity to let a depressed mood run a productive course has been and still is adversely affected by interpersonal and environmental influences.2 Work with transference and countertransference in the therapeutic interaction is helpful in establishing this.

Mode of presentation

I have found many of my own tentative impressions supported, and new conclusions stimulated, by the work of authors in the various disciplines mentioned above, and also by the DSM-III (*Diagnostic and Statistical Manual of Mental Disorders*) of the American Psychiatric Association (1981). Many of these authors I refer to in the course of the book. Sometimes my own observations and interpretations differ from parts of their findings, although other parts may validate my views.

Theoretical terminology I avoid as much as possible because it tends to create distance in the professional reader from his or her own feelings and from those of the patient or friend to whom he or she is listening. It interferes with the empathic understanding of subjective experience. Moreover, technical terms tend to make our writing meaningful only to members of one particular profession and to followers of one school of thought within it. What I have to say can, I hope, have meaning for professionals of many backgrounds who are interested in when and why people, including themselves, may get depressed at any point of their lives; and why this can lead to either good or bad developments. Finally, I do not wish, by the use of language that is too technical, to exclude the educated reader who, without professional involvement in the difficulties of depressed people, is interested in the subject.

My conclusions are documented by cases from my practice and from my personal life, by cases from the professional literature, and by the autobiographical reports by McRae (1986) and Endler (1982). Furthermore, in several contexts I use characters and episodes from Potok's novel (1972) *My Name Is Asher Lev* as an illustration, which by its cohesive detail brings human experience to life more vividly than case material usually does when reported by a therapist or supervisor. The latter is limited by the necessity to conceal identity and by the fact that the therapist to a great extent describes experience observed from without, while in great literature experience is often presented by disguise and displacement of the author's own experience.3

The reader may wonder nonetheless why I do not use cases from my professional practice more extensively than I do. The reason is simple: the cause and character of developmental misfortunes caused by parental behavior or transmitted from earlier generations in the history of most of my own patients is too striking to describe them in detailed context without breach of confidentiality. During the past two decades many of my patients have been members of Swedish mental health professions that are limited in numbers, so that Swedish readers in these professions might be able to identify them despite disguise.

While the format and character of my presentation is not suited for a full overview of the vast literature on depression, selective reference to aspects of a variety of studies will be made where this clarifies my position. In this selection, I am further guided by the wish to give credit to those authors whose work I have found particularly stimulating in my own thinking; and without becoming too comprehensive, to remind the reader of the fact that significant discussions of depression have been published in disciplines other than his or her own profession.

Distribution of contents

In Part I, I develop and exemplify the first three points listed at the beginning of this Introduction as characterizing my approach to being depressed as a basic, potentially adaptive response which can enhance development and creativity, although under certain circumstances it is likely to fail in this adaptive function. I also discuss and exemplify how intrapsychic and interpersonal (as well as physiological) factors can lead to a chronic failure to respond adaptively. Throughout Part I, which develops essential aspects of my views, I refer to the literature on pertinent subjects more extensively than in the following parts of the book which largely apply these views to aspects of development and therapy.

Part II is devoted to developmental questions; whether the depressed response can be seen as appearing in early infancy and, if so, what adaptive functions it can and cannot serve at that stage; what circumstances from infancy through adolescence favor or obstruct a developing capacity to go through an episode of being depressed in ways that enhance growth and creativity. The effect of social and cultural influences on this development is taken up with emphasis on the family as the major, though not exclusive, carrier of such influences.

Part III considers aid to the work of depression: presenting first some behavior during an episode of being depressed on the part of people who are able to tolerate and make productive use of such an episode; then, how members of the depressed person's social environment may be helpful, and how they may judge whether psychotherapy is called for. Finally, two types of professional aid to the depressed – psychotherapy giving relief from acute depression and psychotherapy reducing or eliminating depression-proneness – are discussed with emphasis on mutual learning and increasingly effective communication between therapist and patient, including the role of transference and countertransference.

Part I

The process of depression

Chapter one

Finding a model of normal depression

The resolution of a depression in a work of fiction

> I painted swiftly in a strange nerveless frenzy of energy. For all the pain
> you suffered, my mama. For all the torment of your past and future years,
> my mama. For all the anguish this picture of pain will cause you. For the
> unspeakable mystery that brings good fathers and sons into this world and
> lets a mother watch them tear at each other's throats. For the Master of
> the Universe, whose suffering world I do not comprehend. For dreams of
> horror, for nights of waiting, for memories of death, for the love I have
> for all of you, for all the things I remember, and for all the things I
> should remember but have forgotten, for all these I created this painting –
> an observant Jew working on a crucifixion because there was no aesthetic
> mould in his own religious tradition into which he could pour a painting
> of ultimate anguish and torment.
>
> From *My Name Is Asher Lev*, Chaim Potok (1972:287ff.)

It is often mentioned in psychiatric, psychological, and psychoanalytic literature
– for example, by Winnicott (1964:125) – that depression in the long run tends
to end spontaneously, or that there are spontaneous remissions, but what the
processes are that could explain these remissions is generally not discussed. In
this book, such an explanation is a central topic.

The quotation chosen as a vignette for this chapter shows the emotions of
an artist as he emerges from a depression that was caused by a severe crisis in
his life. In Potok's novel we become intimately acquainted with the development
of a great painter from the time when he is an unusually gifted boy. In this
chapter, after a sketch of Asher Lev's background, I shall give only a summary
of a late section of the novel containing the quotation that opens this chapter.
It illustrates a major theme to be presented: that the withdrawal during
depression can serve to facilitate the resolution of an inner deadlock in
functioning and that the depression disappears when this has been accomplished.

This may help us raise some questions that cannot be answered without our having a model of what is normal, or rather what is adaptive, in getting depressed and staying depressed for some time.

Asher Lev is the only child of a devout Jewish couple, members of a Hasidic sect, whose personalities are marked by the traumatic experiences of violence and loss their ancestors were exposed to over several generations first during Russian and Polish pogroms, then under Hitler and Stalin. He grows up in the culturally intimate and closely knit enclave of an Hasidic congregation of Jewish immigrants in Brooklyn. Gradually he has to face his cultural separateness from the Jewish community at large and from the gentile majority. This fosters deep and loyal ties to his own group, but also overwhelming conflicts when he finds himself different from peers and elders even in his own sect because of his unusual gift for drawing and painting. The full expression of his talent and skill is unacceptable in his religious community insofar as it is forbidden there to portray the human shape, while his art is encouraged by the culture surrounding his congregation. When Asher is prevented from expressing anxieties and conflicts in words, his capacity to express them in drawing and colors becomes in the long run his salvation from the personality disintegration which repeatedly threatens his sanity during his childhood. Gradually, as he becomes an acclaimed painter, his art separates him from his religious group and family even though his faith and affections are unchanged.

At the time of the episode described in the vignette, Asher is a young man. With some emotional support from his mother and some help from his rabbi and two significant teachers, but against hostile objections from his father and many members of his congregation, he has become an accomplished painter. He has succeeded in this despite an extended period of severe emotional disturbance during his childhood. He has finally left home and, after studying painting in Europe for some time, he settles down in Paris to paint on his own. There he finds himself several times and for weeks at a time unable to paint at all. He wanders about the boulevards aimlessly or spends hours in his room brooding inactively. He goes out for only one meal a day – though regularly – and has very limited social contact except during these meals and on the sabbath, at the synagogue. During these periods his mind is frantically preoccupied with a revival and reappraisal of early traumatic impressions of his parents' behavior and of the family history as they have described it to him. He now experiences an ever-deepening understanding of the impact that various events and traditions must have had on his parents. He begins to grasp how this may have shaped their personalities and relationships. In the process, his own attitudes are modified, earlier taboos begin to lift. Each time he reaches a new level of understanding this finds expression in a new sequence of paintings illustrating a particular theme of his own or his ancestors' history as it appears in his latest insight. Each of these intensive phases of painting comes to an end in a further period of inability to paint, a period when old, frightening nightmares reappear as he comes ever closer to a central theme of utter pain. Slowly, he begins to grasp the sources and meaning of his mother's emotional torment to which he has been a witness since the age of six. The nature of her conflicts becomes apparent to him. He begins to see what his own talent and personality has contributed to the hardships of her life. Feverishly he tries to convey her situation in a composition that symbolizes his mother's being torn between the needs of her husband and her son; between her loyalty to her religious faith and her awareness that her son's emotional survival requires that he paint.

Asher then rapidly paints a picture that up to a point illustrates his mother's plight. It almost depicts her as crucified between her husband and her son, but not quite. It is a good painting, but not entirely true to his inner image. As a religious Jew, Asher dreads painting a crucifixion. It will hurt and shock his community. As an artist, he is at this stage of his development convinced that the only artistic symbol that will carry his message in the western world of art is indeed a crucifixion. He is in agony, but then he makes his choice. He recognizes that this is likely to sever his ties to his background, but his honesty as an artist is at stake. He paints "swiftly in a strange nerveless frenzy of energy. For all the pain you suffered, my mama. For all the torment. . . . " At last he dares to be true to himself. The creation of these two paintings also marks Asher's liberation from parental ties too strong, as the end of Chapter 12 will show, to be broken during adolescence.

The successful resolution of unconscious conflict or other impasse that may be reached during the seeming inactivity of being depressed is not always as dramatic and colorful, nor the process as laborious as in Asher's decisive crisis. Yet, to a more limited extent most of us have similar experiences. Aside from this, having spent my childhood and young adult life among creative writers and artists – some of them highly successful – I find Potok's description very true to life.

Questions that may be raised

If as professionals in the mental health field we look at Asher as if he were a real person, we shall certainly ask ourselves how we should evaluate his behavior during these many months in Paris. There is evidence of considerable anxiety, guilt, and conflict in his relationships with his parents. Does this indicate that, if it were not for the absence of loss of self-esteem (Bibring 1953), his mood and behavior should be diagnosed as a neurotic depression, and as such pathological? In as much as there is a history of a serious childhood depression, current social withdrawal, and some temporary impairment of his work performance, is the fact that this current mood and behavior only last several months rather than the two years stipulated by DSM- III (1981:222) the only feature to differentiate it from "dysthymic disorder"? Should we instead apply the criteria presented by Feighner *et al.* (1972:58) and find that Asher clearly does not show sufficient characteristic symptoms to be suffering from depression as a "primary affective disorder"? He is not sufficiently dependent or lacking in self-esteem to fit into Arieti and Bemporad's criteria (1980:63, 156) for "mild depression" either. Yet, although duration and number of symptoms do not seem to qualify Asher for a diagnosis of affective disorder, or any other pathological form of depression, his emotional state certainly goes beyond the sadness, disappointment, or discouragement which at times are seen as sufficient to describe the normal depressed mood.

How then, by existing diagnostic criteria, do we rate Asher's prolonged state of turmoil and bewilderment? What do the realities of his past and current life experiences have to do with his inner upheaval and his outward lethargy? Can one expect him not to have considerable trouble in coping with his circumstances? Do they make him ill? However this may be, when his recurring depressed behavior finally comes to an end, he evidently has discovered a satisfactory way of coping, involving artistic self-expression and maturation. Is that diagnostically significant?

Observations in real life comparable to Asher's experience, and some experiences of my own, have led me to the concept of a potentially adaptive basic depressed response that may lead to a productive (adaptive) outcome, or fail to do so.

Customarily it is deemed that being sad, disappointed, or discouraged, without showing any of the additional behavioral and physiological symptoms that occur in people diagnosed mildly or severely depressed, constitutes the normal form of being depressed. I have not found this assumption to be based on a description of the intrapsychic or social function and adaptive process of being sad or discouraged, nor on what the essential differences between normal and disordered depression consist of, but rather on diagnostic tradition. I find it more useful to take the outcome of adaptive effort as criteria by which to judge whether or not a person's emotion and behavior should be considered disordered.[1] The difficulty for research is that the presence of adaptive effort in being depressed cannot quickly and easily be established. The effort may not reach awareness, if at all, until the problem is resolved. Only then is it possible for the subject of research to account for it.

In deciding whether a person's depressed mood and behavior over a period of several months – as in Asher Lev's case – is healthy or pathological, the adaptive or maladaptive outcome of the crisis needs to be evaluated in relation to the long- and short-term intrapsychic, interpersonal, and environmental provocations of the crisis. In the following chapters I shall try to show what we can gain by using such criteria, and then, in Chapter 10, we shall have another look at Asher's behavior in Paris.

Our disposition for getting depressed and terminology to describe it

What I have said so far implies that I see all of us as endowed with the capacity to react to certain circumstances with feeling low in spirit, with slowing down and withdrawing our interest from some or many of our usual pursuits and commitments. In all of us this may be accompanied by disturbances of physiological functions such as sleep, appetite, and sexual desire. Whether we are members of a mental health profession or not, whether we have ever sought psychotherapy or not, most of us have at times felt like this, while wondering uneasily: "What is wrong?"

It would seem logical that we use the noun "depression" when we refer to the state of being depressed like this in spirit and vigor. In as much, however, as the word "depression" is generally used to refer not only to these common occurrences but also to complex syndromes involving many additional affects and disturbances, I use the term "basic depressed response."[2] Although the basic depressed response may occur simultaneously or in close succession with other painful emotions, such as grief, guilt, shame, anxiety, or anger, the word "basic" is used to convey that I consider the depressed response a discrete emotional response[3] which does not, as do the syndromes or patterns of emotions usually referred to as "depression," comprise any other emotion.

The word "response" implies that the depressed emotion or affect of depression is always elicited by a specific and characteristic crisis, however unconscious the crisis may be at the time it causes depression. The various behavioral and somatic components of the depressed response that I will take up in greater detail in Chapter 3 I call "depressed reactions." When I speak of "depression" I am referring to the total of depressed reactions in a given person during a given time from their onset to their final cessation. I may also call this an "episode of depression." But as much as possible I use instead such expressions as "getting depressed," "feeling depressed," "being depressed," or "staying depressed." Linguistically this is awkward, but it strikes me as the only way to reduce misunderstanding of my meaning that can arise from the fact that the noun "depression" is much more contaminated by connotations of pathological syndromes than the adjective "depressed."[4]

It will become apparent that I call a person "depression-prone" who gets depressed more frequently than people in general and stays depressed longer than others might under similar circumstances. I do so consistently, although it is also customary to call such a person "depressive."[5] I use the term "depressed" to describe a person's mood or emotional state, or the person who is in that mood or state. With the term "depressing" I refer to what causes such a mood or state to arise. An "emotional state," as I use the term, differs from a "mood" by being prolonged, while a "mood" passes more quickly (see Jacobson's discussion 1971:66).

I speak of "productive depression" when at the end of a period of being depressed there is evidence – as when Asher Lev finds a satisfying mode of depicting his mother's tragic situation and his role in it – that some useful learning or maturation has occurred, some behavior has been reorganized, some plan revised, so that following the depressed episode we function more effectively in the attainment of some goal, or become more realistic in setting our goal. I speak of "unproductive depression" when, although the circumstances promoting the depression demand learning and adaptation, no maturation occurs; development is arrested; personality or health deteriorates; and perhaps death is the final outcome. Thus, many instances of what tends to be called "depressive illness" involve, along with additional disturbances, what I call unproductive depression.

Neither any one depressed reaction nor their sum total during a given period of time are in themselves productive or unproductive. Thus, the terms "productive" or "unproductive depression" are abbreviations for "depression with productive outcome" and "depression with unproductive outcome." They are descriptive rather than diagnostic terms. This will become apparent in Chapter 3.

There are, however, many instances where, under circumstances that would normally provoke depressed reactions, neither a productive nor an unproductive course of depression ensues because neither depressed feelings nor much other depressed behavior appears. The "work" of depression, described further on, cannot proceed. Instead, should defenses like denial (or disavowal, see Basch 1983b), reaction formation, or idealization not suffice to prevent the discomforts of being depressed, social or sexual overactivity, overwork, addictions of various kind, or overdependence on medication may appear. These conditions I refer to as indicative of "avoided depression."[6]

Causes for delay in the conceptualization of normal depression

The thought that depression could ever be considered productive in any sense of serving a useful function is not a customary one. When after having been depressed we find ourselves relieved from feeling incomprehensibly slow and ineffective, we often feel new vigor, have some new ideas or plans, or we suddenly understand what has been wrong, we may find that we actually have more cause than we earlier recognized for anger, grief, regret, humiliation, disappointment, or other discomfort. Or we may see that in an important issue we may have been barking up the wrong tree. Such insights are accompanied by the feelings appropriate to whatever was the cause for the hidden discomfort. Since our depressed mood and symptoms have vanished at that point, we may not see them as connected in any way with our new ideas and plans, our recovered vigor, or with our new insight into our situation. We may tell ourselves that having recently been depressed was "just one of those things" – uncontrollable, incomprehensible, a nuisance, but fortunately transitory and better forgotten.

Consequently, when we use the noun "depression" we rarely think of those episodes of disquieting, incomprehensible, low moods that resolve themselves into a reorientation of fresh vigor. We are not familiar with the idea that becoming depressed under certain circumstances could be as vital, universal, and adaptive an emotional response as the emotions of anxiety, grief, or anger are in their own appropriate context. We are not reminded by the word "depression" of a specific type of problem with which the basic depressed response is uniquely suited to help us, as anger or grief do with other problems. Instead, we are likely to think of depression as something "sick," as some undesirable weakness.

Hartmann (1939:6) wrote that "a healthy person must have the capacity to suffer and be depressed." Sandler and Joffe (1965:89) wrote that "there are circumstances which normally and appropriately bring about feelings of depression and we would look for the existence of pathology if such reactions did not occur when they would normally be expected." And yet, we have in our reservoir of mental health concepts no model of normal depression that shows which circumstances can be expected to cause an adequately functioning human being of any age to get depressed – instead of reacting with anger, anxiety, or grief; nor one which shows the function which this emotional response and its symptoms may serve. But, as long as we do not have a model of what would happen if depression were running a healthy course – productive of insight, growth, and reorientation – it is a confusing task, indeed, to sort out potentially productive from unproductive aspects of the responses we observe in a seriously upset person seeking help for depression.

One can discern a number of reasons why cause and function of the universal basic response of depression has only in recent decades begun to attract the attention of members of the mental health professions, including researchers, while the vast literature on the subject of depression almost exclusively deals with syndromes associated with mild or severe disturbance of personality or physiology, where for good reasons despair and depressed reactions are prominent symptoms.

When help is sought from a psychotherapist, from a counselor, a minister, a physician, or a clinic, by or on behalf of a person who suffers from acute and persistent depression, the depressed person will often not only feel low in spirit, be unsettled in some physiological functions, and withdrawn from his or her usual interests and activities – that is, be literally "depressed." Frequently, he or she will also report or show a great deal of other painful emotions such as anxiety, grief, guilt, shame, or resentment. It may also become apparent that this person is handicapped in his or her behavior by severe conflicts, by many inhibitions, and by stereotyped thinking. Even more pronounced somatic disturbances may be part of the picture. No wonder that the acute need for help on the part of such patients has absorbed the interest and occupied the imagination of the helping professions at the expense of any curiosity about the normal and useful aspects of our capacity to respond to a specific stimulus by getting depressed.

Moreover, in a competitive industrial, technocratic, and combative society as ours, it is an unacceptable thought that the depressed affect causing us to slow down and withdraw into ourselves could be useful and necessary to our personal development and to our adaptation to change. In business and industry, in military service, and in public education, where human activity is conducted in keeping with rigid time schedules, only physical disability is – grudgingly – tolerated as an excuse for deserting one's desk, one's machine, or one's platoon during working hours. The employer, superior, or teacher is unwilling, and the employee, subaltern, or student is afraid to consider whether the slowing down, the insomnia, the withdrawal, the entire malaise of depression might not be a valid alarm signal telling us and those around us that all the time and attention we can muster should be devoted to some crisis within ourselves. Only few of us get a chance to discover that this withdrawal and preoccupation might be time and attention well spent, even in the employer's long-term interest. The mood of depression may signalize that it would be better to engage only in routine activity or even stay at home, to attend to our unattended crisis until we have unraveled what it is about and how it can be remedied.

In modern life being depressed is frequently suppressed by diversion or medication. It is only when we have an accident, develop a virus or other infection, and hit our bed with a sigh of relief, or even collapse with a heart attack, that we begin to recognize – if at all – that it was the necessity to communicate with ourselves in peace and quiet that got us into that prostrate position in the first place. For, once the acute physical distress has subsided, the prostrate position very often helps us attend to our inner crisis at last, whereupon we recover.

A further reason for the general hesitation to examine the depressed affect as a normal response serving an important function in our coping with specific circumstances has been described by Hazelton (1984). In her sections "The pressure to repress" and "Feminizing depression" (pp.52–62) she refers to literature and interviews suggesting that in western society, and particularly in the United States, all depression has long been seen as typical of the "weaker sex" who may indulge in it but are not expected to be aggressive. For men, on the other hand, who are expected to be more mature and capable adults than women, it is acceptable to be aggressive, while becoming depressed is atypical and a failure. Research revealing the fallacies of these prejudices is only a recent development. Broverman et al. asked (1970) academically and clinically trained psychologists, psychiatrists, and social workers what they saw as constituting mental health, and found them convinced that mental health consisted of behavior and attitudes typical for men in our society whom they deemed more mature and capable adults than women. Mental health in women was not judged by the same criteria. In order to live up to these social attitudes prevalent even among mental health professionals, men may have to resort to a variety of means to defend themselves against depression, because it is considered female and weak. Such defenses may be aggressiveness, drinking, or other addictions, and restless overexertion, all of which may promote somatic disease. These facts, apparent in criminal statistics and in hospitalization rates for addictions and somatic distress typical for men, are to my knowledge rarely taken into consideration in conclusions drawn from the preponderance of women in the treatment and hospitalization for depression.

Another factor that may have contributed to delaying the development of a model of normal depression is the following. Feeling depressed for any length of time is not only disapproved of in our society, but it is a very disquieting state of mind. As will be discussed in Chapter 3, the depressed response is aroused by something in ourselves not functioning to our satisfaction, but without our being fully – if at all – aware of just what is wrong and why. Feeling depressed is an alarm signal – but being unwelcome, it is often denied.

This creates a dilemma for students of psychological processes. Despite some exceptions and regardless of whether one is honest about it, whether one ignores it or hides it, most new insights into psychological processes are motivated by and rooted in the scholar's own experience and introspective capacity. Yet, depression creates a problem in that respect. Although hidden in their meaning and purpose, some symptoms of claustrophobia or agoraphobia, for example, tend to be touched off by the displacement of more basic anxiety on to tangible and often repetitive environmental circumstances that can easily be recalled. This can be helpful in recalling the symptoms as well if one wants to review and study one's own experience of phobia. The mood and physiological symptoms of depression, on the other hand, may on different occasions be brought on by the intrapsychic frustration of widely divergent efforts which, at the time we become depressed, are not within the range of our awareness. As I will take up more fully in Chapter 3, once we have become aware of the nature of the current frustration, another emotion, the one appropriate to the now conscious specific crisis, has taken over and the depressed mood has vanished. Its distressing quality cannot be recaptured in the way the emotions of grief, anger, or tenderness may be felt again if we vividly recall the events that have stimulated them on a certain occasion. We cannot make ourselves become depressed again until there is fresh, disquieting cause within.

No wonder that the threat of so uncomfortable, intractable an affect is ignored and specific instances are often forgotten rather than studied in ourselves. What is more, these characteristics of the depressed response create problems not only for self-observation but also when, as therapists, we try to observe the process of depression in someone else. In the latter case, the difficulty is compounded by the fact that the feelings and behavior of different observers may elicit different feelings and behavior in the observed person.

In addition to the socio-economic and cultural prejudices; to the urgency of our patients' needs; and to the wish of students of depression to ignore depressions of their own, a further factor tends to influence their focus in studying depression: the theoretical traditions and clinical practices of their profession, and the skills with which their training and practice have equipped them. Such traditions and preconceptions tend to influence the structure and focus of research as well. As Hill has put it (1968:446):

> Those who have been responsible for the advances in theory have built concepts which in all good faith they believed to have been derived from their observations. But in the explanatory hypotheses about the nature of illness with which they ended up, they were as much influenced by the current concepts about the nature of disease and the scientific and medical ethos of their time as they were by their clinical observations. We are all subject to this criticism and must accept the limitations which our current culture imposes upon us.

The uneasiness mental health professionals are left with about what is healthy or pathological, acceptable or unacceptable about being depressed has left us with the vagueness of the term "depression" which in its connotations comprises the normal and the abnormal, the basic affect, and complex syndromes. It has left us with the ambiguity of the term "depressive" which, according to Webster's dictionary, connotes "tending to depress" and "characterized by depression." Thus, "depressive" has both an active and a passive connotation. Provided one does not ignore the existence of normal depression altogether, the multiple connotations of both terms make it difficult to know exactly what an author or speaker has in mind when he uses them, and hard to convey one's own meaning without risk of misunderstanding. Unfortunately, if one were completely to abandon these established though obscure terms, one's readers would not realize that one was talking of any aspect of what they themselves tend to call depression. Consequently, I have been forced to restrict myself only to modifying certain terms, rather than changing them entirely. These modifications, however, deserve the reader's attention.

A different approach

To summarize, depression has been viewed and examined mainly as one or another type of mental or emotional illness or deviance and as caused either by heredity; or by faulty personality development that prevents coping with specific intrapsychic conflicts or prohibitions; or by some unexplained inability to cope with social stress; or by biochemical substances disturbing normal neurophysiological processes. The validity of these views in many individual cases of more or less severe and persistent depression I do not deny. As already stated, my approach differs from the more customary one of focusing on symptoms, insofar as I first examine our universal capacity to respond to a specific type of difficulty with a specific emotion, the basic depressed response, and try to determine what function or functions this response serves if all goes well. Having concluded that the basic depressed response can facilitate our arriving at a better grasp of the difficulty to which we are responding and of what can be done about it, and how it may serve to solicit needed social support, I proceed to examine what may prevent that emotion from serving its function. Why and how may personality development lead to the unsatisfactory interpersonal relations that in depression-prone persons interfere with the effectiveness of their personal choices and with their arousing adequate support? Rather than trying to fit my model of the universal depressed response into any accepted theory of personality I have developed it from examining how depression is subjectively experienced.

Many of the points I will make in my discussion have been made by other authors in professional papers and books, and also in some books for a broader public. A number of points, however, I consider my own, such as the significance of depression in facilitating our communication not only with others but also with ourselves; the development of this function from infancy to maturity; the discussion of the specific cause of the basic depressed response; the detailed differentiation of these features from the causes and functions of other emotions, particularly from those of grief in response to loss, disappointment, and loneliness; and the differentiation of "productive" from "unproductive" depression.

It is my hope that my discussion will arouse in colleagues and other readers a fresh curiosity and a willingness to reconsider what our cultural attitudes and our scientific and therapeutic traditions have caused us to feel and think about being depressed ourselves or seeing depressed behavior in others. Scientific research is making rapid and admirable strides in the examination of emotions and their impact on behavior. And yet, research projects are in their definitions and structures necessarily affected by attitudes, traditions, and established criteria. A shift in attitudes could facilitate new explorations providing the tools for insights far beyond my contribution. Should the reader decide to give me a hearing, my contribution could provide stimuli for ferreting out new facets of the phenomena of depression.

Chapter two

Cause and function of emotions in general

Emotions are subjectively experienced states and always related to a concept of self vis-à-vis some particular situation.

Basch (1976:768)

I believe that emotion cannot be understood or even adequately researched without asking about the cognitive factors underlying the emotional reactions. . . .emotions reflect the continuing nature of a person's or animal's commerce with his environment and the way this commerce is evaluated.

Lazarus (1977:145)

Basic assumptions

My view of depression rests on a few basic assumptions. One of these is that our emotions and our cognition are as closely related as two sides of a coin. What we perceive, what we think, what we remember, and what we conclude from our observations arouses emotions. Our emotions, on the other hand, cause us to think and look for information. They color our memories and our conclusions.

The second assumption is that we are endowed with the capacity to respond with specific emotions to specific experiences, and that each emotional response can serve the adaptive function of coping with the provoking experience. By this I mean that each emotion tends to elicit specific behavior in us that in a normally functioning person enhances maturation, thriving, and survival. In the wilderness in which the human race developed its current genetic characteristics, individuals who had the capacity to respond to dangerous or otherwise significant circumstances with an adequate set of emotions, and acted accordingly, had a better chance to survive, to have children, and to raise them than individuals who were deficient in that respect. Therefore, the hereditary traits of those who had this capacity could be passed on to us through countless generations over millions of years. That is, we have inherited these characteristics phylogenetically or, in Darwinian terms, through survival of the fittest.

This point of view I owe to the acquaintance with Bowlby's "attachment theory" (1961,1969). From the observation of children's responses to separation from their mother or mother substitute, Bowlby developed a theory that explains the nature and origin of the reactions of children and adults to separations from, or loss of, partners in significant relationships. Bowlby emphasizes that during the first year of life a child tends to become very attached to one person – usually but not necessarily the mother   and to behave in such a way that his or her responses tend to maintain proximity to that person whom Bowlby calls the child's "attachment figure." To this person a child turns with all his or her major discomforts, in preference to being comforted by anyone else. For this person a child develops his or her most tender feelings. By this person a growing child becomes most eager to be accepted and understood. From about six months to about three years a child becomes increasingly inclined to keep track of his or her attachment figure's whereabouts and accessibility, and resists separation from that person by protesting, crying, clinging, and pursuing. After a separation of uncomfortable length the child becomes inclined to respond with anger and increased anxious clinging. Later, this pattern diminishes only slowly and never disappears completely. Bowlby calls this behavior pattern "attachment behavior" and, for the reasons stated in the preceding paragraph, sees it as transmitted to us phylogenetically as an "instinctual behavioral system."

My third assumption is that each emotion, whether pleasant or unpleasant, is elicited by our conscious or unconscious judgment concerning the situation in which we believe we find ourselves. This judgment or appraisal I call the *cause* of the emotion.

The subjective experience of each emotion is accompanied by its own repertory of physiological change which in part tends to be visible, at times also audible, such as bursting into tears or laughter, getting hot or cold, red or pale; or a change in the rate of breathing or heartbeat; in other words, responses usually referred to as affective. At the same time as the impact of our situation elicits these physiological symptoms of our emotion it is likely to elicit behavior that is relevant to the cause of the emotion. The emotion itself, the cognitive processes that promoted it, the cognitive processes the emotion promotes in turn, the physiological changes, and the behavior connected with the emotion may combine to improve the situation at hand. In that case I speak of the emotion having served its *function*. I use the expression "serving an adaptive function" approximately as Bowlby does (1969). The term implies that being equipped with a given form of reaction tends to facilitate survival, even though this may not hold for a given individual under special circumstances. The individual adapts or does not. The response or process that makes this adaptation possible is or is not serving an adaptive function in a given instance. How various emotions serve their function, each in its own way, will be discussed more fully in Chapters 6 and 7. This chapter shows only briefly how this operates in the case of grief, anger, fear, and tenderness.

Further terminology

Before proceeding with this description, however, I need to make as clear as possible how I use the terms "cognition," "thought," "emotion," "affect," "feeling," "distress," and "information processing."

First of all, I distinguish between "affective," "emotional," and "cognitive" aspects of our functioning, although they are actually inseparable and interdependent.[1] I describe as "cognitive" those processes that help us register – consciously or unconsciously, verbally (conceptually) or non-verbally – what goes on within ourselves or in the world outside ourselves. They help us establish what meaning these observations may have for us; store them in our memory, or discard them as too insignificant to remember; compare different perceptions and organize them into categories; decide what we may expect, what we need to seek or avoid; and so on. In other words, the cognitive processes, as I use the term, include perception, thought, and memory, but cover a wider range of processes. Generally, when I speak of "thought" and "thinking" I mean a process that has reached awareness and requires the use of words or intentional signs or symbols to be communicated. When I have unconscious processes in mind I try to avoid the words "thought" and "thinking," although that is by no means easy. Instead, I may speak of "unconscious sensation," "unconscious responses," "unconscious perception." What upon reaching awareness becomes a thought, a fantasy, an image, has before reaching awareness been some "information" on the way to awareness, or been withheld from it.

In the literature on affect and emotion many authors tend to use only the term "affect," others only the term "emotion," although both groups may refer to the same phenomena. Basch, on the other hand, presents (1976:768–71) a very helpful differentiation between the two terms, which I follow.[2] When I speak of "affect," I mean pleasant or unpleasant sensations aroused by specific circumstances or stimuli, sensations that are accompanied by inherited and universal, automatic, physiological patterns of reaction. By "emotion," I mean the combination of the affective responses elicited by the circumstances in question with the specific feelings aroused by our *awareness* of the meaning we ascribe to these circumstances. When discussing the position of other authors, however, it is often most suitable to use their terms.

When, colloquially, we use the word "feeling," we are likely to mean the experiential components of an emotion – that is, a conscious sense of joy, grief, hate, and so on about the meaning we see in the event that provokes our emotion. This is how I use the word in my writing. In general, the word "feeling" does not, as does the word "emotion," refer to the full scale of physiological affective manifestations that may accompany our feeling response to an event. Furthermore, with the word "feeling" we primarily refer to our own inner perception of how we react to a situation and what it means to us, while "affect" and "emotion" are terms we or others use to describe from without the effect of that meaning on our behavior.

By "distress" I mean acute, unspecified emotional discomfort, or in other words, being miserable, unhappy. This may be due to various unpleasant affects and emotions, singly or in combination, such as grief, fear, anxiety, helpless anger, hopelessness, and so on; or due to physical frustration, pain, or nausea. I use the term particularly in Part II, when I speak of infants and children who cannot tell us what causes them to feel so miserable. In speaking of older children or adults I will break distress down into the different emotional responses that may be its content.

Both our cognitive, our emotional, and our affective responses are the result of what I shall refer to as "information processing." While this concept has elsewhere been used in psychology,[3] Bowlby (1969) and Peterfreund (1971) have independently introduced it into psychoanalytic theory, where I first encountered it. In that context it implies a complex series of biological processes causally related to our experiencing affect, impulses, phantasies, thoughts, feelings, memories. These complex processes involve behavioral control systems and mechanisms of varying complexity which operate at different developmental levels of the organism. They occur often exceedingly rapidly and largely, though not always, unconsciously. They underlie all appraisals and choices we make.

Cause and personal, as well as social, function of emotional responses[4]

Now we can proceed with a brief discussion of cause and function of such responses as grief, anger, fear, and tenderness.

Grief is usually caused by our judgment that we no longer have access to a person or situation that hitherto has been experienced as essential to our well-being or to our hopes for the future. Or we find that such a person or situation, although still accessible, has changed drastically so that the effect is equally distressing. Grief is a significant component of mourning, though it is not all of mourning. The stress inherent in the experience of grief mobilizes in us many efforts to test whether what appears lost or changed can be retrieved, replaced, or in some way substituted for. As our early efforts to search for or replace what we have lost are failing, there will be renewed grief mobilizing renewed efforts, until the reality of the new situation becomes better understood and accepted, with the result that different aspirations emerge and personal equilibrium is gradually restored. Freud (1917) coined the expression "mourning work" for this process, which I consider to be the *personal aspect* of the function of grief.

At the same time, the behavior prompted by grief – our wailing, our tears, our complaints, our sighs, our posture, our poor sleep, our lack of appetite, our preoccupation with memories, and so forth – tends to stimulate persons around us to assist or protect us during at least part of this crisis. This I see as the *social aspect* of the function of grief. The combination of these two aspects is likely to increase our chances of surviving and thriving in the long run, despite a significant loss. But in infants and young children only the social aspect of the function of an affect can be served, inasmuch as they lack the cognitive and emotional development for its personal aspect to be carried out.

Anger strikes me as an emotion pertaining to an entirely different appraisal of a situation. The judgment is: someone is acting, or circumstances are conspiring, in a way that is not only frustrating, disappointing, or injuring me, but it is done in a way that is unnecessary and should have been avoided. We are less likely to get angry, however distressed we may be, if we find no one to blame, as perhaps when a beautiful oak in our garden is destroyed by lightning; but we may get very angry when anyone in particular, including ourselves, can be blamed for some damage to our garden. Realistically, we may be in error about who is responsible for what has happened or is about to happen, but while we are angry our judgment includes a belief that there is a culprit and who it is, even if we are not fully aware of this idea.

The function of anger has also two aspects, a personal and a social one. In personal terms anger can speed up thinking and action. Combined with the sense of certainty about who and what is to be attacked and stopped, this increases our chances to defend ourselves or others effectively, to express our demands and complaints clearly, or to meet emergencies. Yet, it does so only provided that the anger is neither overwhelming, nor disproportionate to the external occasion, nor interfered with by other emotions. In social terms, the function of anger is served by our visible affect. The changed expression of our eyes and voice, our reddening face or extreme pallor, our swelling blood vessels, the baring of our teeth, or our rapid movements may convey to an opponent that it may be safest to take flight, give in, agree to negotiate, or at least proceed more cautiously. As Bowlby has pointed out (1973), even a child's anger can have a coercive effect on its parents.

When I speak of "anger," then, I have a specific affective or emotional response to frustration in mind. I do not use the term to mean "aggression," in the sense of a basic *drive* toward self-assertion, dominance, and destruction, or in the sense of angry, destructive *action*. Whether an aggressive drive should be postulated as part of human nature or not is not relevant for a discussion of the basic depressed response as genetic equipment and subjective experience. Therefore, the issue will not be discussed in this book.

Fear is the emotional response that accompanies the judgment that a particular person or group of persons, an animal, or a set of circumstances, like an approaching hurricane, is about to injure us in ways we are insufficiently prepared to deal with unless we can escape or – if the injury is to come from man or animal – avoid being noticed. It is the reaction to the perception of a

22

specific and imminent danger. Again, the function of fear has two aspects. Fear may cause us to run as fast as we can without our wasting time on irrelevant preparations. If running is impossible or useless, being "frightened stiff" may facilitate our remaining more immobile and thus less noticeable than we can normally manage. This represents the personal preparation we owe to the emotion of fear in meeting danger. If we can neither escape nor remain unnoticed, the signs of terror in our appearance may reassure or pacify a human opponent and reduce his motivation to attack or destroy us. Thus, the social function is served.

Feelings of tenderness, on the other hand, are awakened by our finding a child, an adult, or an animal a suitable object to please, caress, protect, and comfort; or suitable to satisfy our wish to be protected, comforted, or caressed. These feelings help us recognize with whom, for one or another reason, we want to maintain proximity. They become apparent to others in the expression of our eyes and the tone of our voice, even if we restrain the impulse to caress or use endearing words. This tends to arouse corresponding feelings toward us in others. Again, the function of the emotion is served both in an intrapsychic or personal, and in a social way.

This brief sketch of cause and function of such emotional responses as grief, anger, fear, and tender feelings can serve to show that our emotions and their cognitive components are of vital importance in our total equipment for thriving, maturing, becoming creative, and surviving. They guide us when we have a choice in selecting partners for significant relationships: friends, mates, employees, employers; teachers, physicians, counselors, and other protectors. They help us develop and maintain good relationships, or get out of bad ones. They help us make the best of a relationship when we have had no choice in who the partner is, as between parents and children, and in some settings of learning and teaching, of employment, and of therapy; and as a rule, in the military. They help us adapt ourselves to the many changes to which we are repeatedly exposed: changes in ourselves that result from our maturing and accumulating experience, or from illness, accident, or ageing; as well as changes in partners to significant relationships, and in other aspects of our environment. Finally, our emotions are as significant as our cognitive responses in our studies, our work, and our practical decisions.

From what I have said so far, it should be evident that I am approaching the issue of emotions from a psychological and experiential vantage point. I am focusing on how we subjectively experience our emotions, how we appraise the situation that arouses our emotions, and what we gain from responding with a particular emotion rather than with another or without emotion. This approach in no way rules out the significance of experimental research in psychology or of neurophysiological research. On the contrary, only when all findings begin to point in the same direction can we trust that we are on the right track. Only neurophysiological research can discover how psychological responses are either implemented by, or cause, physiological processes, or both.

Some pertinent literature

My concepts of the cause and functions of affect and emotion in general and of the depressed response in particular have grown from my introspective and clinical observations, from my acquaintance with Bowlby's work, and also from my study of other literature on the subject, mainly but not exclusively psychodynamic. In ways that can no longer be traced, the development of my thinking has been influenced and stimulated largely by papers and books published in recent decades, beginning with Bibring (1953). I have encountered most elements of my views in the work of at least one or of several authors but most in the views of Basch (1975, 1976) and Bowlby (1961, 1969, 1973, 1980), both of whom have strongly influenced my thinking. But I have found no one to combine all these elements into a comprehensive model of a normal depressed response with emphasis on the experiential aspects of its processes. As will be shown in Chapter 6, I do not accept sadness as such a model. Nor do I agree with Fenichel's view (1945:106) of depression in his statement that "Guilt feelings that accompany the performance of a misdeed" are the normal model "for the pathological phenomena of depression."

I have followed Bowlby's work since 1971 and have been continuously aware of its influence on my thinking. Basch's papers I first read in 1977, and then again when I revised the first draft of my chapters on affect, emotion, and cognition. His discussion (1975) of the adaptive role of depressed affect in the developing organism is presented on a high level of abstraction, largely, though not exclusively, on the basis of physiological processes. None the less, by implication it confirms major features of my concept of the basic depressed response to be described in Chapter 3, except for one point. While I also emphasize the role of the depressed reactions in facilitating communication with the self – that is, their role in facilitating the "ordering" function of the brain in information processing, as Basch would say – he only stresses that communication with others is achieved by the behavioral signals of the depressed affect. To Basch's discussion of affects (1976), I have already referred in note 2.

The third major influence on the development of my theoretical awareness has been exerted by Peterfreund (1971,1983), particularly with regard to the conceptualization of learning and of the therapeutic process.

Aside from other papers by the two authors, I found Sandler and Joffe's work on the subject of the depressed response in children and child development (Sandler and Joffe 1965; Joffe and Sandler 1965) supportive of my thinking and helpful in clarifying my conclusions. An example is their statement (Sandler and Joffe 1965:90):

> It is our belief that if depression is viewed as an affect, if we allot to it
> the same conceptual status as the affect of anxiety, then much of the
> literature on depression in children (and ... adults) can be integrated in a
> meaningful way.

Other statements I found challenging, for example the following:

> The basic affective state which we are considering ... is what might be described as a state of helpless resignation in the face of pain [1965:92]. ... While it is clear that ability to tolerate frustration and the depressive affect which may be associated with it is an important one in development we do not subscribe to the view that the very experience of depression is, *in itself*, a valuable one. We would rather stress the importance of overcoming disappointment and mental pain in a healthy way [1965:95].

As I see it, the depressed response is in certain circumstances the appropriate – that is, healthy – way of overcoming turmoil. As will become evident further on, rather than seeing resignation as an inherent part of the basic depressed response, I agree with Winnicott who finds (1964:124) that "the presence of the depressed mood gives some ground for belief that the individual ego is not disrupted and may be able to hold the fort, if not actually come through to some sort of resolution of the internal war."

In reading papers by Engel (1962,1972) and Schmale (1973,1975) I found myself in agreement with many of their views, particularly with Engel (1962:96) on the role of affects in communication with self and others, and with Schmale and Engel on the adaptive function of "conservation-withdrawal" (1975:196). But I do not agree with their view that giving-up is characteristic of the *affect* of depression, although it is significant in many *syndromes* of depression.

Schur finds (1969:651) that "all affects consist on the one hand of a cognitive process, and on the other of a response to this process, although the extent of the cognitive component varies with different affects." This is in keeping with the conclusions I have arrived at on a different road.

Brenner says (1973:11),

> As Fenichel (1945) points out, the precipitating factor, not only in depression, but in any psychoneurosis, is often unconscious, i.e., unknown to the patient himself. It seems to the patient that the onset of his symptoms is wholly inexplicable, that nothing happened in his life to precipitate them. Thus the attempt to distinguish reactive depression from primary mood disturbance is based on an inadequate appreciation of the importance of unconscious factors in mental life.

I agree, but I find this to be true even of normal depression. I also agree with Brenner's view that while anxiety "is unpleasure associated with the idea that something bad is *about to happen* [1975:11ff.]. ... depressive affect is unpleasure associated with the idea that something bad has happened" (1975:10). Only I find Brenner's concept of "depression" too comprehensive, inasmuch as it includes grief, loneliness, shame, and all sorts of misery and unhappiness in the bad that is thought to have happened (1974:542; 1975:10).

Additional literature focusing on depression more than on affect in general will be referred to later.

Except for the early work of Seligman (1975), I became acquainted with the views of behaviorist and cognitive psychologists only when I found it necessary to compare my position with recent developments in disciplines of the field of mental health other than psychodynamic psychotherapy, particularly those emphasizing psychological aspects of depression. I found that, while focus, method of study, and terminology among the authors in the different disciplines and schools of thought may differ greatly from mine, there are, nonetheless, considerable parallels in many of their and my conclusions. Although, as indicated in the Introduction, I shall not give a full review of the literature, I shall continue, in suitable context, briefly to indicate significant parallels and differences between my position and that of some other authors.

Chapter three

Cause and function of the basic depressed response

In psychiatry depression is usually considered a disease. A more fruitful approach to our understanding of this reaction may be to examine depression as an indicator or manifestation of disequilibrium and not as a disease per se.

Pollock (1975:370)

... the universality of the reaction implies that, rather than being an intrusive, alien, and destructive element in human affairs, it may have adaptive purposes, which may go wrong under various circumstances.

Salzman (1970)

Overt features – the depressed reactions

In the preceding chapter I made the following three assertions. Each affect or emotion tends to elicit specific behavior in us. In a normally functioning person this enhances thriving, maturation, and survival. Until further research clarifies these issues, it is useful to consider the basic depressed response an affective response or emotion distinct from, rather than composed of, other emotions. Now we must examine the observations on which these assertions are based.

The readily observable components of the depressed response that I call "depressed reactions" are the following: a lowered overall mood; a reduction of initiative; some withdrawal of emotional and cognitive responsiveness to what we otherwise react to readily; an increase of preoccupation with a few specific concerns – often, but not necessarily, introspective; a sense of, or actual slowing down of reactions, or some other difficulty in applying ourselves as we wish or expect, including a selective disturbance of recall and concentration; some increase in vulnerability and irritability; some pervasive sense of perplexity at our inability to act or achieve in some particular way – a perplexity that may, but need not, acquire some quality of helplessness and hopelessness; feelings of tiredness or lack of energy without concomitant physiological disturbance to explain them; some change in our customary patterns of sleeping, eating, drinking, and sexual responses: perhaps loss of sleep, restless sleep, change in character of dreams, or sleeping more deeply or longer than usual; perhaps loss of appetite, finding food tasting or smelling differently; eating or drinking more avidly (perhaps as a defense against the depressed mood); probably lack of sexual interest (or perhaps excessive need of sexual satisfaction as a defense). Not all these reactions need be present in what one might see as a depressed response, but there will surely be more than one or two.

The question arises, of course, whether the basic depressed response is an affect or an emotion. Most of the reactions I have enumerated are clearly affective: the slowing down, the reduction of initiative and interest, and any changes in physiological function such as sleep, appetite, and so on; and the change of mood unless its cause is understood correctly.

The consideration whether the depressed response is at least at times also an emotion, I shall postpone until I have described the response more fully, with some illustrations.

The question has been raised by colleagues, whether in including physiological features in my concept of the basic depressed response I am not describing a mild affective disorder, rather than normal depression. After all, these characteristics are included in all definitions of mild as well as severe affective disorder – as, for instance, in the definitions by Arieti and Bemporad (1978), Beck (1967), DSM-III (1981), and Feighner et al. (1972), to name a few. My answer is, that mild and severe forms of affective disorder quite naturally involve increased or distorted features of the affect in question. Normal grief, fear, anxiety, and anger all have their affective components that accompany the psychological experience, without our considering all crying and sobbing, lying awake in sorrow or worry, trembling with fear, or raising our voice in anger, as indications of pathology.

The emotions of grief, fear, anxiety, guilt, shame, or anger often appear in combination with the depressed response, but for the following reasons I do not count them as depressed reactions: first of all, when they appear in states of depression one can on closer examination establish that each of the accompanying emotions may have been elicited separately though in the same context in which depressed reactions were also elicited. For instance, a widow may grieve as a result of her pining for interaction with her husband, while her inability quickly to cope with unforeseen massive social and economic change following her bereavement may provoke a depressed response. These are two simultaneous but separate responses to two separate aspects of her widowhood. Not all hardships likely to cause grief necessarily cause us to be depressed as well, nor vice versa. Furthermore, feelings of grief, anxiety, guilt, shame, or anger may be reactions to our finding ourselves depressed instead of active and effective, and to our failure to grasp why this should be so. In that case, these other feelings are a consequence, rather than an integral part of, being depressed.

Or we may be reacting in any of these ways to the fact that our being depressed is not understood and tolerated by those around us.

Examples of overt and hidden features

As we turn to the issue of hidden disturbances and hidden remedial efforts behind the overt depressed reactions, two examples (Gut 1982) taken from outside the consultation room may help us.

1 A successful, inventive, and productive biochemist, Albert, whose personal life is harmonious and satisfying, was asked whether he ever gets depressed. He answered, yes, he did. When he worked on a new project to test a new idea, he would follow some research design that he considered appropriate to the task on hand. When he didn't make headway as expected, he continued to apply his plan of action in every possible way that might yield results. But finally, when he still got nowhere, he despaired of it. Asked how he felt when the sense of despair subsided, he said:"Well, I see an entirely different way to tackle the problem, or else, I have recognized that the project was unrealistic, or at least impossible to carry out at the moment, and so given it up."

As I hope to show, this description contains, between the lines, cause, process, and outcome of being depressed. The second example shows, in addition, some of what I call the "work of depression."

2 A psychotherapist, Bertha, described the following episode. She was working with enthusiasm on her doctoral thesis. During the last weeks of meeting the deadline for sending the draft of an important chapter to her thesis adviser in advance of a scheduled conference, she found herself excessively tired. During these weeks she had some fleeting thought that she was not the adequate therapist she had thought. She suddenly began to wonder whether her work with patients would leave her enough time and energy for the continued research she wished to engage in. This did not keep her from making her scheduled trip to her university town to see her adviser. The conference proved very stimulating and kindled a number of fresh ideas. Some revisions were suggested. She left with the conviction that her research could become more conclusive than she had dared hope. Nevertheless, by the time she returned home, the feeling of exhaustion had returned. When she tried to resume work on her research data and prepare the revisions, she felt out of touch with the subject. It felt as if she could not possibly recover the enthusiasm or the necessary endurance to start all over again examining and re-evaluating her data.

Bertha began to realize that her fatigue might be a form of depression. In that case, she wondered, what could be the cause of being depressed? She decided that it might be best not to strain but to give in to the sense of depression as much as circumstances permitted. She dropped work on her thesis and cut down on activities other than her commitments to patients. Her husband was sympathetic to her need to be by herself more than usual. Yet, she found herself staying up evenings later than necessary and sleeping less soundly than usual. One night, unable to fall asleep, she found herself engrossed in thinking about some puzzling sessions with a patient. Normally this would not happen at night. Yet, it happened again a few nights later, and then a third time with some anxiety. At that point she realized that her being depressed might actually be the signal of a crisis not in her research or writing, but in her activities as a therapist.

In her community, Bertha had no access to experienced supervision or consultation. She had completed her formal training in psychotherapy only a few years before. During an earlier visit to her university she had consulted a more experienced therapist in that town who had been highly recommended as supervisor. They had discussed the two patients Bertha found most difficult. She had been impressed with the guidance she had received. At first, the measures she took as a result seemed to yield excellent results in the movement of both cases. Then, acute and unexpected problems arose. Bertha didn't quite know what to do since she did not really feel at home with the approach the consultant had suggested. She tried some hit-and-miss measures, but was not quite satisfied. Under the pressure of the deadline for the manuscript, and temporarily fascinated by that work, she had let things drift with her patients, hoping for the best. As she now turned her full attention to the consultation and its consequences she realized that, in order neither to disturb her work on her thesis nor to postpone the scheduled conference on it, she had brushed over faint doubts and disappointment about the encounter with the consultant. She was uncertain: had she failed to give an adequate account of her work to the consultant; or had the consultant failed to make his own meaning clear; or could his technique or approach be unsuitable for Bertha's personality? After some intense feelings had surfaced about her consultant, her patients, and herself, including insight into a reaction of countertransference, Bertha concluded that she ought to discuss this with the consultant. Should that discussion fail to be helpful, she would consider other steps for getting help with her patients. She decided to schedule an extra trip to her university town and made an appointment with the consultant. On the following day Bertha found herself deeply engrossed in the work on her thesis. Insight into her reaction to a patient and to the consultant eliminated the depression.

What do these two episodes have in common? Both the biochemist and the psychotherapist came to a deadlock in a meaningful endeavor. Unexpectedly they were at a loss what to do next. Whatever they tried to do to get going again was unsatisfactory. Yet, they could not understand why this was so. Only, after some days or weeks of being depressed with reduced activity they suddenly saw what was causing the deadlock and found a new way to achieve their aim. In Albert's case, the cause of getting depressed was his moving in the wrong direction with a creative project. In Bertha's depressed response the cause seemed at first also to be a flaw in creative work, but when her being depressed resolved itself it was evident that its cause had been unsatisfactory communication with the therapist she had consulted. Breakdowns in communication with significant partners or in any other significant performance are aspects of life that are most likely to be at the root of depressed reactions and the process they tend to initiate. This was also illustrated by the period in Asher Lev's life reported at the beginning of Chapter 1.

The process of depression and its five phases

Analyzing such incidents in greater detail has led me to see the events of a depressed episode as a process involving five phases (Gut 1982). The first two phases are prerequisites for a depressed episode to develop, although it need not develop. Only in combination with the third phase do they contain the emotional and cognitive circumstances that precipitate the depressed response with its various reactions. This combination constitutes the *cause* of the depressed response. The last two phases involve the process initiated by and maintained during the course of being depressed: its *work* and the course it runs to a *productive or unproductive outcome*. The *process of depression* includes all five phases. These should not be thought of as a rigid sequence. More than one of them may be active at the same time.

Prerequisite for becoming depressed, and in that sense the *first phase* of the total process of depression, is our striving to reach some significant goal by applying our personal resources: our body, our mind, our skills, our interpersonal responses. Striving and goal may either reach awareness or remain unconscious. Without them we are not vulnerable to becoming depressed.

The next prerequisite to, and the *second phase* in, the process of depression is our finding that expected progress toward our goal is not achieved by the means we apply. Either it proves impossible to act as we intended, or our method yields no result when applied. Yet, we do not grasp the reason for this failure. Our frustration is compounded by our inability to comprehend what is causing the impasse. Again, some parts of this may be conscious, but most of it is not. What we are most likely to be aware of at this stage is a sense of diffuse perplexity.

I prefer the term "perplexity" to the term "helplessness" which, since Bibring's paper (1953), is so generally used to describe a typical quality of the depressed mood. To me, both terms imply a sense of inability to carry on with an intended activity, a sense of being – at least for the moment – paralyzed in some respect. Yet, there is a difference. To me, the term "perplexity" implies also a sense of unpleasant surprise at the interruption of our functioning, and a continuing curiosity, a desire to find out what has brought our functioning to a halt. But this is not strong enough to be seen as an affect of surprise or curiosity, which is why I speak of a "sense." Perplexity implies an unbroken unconscious effort to overcome the interruption of functioning. "Helplessness," if not qualified by the attribute "temporary," often connotes giving up or having given up. As will become apparent in the course of Chapter 9, this tends to be the case only when depression fails to become productive. Helplessness and hopelessness with regard to our ability to carry out an intended activity provide *cause* for the depressed response, but are not *part* of the response itself. They are part of the depressed person's total experience of the moment: it is depressing not to know why we fail to carry out an intention and not to know what we can do about it.

In *phase three*, an intense, largely unconscious preoccupation takes over, which, were it conscious, we would consider a desperate effort to discover what could possibly be wrong with the methods we are applying; with the pertinent information we have available; with the conclusions we are drawing from the available data, including our view of ourselves and others; or what could be wrong in our environment to account for the deadlock. The uncomprehended obstruction in pursuing our goal is experienced as disquieting.

If the frustration in phase two of our longing to attain a significant goal through our own efforts leads to the disquieting sense in phase three of being inexplicably ineffective, feelings of disequilibrium and urgency arise. In *phase four*, they mobilize efforts in us to remedy the situation by devising new solutions. Most of this remains outside awareness but is signalled on the surface by depressed reactions. Disturbances of sleep and appetite, the inexplicable exhaustion, the slow-down of overt activity, the withdrawal from activities not pertinent to the inner crisis, and other depressed reactions are consequences of the hidden experience of ineffectiveness and of the effort to overcome it.

If we do not suppress depressed reactions by medication, alcohol, other narcotics, or restless activity, or ward them off by mechanisms of defense, they can, as *phase five*, facilitate more intensive information processing than would be necessary if our intentions could be carried out more readily. The aspects, or results, of information processing I have in mind here are the following: comparison and integration of fresh perception with earlier perceptions stored in our memory; comparison and integration of recently reached conclusions with long-established beliefs; and their revision. This also includes the integration of values and expectations with our evaluation of new events that disavow them. In addition, depressed reactions can make it easier for unconscious responses to make their way into awareness.

More specifically, dreams during the often disturbed sleep of this phase sometimes offer clues. Or, while we are lying awake during quiet hours of the night, trains of thought may, at last, yield a conscious experience of grief, anxiety, or anger and its causes, or allow some significant recollection or some ignored perception to come into focus. This we have seen in Bertha's experience. Fatigue may force us to rest, with our attention turned to free floating association; and to wait. Or the anxiety aroused by the total process of inner change – or failure to change – may motivate us to seek aid by talking to a trusted person whose responses may stimulate or reorient our mental activity. All this I call the work of depression. It can be seen as a partly conscious but mainly unconscious search for answers to a riddle. It can lead to our becoming conscious of our intentions, which is especially important if unawareness has contributed to the impasse. It can lead to our discovering new means of carrying out our intentions, or to the recognition that we should abandon our goal as impossible. This type of outcome we see in Albert's occasional depressions. When one or several answers to our perplexity have been found, so that the original intent to act can be carried out or alternatively abandoned, the conscious or unconscious sense of dysfunction subsides and with it the symptoms of depression. There is nothing left to provoke depressed reactions. The process has succeeded in serving an adaptive function.

I have been asked why getting depressed was so vital, why its function of achieving reorientation of purpose and methods could not be achieved as a result of anxiety, guilt, and anger alone keeping us awake a few nights, or causing us to stay at home for a weekend, which would suffice for a quick-thinking person to restructure his or her life. As will become clearer in Chapters 6 and 7, when I compare cause and function of various affects with those of the depressed response, the person who is close enough to grasping the implications of his frustrating situation in a few harassing nights or during a weekend does not get depressed. It is only when the task of reorientation is too complex to be handled successfully by usual efforts; only if some aspects of the problem are unknown, repressed, or disregarded for some reason, the depressed response will automatically appear. It is not a matter of choice.

Consider a simpler automatic response of slowing down that is not a matter of getting depressed and yet a related mode of our natural functioning. When we suddenly realize that we don't know where we left keys we need to get into our car or our home, that they aren't where they ought to be, we are likely to stop short for a moment in what we are doing or saying at the time. Our mind is caught up in the concern of how to get our keys, even if that may cause us to be inconsiderate of a person to whom we should be talking or listening. Or think of driving on a motorway to visit someone, when we realize that we left that person's address on our desk and are not sure whether we will recall it or how else to get it just then. At that moment it will take an effort not to step on the brakes automatically despite the high speed of the surrounding traffic. The impulse is to stop, think, and if necessary turn around. Anger or anxiety in relation to the stupid error will appear some moments later, but the first reaction is our wanting to forget about the traffic and concentrate on the question: what shall I do?

A typical failure of the work of depression

It should, of course, suffice to speak of the depressed response serving "its function" without adding the term "adaptive," but at times the latter can be necessary. It is the basic function of the depressed response to facilitate intensified information processing concerning a specific problem. This, in turn, can result in insight, improved communication, and restored equilibrium. But from this basic function, being depressed can become diverted toward serving a defensive function instead. It is important, however, to note here, that although frequently encountered in the consultation room, defensive use of the depressed response is not universal for all depression, not even for all depressed reactions in our patients.

As an example of the basic function of the depressed response becoming defensively diverted, we may think of a woman who, like many others, has grown up in a family and social climate where her angry reactions as a child were responded to with rejection or punishment, while tearfulness, apathy, tiredness, and withdrawal were tolerated; and physical symptoms perhaps attracted care-giving attention. In response to stimuli to which it has not been safe for her to respond, as others might, with anger, contempt, or even laughter, such a woman will switch automatically into a depressed mood with its physiological components. She will have learned to do so without awareness of the switch. Being unable to become aware of anger or contempt, or to express such feelings, presents a normal cause for depressed reactions. In her case, however, the depressed response may actually serve as a defense against the risk of recognizing and revealing her true self.[1] The depressed response may serve to maintain denial instead of facilitating intensified information processing leading to insight. In a child such a defense can actually be adaptive, if it prevents parental rejection and thereby protects many of the child's potentials for development. In an adult, on the other hand, this is usually no longer adaptive. The diversion of the function of the depressed response toward defensive purposes interferes with the work of depression and prevents the normal function of depression from being served. This can happen in a variety of ways, but here is only one illustration.

Carola was handsome and intelligent. She was single. In her late twenties she sought therapy because she had no desire to live and had been depressed most of the time as long as she could remember. She felt alive only "through a man" and that made her too vulnerable. Recently, after having enrolled in a professional training course, she had found that she could not concentrate on her studies enough to prepare for exams.

For the point I wish to make here I am only selecting one pattern in Carola's difficulties. How such difficulties tend to develop in specific family environments will be discussed in Chapter 13. Carola did not carry within herself the experience of a stable relationship with a trustworthy, understanding, responsive, and sharing other. She had no basic trust,[2] no self-reliance or self-respect. She thought she did not know who she was or what she really wanted. In the course of therapy she gradually discovered that, if she wasn't taken care of by another – something she kept aiming at for quite some time, without achieving it – she at least needed approving people around her all the time, if she was to get the energy necessary for taking care of herself. Left alone for any length of time, she felt despair and could not keep her apartment or business in an order that would enhance well-being.

Carola expected in a close relationship with a man or woman to be taken care of on her own terms, in ways satisfying her own needs and tastes, but she didn't know how to explain these wishes or how to object frankly to their neglect. Despite her initial idealization of new friends and lovers, she soon became disappointed. Carola took for granted that, whenever a misfit appeared in a relationship, this was due to one partner being bad and wrong, while the other was right and good. This was how she had been dealt with by her mother – Carola invariably being the one who was wrong – and how her parents viewed all others, particularly their spouse. Thus, when a new relationship, into which she had plunged quickly and excitedly, began to cause frustrations, Carola began to expect that she would soon be found wrong, which she feared might be justified. She was so terrified of meeting contempt, rejection, and desertion as a consequence of her possible shortcomings, that she quickly had to "make the other one bad." Then she "cut off" and became depressed. By this she meant that she didn't want to live and that she felt apathetic and defeated. Her grief, on the other hand, was short and limited, and there was only some resentment but no hot anger. Neither having an "inner companion," as she later called it, nor anyone in real life in whose presence she could fully grieve or rage, she could not have tolerated the sharp pain of grief, of frustration anger, and the full awareness of her loneliness. Being depressed was easier to bear.

When a circle of reliable women friends had developed, Carola, after long distrust and hesitation, allowed herself to discover that at least her therapist did not vanish but was still there and the same when exposed to anger and reproach. Then, Carola could let herself notice that, when she was really angry underneath about some disappointment a meaningful person was causing her, she tended to get depressed instead.

Carola certainly had valid cause for getting depressed in this context: she was yearning for a close, stable relationship and genuine sharing, but did not grasp what in her expectations, her choices, and her behavior defeated her aspirations. But when the defeat became apparent, she had cause for grief and anger at the same time, which in its accumulation was so painful that until secure support was found and trusted, she could not let herself discover what effective work of depression might have revealed: that indiscriminate involvements were unlikely to lead to desired results; that the chances of fulfillment were not as many as she wished; and that lonely grief and anger are part of life. Staying depressed was the lesser evil until more self-reliance and better relationships had slowly been acquired. Until that time, her depressed episodes served a defensive purpose better than they served their adaptive purpose.

Defensive use of the depressed response has been overemphasized in the professional literature at the expense of studying the adaptive function of the response. Therefore, it is useful to bear in mind that defensive use of a basic emotional response is by no means unique to depression. Many emotional reactions can serve as defenses against other emotions. In a given person aloofness may replace attachment, contempt may replace envious admiration or vice versa, anxiety may substitute for anger, and so forth. Take a boy who grows up in a family or social climate where grief, fear, clinging, or depression in boys and men is treated with ridicule, contempt, or rejection, if not outright cruelty. He may learn to switch into a stance of angry assertiveness in response to any experience that, without such defense, might stimulate tearful, anxious, clinging, or depressed behavior. Yet, even though they can be used defensively and in this way become part of pathology, responses of dislike, anxiety, or anger will commonly serve useful functions. The same, I find, holds for getting depressed.

Productive work of depression

In our patients, our friends, and ourselves we can often observe that more or less persistent depressed reactions vanish upon the emergence of grief, resentment, longing, fear, or other strong feelings. Their emergence is connected with significant thoughts and memories or new information now having become linked in a new way. Some of this linkage has also reached awareness. In considering these processes we must bear in mind that awareness – or conscious process – is like the tip of an iceberg: most of the results of the information processing that causes us to feel, think, and act never reach awareness. Also, before reaching awareness most of our perceptions are either discarded as irrelevant or stored in memory. How readily the latter can later be collected from storage depends on many factors, including the nature of the feelings they would arouse on reaching awareness. Therefore, in new or complex situations, not all potentially available data of relevance are quickly available. It may take time and intense effort to make them available for linking with other data. Defensive repression can, but need not, be the cause for delay in linking. When the necessary linking finally has been achieved a burst of emotion may occur. Suddenly we grasp why we have been perplexed: we had not realized that we had cause for grief, for anger, for longing, or perhaps even for pride – which in places such as Sweden is rarely acceptable. Now the appropriate emotion is felt and we cease being depressed. Actually, the linkage that resolves the depression does not even need to become conscious and elicit emotion. At times a depression subsides upon a burst of meaningful action without conscious recognition of why we became depressed or why we now are happily active again. This is particularly likely to be the case when primary process has played an important part in the work of depression, as we shall see in Chapters 11 and 12.

Let us now turn back to our examples to see what we can find there of the work and productive outcome of depression. In the case of biochemist Albert, we do not know in any given instance the detail of his feelings and thoughts at the time when his depressed response subsides. His general description can nonetheless be used to demonstrate what I consider a sequence characteristic of being depressed productively. The change that restores him finally to a satisfactory sense of effective functioning and initiative is either the insight that his problem is insoluble – at least, for the moment – so that he feels free to abandon it, or the insight that the method with which he approached the problem can be replaced by a better one which he now finds promising. Here one should consider whether what he calls "despairing" might be no more than disappointment, that is, the pain of recognizing the discrepancy between an earlier view of the situation and the revised view which the fruitless efforts have forced upon him. Disappointment is likely to be part of his experience, but the total process has to be seen as more complex. The total production of this man shows not only creative imagination, but suggests as well a great deal of perseverance, independent thinking, self-reliance, ambition, and the capacity to be realistic. A person with such characteristics may well become so engrossed in a phase of his work, so set upon trusted, tested techniques of his own, that the possibility of alternative techniques or of a flaw in his basic hypothesis may not get a chance to emerge. Anything that could be useless diversion is screened off effectively. Thus, no alternative approach is readily available for a time when the reality of his getting no results hits home. Hence the paralyzing sense of perplexity or hopelessness which I believe the statement "I despair of it" implies. Disappointment alone would cause sadness or anger rather than this type of perplexity. As a result of despairing, however, his preoccupation with a specific line of thought is relaxed. Consequently, perceptions previously screened off, hypotheses connected with earlier experience, and fresh conclusions can now be integrated in a new plan. In other words, having relinquished his investment in his original approach to the project, Albert can now permit hitherto excluded information to be included in processing.

In this instance, the depressed response is a symptom of a mental effort failing to reach its goal, but it becomes at the same time instrumental in the redirection of effort, whereupon frustration and perplexity cease. Being depressed becomes productive when efforts in the wrong direction are brought to a halt. Then it becomes possible for more realistic goals and methods to emerge.

Psychotherapist Bertha's account gives us more detail of the observable manifestations of the process. Understanding her patients is important to her (*phase 1*). A disturbance in her functioning with patients (*phase 2*) is signalled early by her fleeting thoughts of self-doubt, and her becoming exhausted despite the pleasure and stimulation provided by her writing. But these satisfactions and the commitment to meet her thesis adviser are diverting Bertha from her warning signals. In the meantime, the disturbance deepens. After the consultation, with the immediate pressures of work on her thesis relaxed, the increasing disturbance pushes toward the surface more clearly with the alarm signals of new depressed reactions: loss of involvement in her scientific project, disturbed sleep, a need to withdraw from activities irrelevant to the hidden crisis, such as social and marital contacts, and some other pursuits. There is also a growing awareness (*phase 3*) that something is wrong, but what? Bertha is able to accept her reactions as significant signals and to listen to them (*phase 4*). Attention to them facilitates the gradual emergence of answers to the puzzle (*phase 5*). Finally these answers add up to her grasping what has gone wrong with her therapeutic work.

These two examples show that depressed reactions are not necessarily promoted by the magnitude of a task to which we are applying ourselves, but rather by the experience that some measures we are intent on using now refuse to yield expected results for reasons we vainly struggle to grasp. Bertha didn't know why her efforts to follow her therapy consultant's suggestions led to complications, nor was she aware of the extent to which the deadline for her writing had prevented her from taking appropriate measures to remedy the therapeutic deadlock. This role of frustrated current intent, more than disappointment in a long-term goal, is also illustrated by Jacobson's (1971: 67) example, John, of what she calls a "normal depressed mood."

> This young man is attracted to a girl who shows uncommonly inconsistent behavior toward him. He is upset and moody as long as he believes that there must be a way to win a more consistent response from her, and he tries to adapt his behavior to the task of bringing this about. When he finally recognizes that her behavior toward him is due to a fickle disposition on her part which he cannot change, he loses interest and the irritable, depressed mood disappears.

Depression lifts when it becomes possible to carry out a formerly inhibited next step toward a significant goal, when a more suitable next step is substituted, or when the goal itself is reached or given up so that the intended next step becomes redundant. As long as we experience ourselves as functioning adequately, we are not depressed. This would explain why men like Bettelheim (1960), Frankl (1963), and others who had a secret plan for survival did not succumb to depression in concentration camp. Focusing on one step at a time, such as getting one piece of bread a day, breaking a golden filling out of his own mouth to bribe a guard, concentrating on the psychological patterns of guards to be dealt with, or memorizing a sentence for a future book, could keep a person going. It also explains why many refugees from Hitler's Germany, who prior to persecution and flight had suffered from chronic or frequent depression, and later became depressed again, were free from depression during the period when they had to concentrate their attention on practical measures to establish themselves in the USA. The latter was for the time being their major goal and usually one they were able to reach.

Now we can return to the question whether the basic depressed response should be seen as an affect, or even as an emotion. It seems to me that very often it remains an affective response without awareness of a specific experience. This seems to be the case in Jacobson's example of John. But both Albert and Bertha, and gradually also Carola, were aware of the fact that they were troubled by some inner deadlock or confusion, and of being at a loss to understand it, and perplexed. This, then, has become an emotion.[3]

Chapter four

Influences on the course run by depression

The facilitating environment is necessary, and without it being good *enough* the maturational process weakens or wilts.

Winnicott (1964:123)

The basic depressed response and personality disorder

In response to the thoughts and examples contained in the preceding chapter, colleagues have repeatedly told me that they well recognize my description of depressed episodes in the course of a creative enterprise. They have had such experiences themselves. But some of them doubt that the process I describe could also apply to cases of "severe depression."

I agree that there is a vast difference between the behavior of the people I have described so far and the behavior, including thoughts, feelings, and defenses, of the patients these colleagues have in mind when they raise objections. If we describe severe disturbances in psychological functioning as "depressions" simply because such disturbances tend to promote and maintain frequent or severe episodes of depression, then these objections are justified. By promoting unfavorable circumstances and by impairing judgment, many disturbed behavior patterns do give a person frequent occasion to become depressed and cause the ensuing work of depression to fail. But although they are part of the various clinical pictures referred to as affective disorder or depression, these disturbed behavior patterns themselves are not part of what I describe as the basic depressed response, nor of the process of depression.

Often, when depression is discussed in the literature and case examples are presented with astute observation of human behavior, it is mainly the disturbed behavior patterns of the depressed person that are described in detail, and the life history that caused these patterns to develop. It is less common to describe the specific intrapsychic experience, and its subjective appraisal by the depressed person, which has provoked the basic depressed response at any given time. By many it is taken for granted that the personality structure of a person diagnosed as "depressive" causes him or her to respond with depression to frustrations that can be observed from without. This may be so, but it needn't. The depressed response is evoked by the failure of an effort and the meaning this has for the depressed person. This failure and its meaning may be apparent to an observer, but more often it is due to strivings that are not apparent. In these descriptions, the function which an episode of being depressed actually serves or fails to serve for a person in a given situation is rarely considered. As long as we lack a model of how and why depression tends to come on, how it proceeds, and what it leads to in a normally functioning person, the approach I have just described is understandable, though it is not illuminating. As we saw in Carola's case, it is likely that there is normal cause for *getting* depressed, but what goes wrong is the *work* of depression, which remains unproductive for defensive and other reasons, so that unrealistic goals or methods do not become revised.

Partially productive outcome in severely disturbed personality

In the chapter "Acting out and the urge to betray in paranoid patients," for example, Jacobson (1971) gives us a vivid description of a man whom she describes as brilliant and creative but paranoid.

> Mr V. was a rather extraordinary, but severely paranoid man in his thirties, who suffered from alternating states of hyperactivity and paralyzing depression. When he was in high spirits and in a somewhat grandiose state of mind, this patient would be flooded by numerous new and interesting ideas. He would then start a series of promising enterprises. For such purposes he would establish suitable associations and look for collaborators whom he regarded as "good tools for the execution of my plans." But it was not long before he developed paranoid conflicts with these collaborators. As soon as they failed to live up to his expectations and demands or objected to his provocative behavior, he felt hurt, let down, exploited, and, finally, cheated and persecuted. Sometimes he made sufficient concessions to terminate his project successfully. Under less favorable circumstances, he became so frustrated and enraged at his supposed adversaries that he relinquished the whole project and immediately concentrated on another enterprise in an entirely different field. If problems of a similar nature developed in this project, too, Mr V. became profoundly depressed and retreated completely from all work. Weeks or months later, as he emerged from his depression, new ideas began to spring up in his fertile mind. Then he would embark once more on new daring enterprises, again in different settings. Despite his illness, Mr V.'s achievements in several fields of work had actually been so outstanding that he had already attained prominence and the reputation of being an erratic but exceptionally gifted man. (1971:304)

41

Jacobson then describes very convincingly how unfortunate family relationships in Mr V.'s childhood and adolescence had led to his compulsion to use in work relationships a pattern of intrigue in which he acted out the roles of destructive aggressor and victim at the same time.

Jacobson speaks here of "paranoid depression," but I would prefer to call it depression in a paranoid man. (Others might diagnose him as manic-depressive.) We are given a general picture of his consciously perceived circumstances at the times he became depressed. It appears that they were connected with disappointment when, having alienated his co-workers, he failed to carry out a project. But it does not really become clear what accounts for the differences in his affect on such occasions – why did he get angry at times, why severely depressed at other times? Did he get angry when he felt reasonably assured that the failure could be attributed to others, but depressed when he had doubts and dimly felt responsible himself? At any rate, this does not appear different from what normally causes depression: in all of us the depressed response is touched off by our conscious or unconscious judgment that for reasons we cannot grasp at the time, significant intentions of ours fail to get carried out. The intentions may relate to a creative project or to a wish to communicate effectively with partners in significant relationships. Mr V. had difficulties in forcing his co-workers to follow his bizarre leads and in carrying out his projects without submissive partners.

I repeat, the difference between the arousal of the depressed response in a paranoid man like Mr V. and its arousal in a normally functioning person does not lie in the cause of depression as such – the uncomprehended failure of a specific operation within the self – but only in the choice of goals and methods, and in some of the reasoning that leads to the disquieting conclusion: "Something is amiss, but what?"

Not only was the cause of the depressed response the same in Mr V. as in everyone else. It also seems that, partially, the work of depression served a function for Mr V. insofar as, though only slowly, it led to his finding new ideas to work on and thus restored, despite repeated frustrations and disappointment, the grandiose feelings he needed to become creative. Due to his deeply rooted paranoid patterns and acting out, however, and due to whatever defense he was using, his depressed states failed to facilitate insight into, and changes in, his relationships. To that extent they remained unproductive and he remained prone to become depressed again for the same reasons.

The work of depression can become partly or wholly productive in states of being severely depressed under greatly varying circumstances in greatly varying personalities. In Mr V. serious cognitive and emotional disturbance led to recurrent periods of being severely depressed. He was treated by an experienced psychoanalytic therapist and diagnostician whose description is based on long professional acquaintance with the functioning of his personality.

We can find equally convincing illustrations of my point in the characters of great fiction.

Largely productive outcome of a major life crisis in a vulnerable person

Let us now turn to Potok's description (1972), in the novel *My Name Is Asher Lev*, of the severe crisis in Asher Lev's mother, Rivkeh's life when she loses her only brother, Yaakov. In the course of the novel we also get Asher's detailed introspective account of how his own depressions developed. This shows how intimately Potok is acquainted with cause and process of depression. Therefore, we can rely on the validity of his account when Rivkeh's despair is described from the perspective of an adult son's recollection. From age six Asher has been a witness to his mother's crisis and to her way of coping with it. His knowledge of her early history is presented as limited, but one cannot help drawing a number of conclusions nonetheless.

Rivkeh is the youngest of three children. Her sister is eight years older and a mother of four children at the time of Yaakov's accidental death. Their parents were born in Brooklyn and brought up in the Hasidic congregation to which the Levs belong. They had high status in the congregation. Both were killed in the same car accident when Rivkeh was a young child. While Asher has heard a great deal even from his mother about his father's family history, it is evident that she has hardly spoken of her own. Rivkeh and her sister, Leah, are not close. That Leah does not understand Rivkeh's situation and feelings is evident from their interaction when Leah, who is living in Boston, comes to visit after Yaakov's death.

We know nothing about Rivkeh's experience with her parents. After their death, no close ties have developed with the relatives who took responsibility for the orphans. But Rivkeh and Yaakov, two years her senior, have been very close. Yaakov had the role of teacher and protector all through the years. This may be one of the reasons why Rivkeh could knit a close bond to Asher's father, Aryeh Lev. He was a member of the congregation and seven years her senior. He was an infant when his father was killed by a drunken Russian peasant. Thus, Rivkeh and Aryeh have important features of background and early life history in common.

Rivkeh was married to Aryeh Lev after graduation from her Jewish high school at age eighteen, and gave birth to her only child a year later. She was not able to bear further children. We gather from Asher's description that his mother has no close ties to the relatives the family associates with on holidays. No women friends are mentioned. Little Asher has no playmates other than his mother, who seems to repeat with him the role Yaakov has had in her own life. She is a responsible big sister to her child, an affectionate and obedient wife to her husband, and a conscientious housekeeper. She is deeply religious and very intelligent.

Rivkeh's life, then, is centered on two men of her own generation and her little son. All emotional support she needs to function in this way comes from her husband and her brother. A great deal of her husband's energy and interest, however, she has to share with his devoted work for the Rebbe, the leader of the sect.

As a boy and with his widowed mother Aryeh was brought to the United States by the Rebbe, now the rabbi of his congregation. Under the Rebbe's supervision, Aryeh's education was planned to make him an assistant to the Rebbe in his national and international services to scattered Hasids. Thus he now relates to the Rebbe not only as a religious leader but also as an awesome father figure. Traveling for the Rebbe, Aryeh is away from home a great deal. But Yaakov, living near his sister, visits several times a week. He cheers mother and child with songs and pleasant conversation. He has begun to travel for the Rebbe, too, but is mainly attending graduate school to become a university teacher of Russian affairs. He is out of town on a mission for the Rebbe when he is killed in a car accident, twenty-seven years old.

To the news of Yaakov's death Rivkeh reacts with continuous screaming until the Rebbe enters the apartment. She is taken to a hospital. She returns home after about a week, skeleton-like in the eyes of her child and completely withdrawn. At first she remains secluded in bed. Then she starts wandering about the apartment in her nightgown, unkempt and without the customary wig. She hardly eats and drinks. She starts smoking. Soon she smokes excessively, scattering ashes about the apartment. She is oblivious of her child, her husband, and the newly hired housekeeper, avoiding them all. She also avoids visitors. She sleeps a great deal or lies in bed in a stupor. She is heard talking to herself directing imploring words at Yaakov in a childlike tone. Later, she also mumbles pleas to God and sings an occasional psalm. After some time she begins to sing as with Yaakov's voice and in his manner.

During the early weeks of her stupor she becomes aware of Asher only once. She urges him to paint pretty things. Then she immediately withdraws into herself again, unaware of the child's reply. When Asher comes to her a few days later with a colorful picture he has drawn for her she stares at him unrecognizing. Many weeks pass before Rivkeh for the first time asks Asher whether he is well taken care of, but again her attention span is too short to hear the answer.

Then her contact with the environment begins to improve. She shows some appetite and gains some weight. Some color returns to her cheeks, she keeps herself clean and wears pretty wigs again. She joins her husband and child for their meals. Asher overhears some of her fragmentary conversations with her husband, whom she reminds of his having taught her that it is not right for things begun in God's honor to remain unfinished. It is obvious that she is struggling with thoughts and plans she is not yet ready to disclose. Then, one evening more than four months after her bereavement she emerges from seclusion in her bedroom and demands a talk with her husband in Asher's presence. Shortly but succinctly she declares that Yaakov is dead but that it is wrong to let his work remain unfinished. She wants to enter Brooklyn College in September to take the same course of study Yaakov has pursued. Asher will be attending school by then. She wants to call the college the next morning. Aryeh asks her to wait another day. Rivkeh understands that Aryeh wants to talk to the Rebbe first. With a brief outburst of anger at the Rebbe, she expresses the doubt that he will give permission. Yet, he does.

After that, Rivkeh returns to relatively normal functioning although she does not quite become her former self. She never becomes Asher's happy companion again. She remains anxious and irritable in response to her husband's travels. She is forever in terror of losing him or Asher through an accident. She is an excellent student but overexerts herself with her homework. Asher is left to his own devices. Rivkeh does not relinquish her studies when Asher becomes an increasingly depressed child and when friction develops between father and child.

When four years later Aryeh accepts the assignment to develop new congregations in Europe with headquarters in Vienna, Asher, ten years old and emotionally disturbed, refuses flatly to move to Vienna. It becomes apparent that he would become mentally ill if he were forced to move. The Rebbe decrees that Asher must be kept in Brooklyn. Because of his condition Rivkeh decides against placing Asher with his paternal uncle and for letting her husband travel in Europe alone. Perhaps she also wants to complete her studies. But she misses Aryeh very much. Whenever there is an interruption for some weeks in the arrival of his regular letters, she assumes, correctly, that he is on a secret mission behind the Iron Curtain, and she becomes extremely tense. If Asher comes home an hour late she bursts into angry reproaches. Then she locks herself into her bedroom where Asher may hear her talking to Yaakov. The next morning she apologizes.

It is not difficult to understand the severity of Rivkeh's reaction to her bereavement. With Yaakov she loses not only a beloved brother. She loses a mother and father all over again. She loses the only person with whom she shares significant memories from her childhood and early youth. She loses an important part of her existence. It is likely that as a child she had no adult to help her express and understand her grief, anger, and possibly guilt, at the loss of her parents. The close relationship with her brother is likely to have diverted her from such reactions without helping her to resolve them. Now, all this breaks open again, and again there is no one to help her. The only trusted adult left to her, Aryeh, is very limited in his ability to express his own feelings or to listen to those others try to express. He tends to change the subject instead. But even if he could bear to listen, Rivkeh's life has not helped her become articulate about feelings, either. She has been patient and submissive, not in touch with feelings of anger and protest in herself. After the first shock of her bereavement to which she reacted with helpless screaming, she surrenders to the pressures exerted on her by her environment. Her screaming is replaced by a state of stupor, and when she is not in a stupor she cries easily. Often she needs to withdraw completely.

Not knowing what Rivkeh is thought to experience subjectively it is difficult to draw a line here between grief and the depressed response, but quite early there is evidently both. She is pining for Yaakov. There is the mourning work to be done of recognizing the irrevocability of the loss and the necessity to adapt to it. But how can she do it? Until her bereavement she has obeyed the demands her society and family have made on her. For reasons we can see, but she herself can hardly grasp, she is ill equipped to return, as is expected of her, to her usual wifely and motherly duties. She is left to her own devices to understand what has happened to her capacity to adapt to the expectations others have of her, or to her own. Her grief, anger, and fear are too overwhelming. She feels like a totally helpless, disoriented child. Her incomprehensible and unacceptable helplessness to act as she no doubt expects of herself can be seen as continuously eliciting the basic depressed response. This, in combination with her overwhelming grief and suppressed anger, produces a prolonged disturbance that some may diagnose as a severe state of depression, others as pathological mourning.

Rivkeh's crisis is severe. Her mourning and her depression have pathological features. But if one considers the unfavorable circumstances of her past and present life it becomes apparent that her mourning work and her work of depression are slowly progressing toward an adaptation, none the less. Within less than a month, when she begins to sing in her brother's manner, she is on the only road open to her to adapt to Yaakov's disappearance from her daily life: identification with him in his professional calling. The only close and supportive relationship with a living adult now available to her is that with her husband. But he is often unavailable and frequently in danger. Her plan provides a mode of emotional survival. The intellectual tasks and human contacts connected with the course of study are likely to meet some of the needs her husband cannot satisfy and to divert her from too much protest and anguish. Moreover, it offers her the only sense of closeness to Yaakov in daily living that is still available. These aspects of her decision are not likely to reach her awareness.

As will become clearer through the differentiation in Chapter 6 of grief from the depressed response, this solution can be seen as an outcome of both the work of grief and the work of depression. When in her decision to enter college Rivkeh finds a compromise between her need of Yaakov and her need to function as a wife and – in a limited way – as a mother, the paralyzing aspects of her depression subside. A persistent milder depressed mood and occasional brief recurrence of other symptoms subside only years later, when Asher's increasing independence and emotional strength lessens the conflict between her wishing to satisfy his needs and those of his father; this has been a conflict beyond her power to solve, but apparently she feels she ought to solve it. Her tacit wish to complete her studies has complicated her situation further by causing suppressed anger and guilt. Only when she has completed them and can leave the adolescent Asher with relatives in Brooklyn and in a satisfying relationship with his art teacher can she at last live with Aryeh in Europe in a close union as an equal partner, and accompany him on his travels. At that point the mild depressed mood and occasional symptoms disappear.

Significance of benign conditions

The depressed response diverts our attention from many events and causes us, consciously or unconsciously, to focus on specific difficulties. With the help of this restriction of our attention we have a better opportunity than otherwise to penetrate the nature of our difficulty, so that we may resolve it.

Yet, the effectiveness of the work of depression is dependent on many factors. A comparison of my last two examples (Mr V. and Rivkeh Lev) with the first two (biochemist Albert and psychotherapist Bertha) suggests that productive outcome will occur only when conditions are benign. In this respect being depressed proceeds similarly to grieving after a loss, which will take the favorable course described by Freud (1917) only under the benign conditions of mature personality and satisfactory, stable circumstances. For the process of depression to lead to a resolution of the precipitating difficulty it appears important that we respect the signal from within as meaningful. It is further important that our self-respect should not be threatened to any extent by the mere fact of our depressed reactions. We do not develop reactions that go beyond grieving, being discouraged, or disappointed for tangible reasons, unless efforts to approach some significant goal are falling for reasons beyond our immediate comprehension. If, in addition to experiencing the perplexing discomfort of the depressed response, we were to become tortured by self-reproach, shame, guilt, or anxiety about *being* depressed; unable to accept our reaction as meaningful; and unwilling to listen to its message – then the task of exploring the nature of the crisis and resolving it by new insights would become much more difficult.

An essentially tolerant attitude toward our own reactions helps us make progress in the largely unconscious processing of data that pertain to the deadlock and its potential resolution. Such processing may involve revision and reorganization of many plans, hopes, and apprehensions, and a review of those memories and facts we find relevant. Since the resolution of a period of depression always involves some change, it is important that our thinking be open to a revision of attitudes, that we can abandon strivings, allow an emotional tie to loosen or become tighter. "Depression coming on, continuing and lifting indicates that the ego structure has held over a period of crisis. It is a triumph

47

of integration" (Winnicott 1964:125). In other words, we need the same emotional equipment that Parkes (1972) finds necessary for successful adaptation after a major bereavement. In the latter case our equilibrium is disrupted by the consequences of a significant change in our environment. When we react with the basic depressed response, our equilibrium is disrupted by an unexpected or uncomprehended necessity of changing the direction of a significant effort of our own, or the method we are using to implement our intention. Overcoming the disruption requires in both types of experience the capacity to tolerate change.

One can say that the process of depression, like that of any other affect, is a form of communication, partly to the self about the self and our perception of others; partly to others about our view of them and of ourselves. As, for instance, in Rivkeh Lev's case during the early months of her mourning, the depressed response is precipitated by a perception of insufficient intrapsychic or interpersonal communication. Rivkeh is suddenly deprived of the possibility to talk with her brother while his death makes that need more urgent than ever. She does not understand why this situation should be quite as painful and paralyzing and has no one else to whom to describe this and complain. She finally resorts to talking to him in the manner of her childhood crisis, although now she cannot get an answer.

The capacity for a ready flow of communication within the self not only aids our communication with those around us, but it also tends to reduce causes for, and facilitate productive outcome of, depression. Research into mourning has shown that the capacity as well as the opportunity to confide in a sympathetic listener is invaluable to the mourner in his labors to adapt to the consequences of his loss (Parkes 1972). The same is true for depression, as Brown and Harris document (1978). If we have access during an episode of depression to one or more sympathetic listeners we can obtain their support and guidance in our bewilderment and also use them as sounding boards. Fresh considerations stimulated by what we hear ourselves saying in a dialogue may be as important to the ongoing work of depression as the stimulation that comes from another's comment or question.

Thus, the capacity to trust people, confide our experience to them, and consider their response freely tends to aid productive outcome of depression. Alternatively, the capacity to express ourselves in writing, pictorial means or sculpture, in music and creative dance, or acting, to an actual or imagined audience can also assist our information processing. This becomes very clear in Potok's description of Asher Lev. Trust in the validity of our communication is of great help in resolving a deadlock causing depression.

In my first examples, Albert and Bertha, both persons had sufficient self-reliance to accept the validity of their mood. Both had relationships that made it possible to confide an acute problem to a trusted person with the expectation of a sympathetic hearing, perhaps a helpful question or suggestion. Both were sufficiently rooted in their network of life so that the risk of failing with the problem at hand did not entail a threat of personal or social catastrophe. Both were free from major psychological or physical handicap, free from acute psychological trauma or somatic illness, independent of threatening or inconsistent social pressures, and living in a reasonably familiar social setting. Neither their physical nor their psychological resources were overtaxed by the learning they had to tackle.

Circumstances likely to prevent productive outcome

When, as is so frequent in our society, a person's work of depression remains partly or totally unproductive for a long time I hold that he or she has been and realistically is overtaxed in the capacity to understand and meet some of the demands made on him or her. Early experiences in family relations or the impact of other life circumstances may, despite a person's adequate or rich endowment, have blocked certain intrapsychic and interpersonal patterns of communication that would be necessary for the understanding and resolution of a breakdown in functioning. As in Rivkch's case, childhood traumata and deprivations may have delayed parts of her maturation that would have been necessary for her understanding, accepting, and communicating the nature of her despair. Or the attitudes and needs of persons in the immediate environment may also, as in her case, constitute a threat to successful information processing. Of Mr V.'s current social network we know nothing, but the handicap to adequate work of depression in his personality is obvious inasmuch as he is tied to stereotyped reasoning and compulsive acting out. Alternatively, a person's total endowment – mental and physical – may not qualify him or her to master the complexity of a current problem and to grasp why this should be so. Social and cultural inconsistencies, or rapid changes in the environment, may also have an unfavorable effect on cognition and flexibility. Acute somatic illness or some other physiological process (as, for instance, rapid ageing) may also interfere with the growth and learning that the depressed response might otherwise facilitate. Finally, other genetic factors than mental endowment may affect a person's capacity for productive work of depression, but physiological and genetic aspects will not be emphasized in this book. Genetic factors differ from individual to individual, but whether they become significant depends on the environment in which the personality develops.

Despite the arguments presented so far, readers who have not themselves experienced the pain and anguish that can be hiding behind the apparent cause for getting depressed, nor the clinical experience of seeing this pain and anguish emerge in others during their therapy, may at this point ask: if this thesis about the function and work of getting depressed is correct, if getting depressed is not caused by purely physiological processes, then why do so many people fail to avail themselves successfully of its adaptive function? They fail because too much fear, shame, and guilt has from earliest childhood on become attached to some very significant natural impulses and feelings of theirs. The misconceptions and anxieties involved in having to ward off such impulses and feelings have inhibited their capacity for realistic self-exploration. Therefore, they fear that admitting to themselves or others what they really want and feel would cause intolerable guilt, shame, or other disaster. I hope that my Chapters 8 and 9, as well as Parts II and III, will bring this to life.

Chapter five

Depression as affect, emotion, pattern of emotion, or syndrome

... disease theory is derived from a theory of normal biological functioning.

Wing *et al.* (1974:3)

Tomkins and Izard on categories of affect and emotion

We need now to differentiate the basic depressed response as an affect or emotion from patterns of emotion and from syndromes called depression.

In his important work on affects, Tomkins has presented the "positive affects" (1962) as interest-excitement, enjoyment-joy, and surprise-startle. The "negative affects" (1963) are presented as distress-anguish, shame-humiliation, contempt-disgust, anger-rage, and fear-terror. He sees the face as "the primary site of the affects" (1962:204) and, following Darwin, describes how each of these affects has its universal and generally recognized characteristics of facial expression and posture.

Tomkins considers (1963:126) depression as "a syndrome of shame and distress, which also reduces the general amplification of all impulses." It arises (1963:497) when shame becomes so intense and protracted that a vicious circle develops between increasing shame and depressed mood.[1]

Izard, except for omitting "startle" and substituting for the term "primary affects" the term "fundamental emotions" or alternatively "discrete emotions," discusses (1972) his discrete emotions theory in keeping with Tomkins's observations. His discrete emotions are: interest, surprise, joy, distress, anger, disgust, contempt, shame (shyness, guilt), and fear.[2] He points out (1972:9), however, that "a particular single emotion in isolation from other emotions is rarely obtained in the laboratory, and when it is obtained it probably does not remain the only emotion for very long." Nevertheless, Izard finds his view confirmed by the results of research projects that have identified specific neurophysiological and biochemical characteristics in the case of each of his fundamental emotions, but not in "depression" or anxiety.[3]

I am acquainted only with a limited number of reports of extensive neurophysiological and biochemical research on syndromes called depression, and am not competent to evaluate their validity. It is my impression, however, that research has been concentrating on behavior appearing in complex syndromes of depression, or on reactions to loss referred to as depression, rather than on the *affect* of depression, so that there are no generally accepted findings available as yet. Most researchers appear to proceed as Klerman does (1973:69–70) when he defines normal depression as "sadness, disappointment, or discouragement" prototypically occurring "after separation, loss or bereavement ... especially during those vicissitudes that accompany changes in the relationship between man and his social environment (Freud 1917; Lindemann 1944)."[4] As will become apparent further on, I find this definition applicable only to normal grief or normal mourning (which may but need not encompass a phase of being depressed), but neither to the basic depressed response in itself, nor to the adaptive process it normally initiates and facilitates.

I believe that findings concerning neurophysiological and biochemical aspects of the basic depressed response when functioning adaptively can be conclusive only when the response is not blended with the intense emotional and cognitive disturbances that are part of affective disorders, of syndromes called depression. Thus, one would have to study the depressed response in normally well-functioning and creative persons like my examples Albert, Bertha, and – later in this chapter – Eric, who do not require therapy for the resolution of the hidden deadlock.

The same holds for psychological research. The basic depressed response is not elicited directly by stress as such, but only by the failure of an effort to cope with a situation that may or may not be related to stressful events observable by others. This absence of direct correlation between observable stress and depression I find supported by the results of a study at the National Institute of Mental Health (NIMH) reported by Leff *et al.* (1970). They find in the study of forty severely depressed patients that it may take months of frequent psychotherapeutic interviews with the patient and his or her significant other to establish what stressful events *preceded* the onset of the breakdown. Even so, the authors emphasize, it is not the sequence of stressful events themselves, but the *meaning* they have for the patient *on the basis of the patient's life experience, vulnerability, and interpretation of events*, that appears to bring on the syndrome called depression. Also, their discussion as well as their seven case examples demonstrate that the onset of being severely depressed following the last of several stressful events was clearly related to the patient's loss of sexual and/or occupational self-image, and/or to the patient's reaction, when failing to adapt to a significant change. In other words, it followed a devastating deterioration of the self-image when failing to live up to the ideal self. This was also presented as a core feature in the dynamics of twelve manic-depressive patients described by Cohen *et al.* (1954, reprinted in Frieda Fromm-Reichmann 1959).

We also see that, in depression described as severe, psychotic, and endogenous, the patient reacts with getting depressed to what *normally* tends to activate the depressed response.

Furthermore, I would stress that without a model for normal depression as distinct from normal grief, it is difficult to construct a relevant self-report-scale and formulate instructions to research subjects that will prevent confusion between a mixture of other painful feelings and genuine depressed reactions. Nor is it uncommon to confuse the personality of the depression-prone person with being depressed as a basic affect and process. It is my impression that some such confusion has entered the otherwise carefully designed study by Izard (1972:241ff.) to validate his position, that depression is not a fundamental affect but always a pattern of emotions consisting of distress (sadness, disappointment, and dejection), anger, disgust, contempt, fear, guilt, and shyness (1972:257).[5] I certainly agree with Izard that in pathological syndromes of depression there is usually a blend of grief, anger, guilt, and fear along with important other symptoms and disturbances, and that such a blend is not a discrete affect. I only hold that as a rule this unhappy mixture of emotions and other symptoms will *promote dysfunction*, activating the affect I have described as the basic depressed response, and at the same time interfere with its serving an adaptive function (see Chapter 9).[6]

The issue of conflict and guilt as integral parts of depression

As we have seen, many analysts refer to depression as an affect. But many other scholars tend, as does Izard, to consider guilt over repressed anger an integral part of depression, in which case the latter is no longer one affect, but a pattern of affects. Some hold that it is invariably evoked by an unconscious conflict that remains unresolved.[7] Actually, unresolved conflicts are present in most instances of prolonged or recurring *syndromes* of depression, but are they part of the affect or process of depression? These questions deserve consideration.

The affects of anger or guilt, although seen by these scholars as inherent components of all depression, certainly do not as such slow us down or cause listlessness, as being depressed does. Rather, when these emotions reach awareness they activate us in various ways. Only their failing to become conscious promotes depressed reactions. Conflict, on the other hand, immobilizes us even when it is conscious, and it does so in ways that seem similar to the slowing down of depression. Conflict resembles depression also in the feelings of helplessness and hopelessness each can create.

Let us bear in mind, however, that we ourselves tend to describe our state of mind as a depression mainly when we find – together with at least some general slowing down, some withdrawal from activities, and emotional involvement – a perplexing sense of not knowing what is wrong with us, and some physiological disturbance. A conscious conflict also absorbs our attention and may therefore prevent us from engaging in some usual activity. But this does not cause the other symptoms, and we are unlikely to describe this unpleasant experience as a depression. When we are conscious of opposing impulses or mutually exclusive wishes we resolve the deadlock by actively seeking further information and weighing various aspects of the situation against each other until we become able to make a choice. If we are unable to seek a solution in this way, some psychological difficulty other than the conscious conflict is at work at the same time.

To disguise identity I am in the following example blending data from two different histories.

Let us consider a very serious conflict. During a war, a married young woman, Daisy, receives the news that her husband is missing in action. She keeps hoping and waiting. Two years later she is informed that on the basis of testimony her husband has been declared dead although his body could not be recovered. The couple were married two years before he was called into active military service and although as yet they did not have children they had hoped to have children later on.

Daisy mourns deeply for a long time, with phases of mild depression, and can never quite relinquish the hope that her husband might still be alive. Yet, as years pass by, the desire to have children wins the upper hand. She remarries, although she does not get as deeply attached to her second husband as to the first. Her new husband is devoted to her and to the children, who are one and three years old when her first husband returns. The latter had been seriously wounded and then kept a prisoner of war in a remote area. He is an invalid now but his mother is alive and ready to take care of him. During her second marriage his former wife has at times both wished and feared that he might reappear. Thus, the current conflict does not catch her entirely unprepared. She is overwhelmed by grief and by anger at the authorities for having discontinued the search for her first husband and misinformed her. At first she is plagued by anxiety, not knowing what to do and how she will be able to live with whatever decision she will reach. In the end she decides to stay with the father of her children.

From my experience with people in situations of conflict resembling this, a woman having to choose between two men under difficult circumstances need not respond with a disabling depression in addition to grief, anger, guilt, and anxiety, unless she is prone to respond with depression to heavy demands. Otherwise, depressed features during this crisis will not correspond in magnitude to her anguish and mental pain. Some phases of mild depression will occur at points when she does not yet have a grasp of all aspects that need to be considered, so that she finds herself not making progress toward a decision. In a case like Daisy's, some factors will be in favor of her rejoining her first husband: his past and present plight, their past close tie, and a sense of guilt at having remarried and experienced happiness and security while he was alone and miserable. But their totally different life experience since their separation

54

will have created an alienation which will be a heavy weight against a remarriage, and so will the man's recognition of his poor economic and personal capacity to function as a husband and father. Most decisive for staying in her second marriage will probably be her awareness of her children's needs, her loyalty and gratitude toward their father, and what they have in common as parents and in everyday life. Her grief and some guilt feelings will long outlive her anger and her anxiety, but she will function in her family relations and her work without prolonged and disabling depression.

It is not conflict as such that causes us to get depressed, but only its remaining unconscious and therefore inaccessible for pertinent new information that could facilitate a choice. In instances where unconscious conflict causes depression, the depression will lift when the conflict has become conscious so that it can be resolved, or accepted as unavoidable. In a given episode of depression the existence of some conflict can be a minor feature while another feature is the major cause of being depressed.

Here is a simple example from creative activity. A novelist, Eric, is suddenly unable to go on with his writing. So far he has had a clear vision of his plot and of his characters. Then he runs into an unexpected difficulty. However he tries to describe a certain meeting between two characters, the description does not ring true to him and leaves him dissatisfied, nor does he find himself able to let this scene rest for a while and work on another. After repeated efforts he gets discouraged and depressed, beginning to doubt whether he is adequate to the task of conveying the major message he has in mind with his novel. Ready to give up he puts his manuscript aside in distress. A week later, on a long walk, when he is still depressed, the scenery and lighting evoke memories of an experience he has not thought of for many years. After dwelling on this experience for a while, his mind shifts back to his novel. Suddenly Eric recognizes that there is indeed a misfit between one of his characters and the role in which he has tried to cast him in the scene he has failed to make plausible. Now he sees the link that has been missing and how he must revise the life history and the actions of one character. This involves a good deal of rewriting, but the deadlock is removed and confidence has returned.

It is true that some conflict can be thought to have delayed the author's remembrance of the crucial personal experience and thus delayed the illuminating insight which resolved his depression, but even without conflict we cannot remember at all times everything that has long since lost significance unless some current situation makes it regain significance. The major issue in such a situation seems to be that the author, though dimly sensing that something in his creative endeavor has gone wrong, is at first unable to grasp just what is amiss. Once he grasps his mistake and, consequently, can correct it, the depression is gone.

Patterns of emotion: attachment behavior, mourning

In theory, it is easy to differentiate various affects and emotions according to their apparent facial expression, or alternatively to their cause and function, along with their typical physiological symptoms. In actual life, however, the pleasures and stresses we experience are so complex that we rarely respond to them with only one single emotion at a time, although one may dominate. We may get angry, and feel anxious and helpless as well. We may feel grief, guilt, and shame, and so forth, in many combinations of both unpleasant and pleasant feelings. Certain situations bring on typical combinations, such as the behavior pattern Bowlby has described as "attachment behavior," which involves the combination of love, fear, anxiety, grief, and anger. This pattern, which he describes in detail (1969), serves the function of maintaining proximity to an attachment figure, or recovering proximity after a separation. I find that tenderness actually serves a related function. It contributes to maintaining proximity not only to attachment figures – persons to protect us and give care to us – but also to persons whose attachment figures we are or would wish to be. The cause of tender feelings is the judgment that someone is suitable for the joys of proximity, while the cause of attachment behavior is actual or anticipated loss.

Although it can no longer serve its function, attachment behavior appears even at the time of permanent loss. Then further emotional responses appear in addition to those of attachment behavior in the process of adapting to the painful change. This even more complex pattern is the state of mourning. When I speak of "mourning," I mean the entire laborious process of adaptation necessitated by a major loss or change. As Bowlby (1961) and Parkes (1972) have shown, such a loss tends to touch off in us the entire pattern of attachment behavior – grief, anger, despair, and the urge (Parkes 1972) to search and recover. At the time when the mourner begins to face, consciously or unconsciously, the necessity to go on without the familiar way of life, the inner structure of the personality, organized around that way of life, begins to dissolve, with the result that the depressed response appears and remains activated until the mourner's functioning is restructured in a way suited to the new life circumstances. Bowlby calls this the phase of disintegration and reintegration (1961:334), which he views as adaptive processes. In the course of the total process many mourners respond to their loss also with guilt, others with anxiety. The process of mourning, then, involves a complex but typical pattern of discrete emotions, with each component having none the less its own cause and its own function in coping with separate aspects of a loss or of another distressing major change.

To give an example, I have repeatedly had occasion to observe the impact on his or her parents of a young person's suicide. In the following, a real history is again disguised by features from two similar ones.

This is a mother whose gifted, nineteen-year-old daughter has committed suicide while away from home at college. She knows that the girl went to the student health service of the college and, without giving a history, asked to be admitted to a psychiatric ward because of depression and fear of suicide. She was sent home with some medication and took her life that night. She left no explanatory farewell note, nor do her friends understand her actions. Its motive remains obscure despite efforts to find out.

The relationship between the mother and this daughter has been particularly affectionate and stimulating to both. The mother is stricken with grief. Some of the interests she had in common with this daughter were not shared by the rest of the family, nor does she feel that anyone else in the family needs her quite as this daughter did. She realizes that the child has long had emotional problems and at times she has been concerned about her adjustment, but for more than a year now the girl has appeared more stable than ever before. Thus, her suicide has caught both parents unprepared. Both parents are angry at the physician who failed to admit their daughter to a psychiatric ward. At times, the mother feels intense anger at her daughter for not having turned to her parents for help and for having hurt the entire family by taking her life. At the same time she feels that her preoccupation during most of that year with her own aged mother's terminal illness may have kept her from being sufficiently alert to possible covert messages in her daughter's remarks when they met. Perhaps she could have prevented the suicide if she had not been so preoccupied. This causes guilt. She makes repeated efforts to get information from her daughter's friends. This is a search for better understanding that could restore the currently disrupted sense of closeness to this daughter. She is at the same time very concerned about the impact of the dramatic loss on her husband and the other children, particularly the youngest, a girl who was very attached to this five-year-older sister and tended to emulate her attitudes. This causes the mother a good deal of anxiety. Might she fail with the youngest also, will she prove to be a much less adequate mother than she thought she was? Has her husband perhaps been less sensitive as a father than she thought, or could her youngest be more vulnerable than she knew?

Obviously, such an event would cause a difficult, prolonged process of mourning in a mother. Her grief may never end entirely but rather keep recurring time and again although with diminished intensity and frequency.[8] Yet, the effort to escape its pain will serve a function by forcing her to redistribute her affectionate attention and to remodel some of her interests. Her anger will forcefully remind her that there are factors in a child's personality and life over which a parent has no control. This may serve the function of protecting her from excessive guilt. Both her guilt and anxiety, on the other hand, may alert her to her husband's and her children's acute needs in the current family crisis, and this creates motivation for not losing herself completely in her own grief. She will also be depressed at times, but to its cause and function in such a case I will return in the next chapter. The symptoms of her grief, anxiety, depression, and guilt will at the same time alert her husband, her relatives, her friends, and her children to her need for understanding, patience, and sympathy.

Syndromes as against patterns of emotion

In Webster's *Ninth New Collegiate Dictionary* (1985:1197), the meaning of "syndrome" is listed as: "1: a group of signs and symptoms that occur together and characterize a particular abnormality   2: a set of concurrent things (as emotions or actions) that usually form an identifiable pattern." Inasmuch as the second of these meanings is well covered by Izard's term "pattern of emotions,"[9] I use "syndrome" according to the first definition, even though in the professional literature both meanings are used interchangeably. In other words, I use it to describe a combination of normal affective responses or normal patterns of emotion with affective, emotional, and cognitive responses that are disturbed and excessive, and possibly accompanied by somatic difficulties beyond normal affective symptoms.[10]

Generally, when the term "depression" or "state of depression" is used in psychiatric, psychological, or psychoanalytic literature, this means a syndrome, including excessive components of the basic depressed response, along with grief, anger, anxiety, guilt feelings, hopelessness, and helplessness, often the shame inherent in loss of self-esteem, cognitive disturbances, and other symptoms in varying combinations.

In the syndromes called "depression" we find a great deal of psychological, and at times also physiological, dysfunction. When this dysfunction becomes sufficiently alarming, the basic depressed response will appear as a normal attempt to cope, although, due to the magnitude of the dysfunction and the various psychological handicaps precluding successful work of depression, it may be doomed to fail in its function, so that the depressed reactions persist and become exaggerated. Such handicaps will be described in Chapter 9. Becoming depressed and staying depressed in these circumstances I consider normal. What goes far beyond normal limits in these instances is usually the emotional and cognitive disturbance. Nonetheless, it is necessary to bear in mind that the severity of the symptoms must be considered in the light of the provoking social circumstances in order to determine whether and to what extent they should be seen as pathological.[11]

In closing this chapter, I briefly return to the issue of confusion between symptoms related to a patient's personality patterns and those related to his getting depressed. Perhaps, the accurate and comprehensive perceptions inherent in many schedules for the measurement and classification of syndromes called "depression"[12] will yield new answers when the symptoms, both psychological and physiological, can be organized in relation to the following questions:

1 What in the depressed patient's behavior characterizes a *person* who is prevented by various cognitive and emotional patterns from relating to self and others in a realistic and adaptive way, and is therefore depression-prone?

2 What in the patient's behavior is a normal though unconscious *effort* of that person to remedy a perplexing failure to function, although due to the person's cognitive and emotional handicaps this remedial effort is partly or totally failing?

3 What in all this are powerful affects or emotions *other* than the depressed response which appear simultaneously but for different reasons; possibly emotions that contributed to the dysfunction which became traumatically perplexing and required the withdrawal facilitated by the depressed response?

Means to differentiate symptoms in such a way will not be found easily, but to ask the questions may none the less pay off in the long run. Perhaps if such differentiation becomes possible we will find that what holds these many diverse symptoms together in one diagnostic category is a normal attempt at self-healing that fails to become productive.

Chapter six

The depressed response compared with other affects

A: Grief, anxiety, depression, and anger in loss, change, or isolation

---

... depression is not the same as the mourning process – it may be seen in varied mourning processes, but not in all and not at all times.

Pollock (1978:272)

... when an individual is confident that an attachment figure will be available to him whenever he desires it, that person will be much less prone to either intense or chronic fear than will an individual who for any reason has no such confidence.

Bowlby (1973:202)

Approach to the topic and its semantic difficulty

In the context of this chapter we need to keep in mind my concept of the basic depressed response outlined in Chapter 3: the role of its affective components, the conscious and unconscious appraisal that elicits it, the adaptive function that it normally can serve, and the information process necessary for this productive outcome. Now we can turn to the differentiation of this response from other emotions, although some of them – particularly grief, anxiety and fear, shame, guilt, hopelessness, helplessness, and anger – may appear simultaneously or otherwise in close connection with being depressed. In Chapter 9 I will describe how in depression-prone personality disturbed cognitive and emotional patterns of response interfere with the remedial information processing that otherwise the depressed response would facilitate. Because the physiological expressions of various affects overlap – as, for instance, disturbance of sleep in grief, anxiety, and being depressed; or crying in grief, shame, anxiety, physical pain, or sudden relief of tension – the differences between affects have to be determined on other grounds.

In recent decades comprehensive studies of emotions in general, and of grief, anger, anxiety, shame, guilt, and loneliness in particular, have been published. In this and the next chapter, these particular emotions will be considered only to the extent that this appears necessary for showing how I differentiate them from the affective response of getting and remaining depressed. The focus will be on painful emotions in relatively normal behavior patterns. I say "relatively," because I see no difference between normal and pathological emotional responses in kind, only in quantity, quality, and defensive distortions or substitutions. Grief and loneliness in this chapter, and shame in the next, will be given much more space in my differentiation of emotions than anxiety, guilt, and anger. This has two reasons. First, guilt, anger, and anxiety have been treated more fully in the literature and much earlier than grief, loneliness, and shame. Second, the latter are the most difficult emotions to differentiate from the depressed response, partly but not exclusively because problems in coping with them so often lead to getting depressed.

Responses that adult observers tend to interpret as grief, angry protest, and anxiety, particularly in connection with separation from the attachment figure (usually, but not necessarily, the mother), appear to develop during the first year of life while, as far as we can observe, the development of shame and guilt becomes apparent somewhat later. This is one of the two reasons for beginning my comparison with the discussion of grief, anxiety, and anger in response to separation and loss. The other reason is that grief as well as anxiety are frequently confused with being depressed by grievers, depressed or anxious persons, and their observers alike.

I shall not try in this context to discuss different concepts of emotions used by authors in various disciplines, important as they are.[1] My differentiation remains on a descriptive level and is focused on the subjective experience of emotional responses that can or do reach awareness. This means using everyday language and struggling with the semantic difficulties this entails.

Western languages are rich in words referring to different shades and combinations of emotional experience. Each culture and subculture tends to focus on and emphasize in its language different aspects of emotional responses. Thus, our choice of words in differentiating the quality of feeling and in conceptualizing it is bound to be somewhat arbitrary even when there is essential agreement on theory. All of us have our individual preferences for the words that to our mind best describe a certain emotional experience, a certain composite of discrete affects. We have no agreement as yet on whether, for instance, the word "sadness" implies normal depression, or whether it describes the mildest form in a progression from sadness over sorrow or grief to despair. All we can do is to state as best we can what we mean by our own descriptive words. I shall try to do so as I go along.

Emotions in social adaptation

Hinde demonstrates (1974) that in animals who live in social groups, cohesion of the group, although affected by power dominance, is primarily maintained by the dynamics between two forces: the attraction between certain animals, and at the same time their need for keeping distance to avoid aggression. Between different species, these patterns of attraction and repulsion vary, but always exist in some form. They also vary, within the same species, according to varieties of attraction and repulsion between different categories, such as sex, age, having a mate, having offspring, and so on. The compromise reached between these conflicting tendencies makes the group cohesive, be that a pair, a family, a troop, or herd.

This conflict of tendencies is operative between humans as well. A proper balance between intimacy and privacy, between closeness and distance is of the essence in our achieving satisfactory personal relationships and secure functioning in groups. As Hall (1966) demonstrates, what is too close or too distant varies according to culture and sub-culture. Each culture tends to develop in its members patterns of behavior in keeping with a characteristic appraisal of what is close enough, too close, or too far for comfort. This appraisal stems from where the limits are learned to be running between self and not-self, and consequently, from which point on bodily or psychological contact is felt to become intrusive. Although members of several western nations tend to need considerable space around their person to feel at ease in their housing or their dealings with other persons, members of certain other nations or cultures feel at ease in what would distress some of us as extremely crowded conditions.

In order to develop our innate disposition for both intimacy and distance and for identification and separateness; in order to develop our other potentials and to mature and thrive in life, we do not only need adequate nourishment, shelter, and sexual satisfaction, but also secure and durable attachments to individuals and stable participation in groups. We need stimulation and protection against overstimulation. We need a chance to exercise our physical and mental faculties in play and work, with a balance between freedom and protection. We need the information necessary for understanding ourselves and our human and material environment. We need values, aims, and hopes to guide our decisions. In other words, we are engaged from birth to death in intricate patterns of interaction with the world around us. To manage this we need an opportunity to develop a secure identity, a clear-cut view of ourselves as compared with our view of others. The development of such an identity requires during our formative years the opportunity for communication adequate to our level of development, sufficient stability to minimize the effects of painful changes, and the necessary flexibility on the part of those around us to allow desirable changes to occur. In all these conditions and processes our emotions are as instrumental as our cognitive equipment.[2]

Some affects and emotions are particularly suited to assist us in our dealings with what we experience as the human and non-human world around us; others to assist us in organizing, regulating, and repairing what we experience as our own self. The strength of pleasant emotional experience, such as joy, love and tenderness, admiration, hope, interest, curiosity, pride, and amusement, play an essential role in orienting us to what is desirable, so that we may try to obtain and keep it. But there is no need here to explore and describe their function. They are not activated by the experiences that activate the depressed response and are easily differentiated from it. I will take up only the painful emotions and organize their discussion in relation to a few significant facets of living, although these overlap. In this chapter I take up the emotions aroused most intensely by the severance of attachments or group belonging, and by lack of attachment or group belonging. In Chapter 7 I deal with emotions that significantly regulate our participation in interpersonal relations and group processes: shame, guilt, and anger (although anger belongs as much with loss and loneliness).

When comparing different painful emotions with one another and with the depressed response, I will not only point to the different appraisal prompting each emotion and consider to what extent the emotion is aroused by hardships we attribute to factors in the world around us or to our own nature or behavior, but I shall also examine the adaptive function of each emotion.

Grief upon separation and loss

Losing or missing a significant and satisfactory relationship causes a pain very distinct from other emotional pain, just as a stomach pain feels different from a headache, a burn, a toothache, or a sore throat. Each such bodily pain is not only associated with a different part of the body and with a different function, but it also arouses different apprehensions. The same is true for psychic pain. The pain of loss of partner is very different from the pain of humiliation and shame, the pain of regret or guilt. Subjectively, grieving differs from being depressed primarily by the clarity of images and the flood of vivid memories that are part of the pining during the experience of separation or after a loss is recognized as final. These images are often the happy memories connected with the relationship;[3] but they may also be the vivid, painful recollections of the lost one's final illness that need to be described time and again, or of the hopes that a lost relationship failed to fulfill. Here is an example of happy memories reported to me by a woman in her sixties, Elsa.

She had spent part of her childhood in an aunt's home, separated from her parents. A close relationship with this aunt had continued after the reunion with her parents, and later after her parents had died. Now this aunt had suddenly died at the age of eighty-five. Due to the great distance between their residences, Elsa and her aunt had in recent decades met no more than for a week or two every few years, and correspondence had become sparse although they kept each other informed about their welfare. Thus, Elsa's everyday life was hardly affected by her aunt's death. Yet she was much more shaken than she had expected. Early attachments tend to be very durable even if, due to circumstances and personal development, their depth may have receded from awareness. In the course of her reactions to this bereavement, Elsa became suddenly aware of how many objects on her walls, on her shelves, in her drawers and cupboards, among her clothes and jewels, were gifts received from her aunt during a lifetime. Each of these objects which hitherto had mainly been parts of her household to Elsa, now constantly reminded her of her aunt and of the circumstances when the gift was given. They suddenly revived memories of beautiful shared experiences, while disappointments and misunderstandings that had also occurred but were long since overcome did not become revived.

Usually, the predominance of positive recollections in bereavement is interpreted as a defence against guilt. Experiences like Elsa's, however, suggest a further thought. I have earlier reported Bowlby's view (1961) that attachment behavior – following, clinging, protesting, crying – serves the purpose of maintaining proximity with the attachment figure and is automatically activated when loss is threatened; and that in bereavement, attachment behavior is activated as well, although in that instance it is to no avail. If we adopt Bowlby's view, as I do, the fact that the pain of pining does not dull our memory but focuses it on past satisfactory interaction makes eminent sense. This aspect of grieving makes us keenly aware of what we are missing, what we must try to recover or adequately replace, and should this prove impossible, what we should try to retain and enjoy at least in memory. In this way, the personal aspect of the adaptive function of grief is served. Unless the negatives in the relationship were significant, they are irrelevant in this context.

The sudden clarity of recollections, seemingly long forgotten, gives strength and direction to the relentless search which Parkes (1972) has observed in mourners. The following illustrates the intensity of this search. Almost three months after her husband's death, for which his illness had long prepared her, a widow, Gerda, wrote in her letter of thanks for the condolences of friends and relatives:

"I guess, despite all your tears and violent sorrow, you don't truly grasp at first what has happened. You know it on the surface only, as painful as that may be, but deep inside you can't accept and you don't accept. It must have been almost three weeks after John's death that something began to snap deeper down, when, for the only time since his passing, I had a 'bad' dream: at a great distance, at a place where John had some errand, an enormous avalanche came down like a Niagara Falls of powdered snow over some steep rugged mountains. When the masses of snow had finally stopped pouring down and settled, I tried to discern whether some little dark speck might be visible that might be John, but there was nothing, just white cold snow. – Since then I have come to understand the myth of Orpheus in a vivid way. When you have lost the person you have felt at one with, who gave so much understanding, pleasure, and support – and allowed you to give so much of the same – then you fight with all that is in you against letting go of the illusion that what he gave and what he received can somehow continue to flow to and from you. Like Orpheus you play in every way every string of your being to find the lost response. With your tears and your cries you are trying to reach him, by looking at his pictures and touching things he has touched you seek him, by talking about him and yourself you try not to feel that the one who understood you most deeply is no longer there to hear you. It will take much time to stop trying, but since I am not Orpheus altogether I am also fighting to find new productivity and new rewards, that can make the loss bearable and continuing life meaningful."

Anxiety in separation and following loss

In bereavement, the pain of this intense yearning often arouses the wish to follow the deceased into death, to join him or her in the grave. Furthermore, the experience of nursing a dying attachment figure – spouse, parent, close friend – can arouse a preoccupation with one's own perhaps more lonely, future terminal illness. Along with anger about the new circumstances, the pain of hopeless pining and a variety of other emotions can arouse the intense anxiety that one might be unable to bear this upheaval for any length of time. One of the difficult emotions to bear might be envy of the dead person for having died in the care of a loving mate, rather than in loneliness. Thus, there can be mounting apprehension that one might become unable to function, become ill or collapse emotionally – as some widows and widowers actually do during the first six to eighteen months after bereavement (Parkes 1972). Other anxieties during the total mourning process may be related to the changes occurring in the mourner's social environment subsequent to bereavement. In the case of loss of spouse, for instance, there may be a loss of one's former social association with couples, from which one is now excluded; economic changes; the burden of unfamiliar practical tasks and of single parenthood; and last but not least, the frequent friction and rivalries between members of one's family or other group who mourn the same person. Such anxieties are inescapable in the total adaptive process of mourning. Some of them seem on the surface to be almost inseparable from grief, although they are not.

In my view, the subjective experience of being depressed tends to differ from that of anxiety in the following way. The former slows us down, causes us to withdraw from contact with others into ourselves, so that we may react with open or suppressed irritation when disturbed; but it does not truly paralyze us. Anxiety activates us excessively, causes us to overreact to any disruption or failure so that we either clamor for attention or feel more frighteningly paralyzed than when we are depressed. Often, however, circumstances give us cause for both depressed and anxious reactions. Likewise, personality development can have made us prone to both getting depressed and getting anxious. Then it is difficult for the observer to determine which of the symptoms is elicited by which affect or emotion.[4]

Basic grief and patterns or syndromes of grief

Bowlby speaks (1961:331) of grief as "a peculiar amalgam of anxiety, anger, and despair following the experience of what is feared to be irretrievable loss." Lazarus[5] also uses (1975:65) the terms "grief" and "grieving" for a complex of emotional reactions, as do Parkes and Weiss, who speak (1983:14) of the "syndrome" of grief. In the case of grieving with a productive outcome, however, I find it useful to speak of an emotional pattern of grief, rather than of a syndrome, reserving the latter term for pathology. The combinations of several affective responses typical for pathological grief heavily overlap with such combinations in syndromes of depression. Yet, each of these two types of syndromes has a core component that is distinct from the core component of the other. The emphasis on the *combination* of affective responses implied in the concept of "grief" as a pattern of emotions – as used by the authors just mentioned – is useful for other purposes, but the emphasis on the *core component* alone is necessary for my purpose. Unfortunately, we have no separate word for it. We need a word connoting only the pining with its tears, sobs, and cries, its vivid images and memories, its impulse to talk to the dead one and repeat, alone, those activities one earlier shared. In other words, we need a word to connote only the components of our *reaching out* for what is lost, but excluding anger and anxiety, although under the circumstances the latter two can be as normal as pining and searching.

I propose using the expression "basic grief" for this very distinctive subjective experience of pain upon the loss of a significant person. Basic grief can be conceptualized as the subjective experience that gradually develops out of the innate components of attachment behavior that Bowlby has described as clinging and following. The word "despair," on the other hand, which Bowlby uses, connotes to me an almost unbearable intensity of any painful emotion when its causes are experienced as being beyond remedy.

Differences between basic grief, anxiety, and being depressed

Now we can examine the differences between basic grief and anxiety. We start with the difference of appraisal that arouses the affect or emotion. During the process of mourning we are likely to experience anxieties provoked by more than one factor and its appraisal. One type of anxiety is related to the possible consequences of the social changes following bereavement, divorce, or other separation. This anxiety is independent of and separate from our grief reactions in mourning. Second, as mentioned above, when our belief that something felt essential to our well-being can no longer be reached and enjoyed, this may cause grief sufficiently intense, and a variety of emotions sufficiently conflicting to arouse anxiety that we will prove unable to bear this state. This anxiety is directly related to our grief, but *secondary* to it; it is a consequence of grieving. *Primary* anxiety about loss is aroused when we are not convinced that the loss need occur; when there is still hope, despite the fear of impending loss. Both the primary and secondary anxiety directly related to our loss and our reactions to it serve the personal aspect of the adaptive function of anxiety: they warn us that we may be near reaching the limits of our capacity to cope independently: that we need care, support, and guidance in order to avoid physical or emotional damage.

The main difference between basic grief and anxiety lies in the personal aspect of their respective functions. While anxiety alerts us by sharpening our vision of dangers we want to *escape*, grief sharpens our vision of the type of interaction we want to *attain, retain, recover*, or at least *replace*. Both functions, however, are served only whenever grief or anxiety have reached awareness, so that they can find appropriate expression. The social functions of basic grief and anxiety, on the other hand, are similar: both cause behavior that tends to arouse sympathy and care-giving impulses in others.

Next, we need to examine how being depressed differs from grieving and being anxious.[6] Being depressed signals that in some way we are lacking in awareness of what causes us distress or what can be done about it. Being depressed involves a sense of dullness, a confusion, and perplexity that interfere with our ability to take action toward getting what we want or escaping what we fear. Its function in such context is to enhance or restore our capacity to be aware of our feelings and bear them. Here is an example.

Fifteen years after John's death, Gerda was still active in her occupation but, having suffered further losses through death, rather lonely. Spring that year came unusually late but then was unusually sunny and warm. After a long, dark, wet winter everything seemed to bud all at once. She was surrounded by masses of blossoms and the jubilant song of birds. She didn't understand why she suddenly slept poorly, felt touchy, numb, and lonely, instead of enjoying the beauty and vivid life that surrounded her. Why didn't her work satisfy her as usual? Why did her friends have less appeal than usually?

After a few days it struck her that she had had a similar experience a year earlier when spring was unusually glorious. On that occasion she had suddenly realized what ailed her: her husband was no longer alive to share this beauty with her. Her life's closest companion with whom sharing the beauty of nature was most satisfying was dead. Other dear ones who might have replaced him in this were also dead or far away. None of her currently available relationships had filled this gap. All of a sudden Gerda cried. She also felt protest against the increasing isolation of old age, but mainly she was flooded with memories of togetherness and sharing. She pined again, years after her bereavement.

This was a pattern of grief – basic grief combined with hopeless protest. Now she knew what had lately been wrong, what the beauty of the season made her long for in vain. Late in life she knew that her losses could no longer be adequately replaced and that, therefore, they would cause grief time and again, however active and committed she had become in her new pursuits. The old way of life lived on in her, side by side with the new one. The happy habits once established in her did not die along with their original partners. They wanted to be repeated. This is not unusual.[7]

The numbness, the sense of emptiness and loneliness, on the other hand, that Gerda experienced before she recognized that the beauty of spring was calling to be shared with a satisfactory partner: that was the depressed response. She was too busy with her work to realize that basic grief as well as angry protest might be brewing inside her and clamoring to be expressed. She did not realize that she was unconsciously searching for some impossible solution for her craving for the presence of someone with whom to share deeply, nor that she was unconsciously trying to stop longing for what was missing and could not be replaced. All this unawareness caused depression: time was ripe to feel the yearning again, express it again, and attend to the experience consciously.

Basic grief over a fresh loss, as well as revived grief, can be so painful that we tend to divert ourselves from it after a while with routine activities, with work, with social contacts, new aspirations, new hopes, new plans, new creativity. Up to a point, this is actually how basic grief serves its adaptive function: forcing us to expose ourselves to new experiences from which a new way of life can develop. Diversions can, however, be used too persistently and result in temporary or permanent repression of what must be felt and expressed before it can abate. If a major loss cannot be replaced – many losses cannot – then the specific needs, habits, and desires that after the loss remain unmet will from time to time accumulate to the point where they need new attention. Our resistance to re-experiencing this pain will give cause for the depressed response until the work of depression, aided by temporary withdrawal from diversions, has freed the way for renewed expression of grief and for a period of preoccupation with the satisfactions of the past. These will cause us to pine but at the same time to find pleasure in being vividly reminded of what we have been able to share and how we have been able to respond in the lost relationship. This memory of closeness can be a significant comfort when our new circumstances create isolation and loneliness. Thus, both grief and the depressed response enable us, *each in its own way*, slowly to integrate loss and change into new creative living.

Basic grief, then, is part of our total reaction when we believe that something valuable and necessary to our well-being – to our joy, our contentment, our trust and security, our self-respect, our hopes for the future – is no longer there and may never return, or return only in an uncertain future. This belief may be caused by many different circumstances: a meaningful bond may be severed by death, by migration or incarceration, by desertion, by disillusionment, or even by changes in taste or compatibility that our own development has brought about. Even when our own development, our own wish to desert or divorce causes a bond to be cut off that once was valuable and necessary, this may cause grief. Loss of occupation, of health, and of other significant involvements do so as well.

On the other hand, our tie to a person, our striving for desired work, our efforts to belong to a particular group, may only have been a wish, a hope built on mistaken expectations, or been due to a belief created by deceit or misinformation. Yet, when such a wish or hope is destroyed we lose an emotional investment that until recently has had deep meaning for us and has engaged important parts of our inner life. This also causes grief. So does damage to our self-image. Such factors are significant in the painful turmoil connected with marital separation, as discussed and exemplified by Weiss (1975). Even when a loss is no cause for the painful grief that leads to tears and vivid memories, even when it only causes sadness or loneliness, if that sadness has not reached awareness, this may arouse a mild depressed response.

I have illustrated basic grief mostly with examples of bereavement, although it may be just as severe in cases of desertion or divorce. More generally, one can say that grief is related to a major *change from better to worse*: in disappointment in a significant relationship or group association; in loss of one's home (Parkes 1972), occupation, projects, or beliefs; or in such change in one's body as loss of limb (Parkes 1972).

Hopelessness and helplessness

Hopelessness and helplessness must be mentioned here, because they are often considered integral characteristics of depression. Indeed, in cases diagnosed as severe depression some degree of hopelessness and helplessness is usually evident. In my view, however, they are not symptoms of being depressed but symptoms of a state where the depressed response has no chance to facilitate a productive outcome. Hopelessness and/or helplessness prevent the flexible cognitive and emotional contribution to the improved information processing that is necessary for the remedial work of being depressed. As long as there are emotions of true and lasting hopelessness and helplessness, the depressed response is prevented from serving its adaptive function and must remain unproductive. Unless there is at least minimal hope, trust, and persistence, the depressed response cannot facilitate improved functioning.

Anger

In Chapter 2 I have pointed out that anger is our response when our desires or efforts are thwarted by what is experienced as an agent outside the self. The personal aspect of its adaptive function is to alert us to what is undesirable and how it may be avoided or combated; the social aspect of its function is served by the controlling effect that our affective behavior can have on an opponent. There is some similarity between the causes for the depressed and the angry response, insofar as both are touched off by the frustration of an effort or expectation, but they differ significantly in the perception of what causes the frustration: in the depressed response the frustration stems from some uncomprehended inner dysfunction, while in anger there is a conviction that a specific, tangible, and usually external agent is responsible for the frustration.

A defensive denial of the disquieting perception of uncomprehended, intangible inner dysfunction and of the resulting depressed response can easily lead to anger – that is, to seeking a tangible culprit to be held responsible for the discomfort. The desired culprit may be found either in someone else, or even in the self. In the latter case, one takes the stance that one could and should have avoided frustration; this makes one bad, which may be experienced as more easily remedied or less shameful than being incompetent or helpless.

The defensive denial of realistic cause for anger, on the other hand, can easily lead to seeking the cause for the resulting frustration in the self, instead of in the denied real cause of discomfort. This distortion of perception is likely to provoke the depressed response. These distortions will be taken up in greater detail in Chapter 9.

In conclusion, grief, anxiety, anger, and being depressed are central emotions in our adjustment to living a different life after a significant loss, separation, or disappointment. Grief and anger are mainly concerned with the conditions forced upon us by what we experience as not-self, and with our efforts to influence them. Regret is grief aroused by a conscious idea of having made a poor choice. Depression, when following a major change for the worse, or when due to other causes, is concerned with our perception of ineffectiveness of our own *current* functioning in this context. Anxiety may be a response either to our appraisal of risk of danger in our external circumstances or to our appraisal of some *potential* dysfunction in ourselves. Being depressed serves to restore our functioning by concentration on the origin and nature of the dysfunction. Anxiety, when a response to our own potential dysfunction, does not serve to concentrate information processing on the cause for such a potential dysfunction but rather on its consequences, should it materialize.

Loneliness, grief, and being depressed

Loneliness is the pain involved in the *continuous lack* of emotional attachment or social belonging. Weiss clearly describes (1973, 1982) emotional and social isolation as two different affective states likely to be characterized as loneliness. The experience of loneliness due to *emotional* isolation is the pain of having no true attachment, no one to trust, to love, to care for, to hope for, to lose, or pine for. The experience of loneliness due to *social* isolation is the pain of feeling a stranger when one does not, on a steady basis, have the opportunity of sharing interests, language, culture, or activities with members of informal or formal groups. Both types of loneliness can cause excruciating pain. The pain of emotional isolation is not relieved by participation in a group, and a close relationship does not cancel out the pain of lacking group participation. Her mother's presence in the room is no sufficient solace for a little girl watching through the window her older sister dancing on the lawn with her companions.

The threat of loneliness can make it difficult for a bereaved or divorced person to stop grieving. Many mourners have confirmed to me that, compared to loneliness, basic grief – if not marred by shame or guilt – is still company. It maintains some of the past experience of richness, vitality, and closeness. Once grief subsides in everyday living, this richness fades to be re-experienced in memory when grief is reawakened. This reflection of richness is the reason why a mourner's expression of intense grief often provokes envy and anger in lonely people. I heard a woman at a social gathering say about a widow among her friends: "Why should I have to listen to her grief when I have never had a chance to experience what she has lost?"

The pain of loneliness – the frustration of our basic need for secure individual attachment and secure social belonging in a group – is so hard to bear that it is readily repressed, and then the frustration of hidden and unrealistic strivings to change the situation is likely to produce depression. Loneliness due to emotional isolation can be caused by the inability to form attachments, but also by the loss of a significant attachment or of several attachments. Many of our patients with persistent depression are lonely people and have always or most of their lives been lonely due to both emotional and social isolation. Unfortunately, this breeds shame. Often they have grown up in socially isolated families, with emotionally isolated parents, and have not acquired the self-confidence, or learned the social skills necessary even under favorable circumstances for establishing and maintaining a successful social network. This creates a vicious circle between emotional and social isolation. Such a vicious circle is so threatening a situation that we tend to avoid identifying with it. Consequently, its reality in the life of a patient is often denied even by members of the mental health professions who thereby unwittingly reinforce a patient's conclusion that, being lonely, he or she is worthless and the sole cause of the difficulty. This adds insult to injury.

Even more than basic grief, loneliness arouses in the adult an "amalgam" of anger, despair, and depression. In the child or adolescent, of course, the despair of unbearable and hopeless grief develops much more quickly than in the adult. A child can early lose the courage to seek and try out a new attachment. The child and adolescent are less able, if at all, to comprehend causal connections in his or her situation and reactions than the grieving or mourning adult, and consequently more vulnerable to becoming and remaining depressed.

And yet, in people who have the strength to bear pain without excessive repression and distortion, feelings of loneliness can serve an adaptive function as well.

> We find in our work with the divorced that loneliness fosters a search for something more than a companion or a sexual partner. Loneliness is allayed only by a relationship in which there is assurance of the continued accessibility of someone trusted.
>
> Loneliness may always have functioned to alert individuals to a relationship in which there would be mutual commitment; it may have been selected for because those who possessed the trait were more likely to choose as a mate someone with whom it would be possible to establish a persisting bond. Loneliness may have provided the incentive for forming a partnership that would eventually make more than one person available for child raising.
>
> (Weiss 1982:77)

Chapter seven

The depressed response compared with other affects

B: The role of shame and guilt in personal and group relations

Shame is an emotion insufficiently studied, because in our civilization it is so early and easily absorbed by guilt.

Erikson (1963:252)

... shame and guilt – and the defenses against them – ... fulfill a positive, homeostatic function and serve *family* cohesion and solidarity, just as, on a social scale, shame and guilt serve *societal* cohesion and solidarity. ... But in the family, as in the larger society, this homeostatic function of shame and guilt easily exceeds what is required.

Stierlin (1974: 384)

Identity a guide in socialization

As described in Chapter 6, basic grief, anxiety, anger, and the basic depressed response are the most prominent emotions in our coping with separation, disappointment, loss, and other painful, bewildering change. Shame and guilt, on the other hand, although they can also lead to pathology, normally contribute significantly to the development of what Erikson calls (1950, 1963) our identity. A secure identity assists us in establishing and maintaining satisfactory personal relationships as well as a stable place in a social network.[1] Identity is part of our relating to others; it is an appraisal of the extent to which we are like certain others, or different from them. It becomes the more important, the greater the choice of participation and roles open to us. It is also important for the self-assertion required, when someone tries to withhold a role from us that we believe we can fill. It encompasses our appraisal of cause for shame, guilt, or pride. The capacity to react with shame and guilt can provide us with successful guidelines and stimulation in this development, but if excessive, these emotions can severely inhibit it.

For our image of who we are, as compared to others, we remain throughout life dependent on past, present, and expected future feedback from certain others.

I shall take up further in Chapter 13 how, from complex patterns of early interaction and communication with those who take care of our emotional and physical needs, and from observing their interaction with others, we slowly develop an image of ourselves as lovable or unlovable, useful or worthless; we learn what is expected of us and what we may expect of others.

If we are lucky, we are surrounded in infancy and childhood by people – particularly one or two central, reliable attachment figures – who enjoy interacting with us, who encourage and stimulate us, at the same time as they are not afraid to set limits appropriate to our age and endowment. This fosters a sense of security, positive expectations, clear guidelines for action, and ease in connecting cause and effect. But many are less lucky.

Whatever the actual responses we have met and are meeting in the world around us, all of us construct from our interactional experiences our individually colored models of what we are and should be; of what others are and want; when we have cause to be proud of ourselves or ashamed; and what we may expect of others. Such models of the world[2] derived from a multitude of sources within ourselves and without, and frequently reinforced, shaken, or changed by new experience, are rarely consistent, but there are great individual differences in the degree of inconsistency. We are often unaware of these contradictions. As a result, we are likely to find time and again that we are falling short of being the person we believe we ought to be in order to be loved, admired, respected, or feared by a significant other, by several others, by everybody; or most of all, to be acceptable to ourselves. The painful disappointment caused by the discrepancy between the standards we set for ourselves or accept from others and our estimate of what we really are – in general or on a given occasion – tends to be called shame.

When I speak of "shame," the term covers acute and chronic experiences of embarrassment, humiliation, and worthlessness. What one might call chronic shame is referred to by Alexander (1948) as inferiority feelings. The affect of acute shame has characteristic physiological components: blushing, sweating, and accelerated heartbeat; it is also evident in the avoidance of meeting another's eyes, and a tendency to bow one's head and pull up one's shoulders as if one were trying to disappear or to ward off a blow or kick.[3] In expressing feelings of shame, phrases suggesting the wish to hide are often used, even "I wish I were dead."

Development in theories of shame

Freud sees (1905, 1921, 1931) the function of shame as a socializing force protecting us primarily against socially unacceptable sexual overactivity and perversion, particularly against unacceptable impulses to expose our body and observe the bodies and sexual activities of others (exhibitionism and scopophilia). He sees shame largely as a product of education but also suspects (1905:178) that it may at the same time be a genetically acquired tendency;

shame fosters sexual inhibition but when excessive leads to hysteria. Freud finds (1905) that girls develop shame earlier in response to education, with less resistance than boys, and (1931) that women, due to what he sees as their genital deficiency, are more prone to shame than men. Freud's description (1905:192) of the behavior of young children still holds for the behavior of children today. But cultural attitudes that heavily influenced his comparison of the sexes have changed since his time and are still in flux.

Yet, Freud does not connect the experience of shame, as is increasingly done today, with disappointments at the discrepancy between our actual behavior and our ideal self in areas that go beyond the naked body and its functions. The ideal self, as I use the term here, is a conscious and unconscious model that has developed from an identification with and internalization of admired actual or idealized traits of our attachment figure(s) which gradually have become modified by admired traits of further adults, of peers, or heroes.[4]

Nevertheless, Freud's view that shame feelings are connected with being seen, wishing to look, and with conflicts concerning such wishes in the context of sexual arousal and exposure of the body, is unquestionably valid as far as it goes. What he describes is an essential feature of the earliest development – at least within our culture – of our genetic disposition for the affect and emotion of shame. Only it does not cover the full range of later developments. In infancy we are for quite some time dependent on communication about our mother figure's pleasure or displeasure conveyed to us by her glances, facial expression, tone of voice, and the touch of her arms and hands, often while she is handling our body and its excrements. These impressions are the first clues we receive and retain about our worth and desirability. No wonder, we later remain particularly sensitive to the actual or expected response of others to our physical appearance and the exposure of those parts of the body that early were the object of adult attention, and to how people look at us. This is later reinforced by our discovery that much of our own evaluation of others is conveyed to them, often unintentionally, through the expression of our eyes. Both in childhood and in adult life, gender, sexual behavior, and sexual satisfaction play an important role in the expression and implementation of our striving for acceptance and intimacy in personal relationships, for power, status, and a satisfactory role in groups. Shame is intimately connected with the failure to acquire and retain closeness, a desired role, status, and power – and with our fantasies about why we are failing. Sexual arousal and satisfaction, when arousing shame, is more often than not secondary to – that is, an expression of – these other strivings, rather than the primary aim.

Some of the early anxiety aroused by the feelings of shame when meeting ridicule, contempt, and rejection by others tends to persist in the adult, but an adult can experience intense shame when no one else is or can be expected to become aware of the shortcoming that causes shame. If we do not comprehend but misinterpret the personal and social causes for painful feelings of shame and repress them, we cannot cope with them. Instead we tend to become depressed, usually without productive outcome.

Freud's views on the affect of shame were for a long time not developed further by his followers. The general concern was with the affect of guilt. In recent decades, however, a new trend has been gaining impetus side by side with persistent traditional views.

Alexander (1948), Erikson (1950, 1963), and Piers, in Piers and Singer (1953), were pioneers in showing that shame is as significant as guilt in the development of pathology, and how the two interact. Alexander was first to describe the shame–guilt cycle. Guilt and shame often overlap or elicit each other. Guilt over our actions tends to arouse shame over being the kind of person who will behave like this. The pain of shame may be defended against by turning the helplessness of *being* bad into the more active role of being guilty. Having *done* wrong is a failure that at times can be repaired by making amends, whereas being bad can be overcome only by changing.[5]

Lynd, a psychoanalytically oriented sociologist, is concerned (1958) with the normal causes and function of shame and with its contribution to development, particularly in enhancing the development of identity.[6]

Lewis starts (1971) from a discussion of the normal, regulatory functions of shame and guilt before she devotes herself to an extensive examination, discussion, and illustration of shame and guilt in neurosis. She emphasizes that guilt feelings often serve to substitute for more painful feelings of shame, but that the opposite often follows, so that a shame–guilt cycle develops.[7]

Morrison specifies (1983:316) that "As guilt motivates the patient to confess, shame motivates him to conceal," and "For guilt the antidote is forgiveness; shame tends to seek the healing of acceptance – acceptance of the self despite its weakness, defects, and failures."

Shane, a psychoanalytically oriented educator, presents (1980) the thesis that shame serves an important function in processes of learning, insofar as the desire to know grows from the realization that one does not know, that one is lacking, but that "what is not known is something that one is capable of knowing and should know" (1980:349).[8]

Matthis also emphasizes (1981) the importance of painful experiences of ignorance in the experience of shame, and that this can either "lead to an impasse for personal growth," or "stimulate psychic development and intellectual achievement" (1981:57). Her point of departure, however, is not the student–teacher relationship and the classroom but the situation of girls in our society when, in their development from infancy into womanhood, they meet with prohibitions, secrets, and incomprehensible as well as impossible expectations.

For the role of incongruence and painful ignorance in the development of shame, Lynd gives (1958:47) a vivid illustration from fiction, which I condense:

At the turn of the century, Emmy Lou, a child in first grade, eager to understand and learn, finds many practices in school bewildering. No one has told her why one must get up, when the bell rings. And why is she told crossly to sit down when, in answer to c, a, t, she says "Pussy"; why, when the teacher is pointing with her stick to the kitten illustrating the chart? Then the music teacher tells them that eight dots on five lines on the blackboard are "A, B, C, D, E, F, G, A," but they must be called do, re, mi, fa, sol, la, si: "Always remember the first letter in the scale is do." It is perplexing that now A is not A but a dot. Yet, Emmy Lou dutifully remembers. In the next spelling class she carefully pronounces the letters ADAM as "Dough – d – dough – m, Adam." The class laughs.

Here, a child experiences the shame of incomprehensible failure despite trusting and hopeful effort; and the shame of exposure of this failure.

Wurmser demonstrates (1981) the manifold variety of causes for and contents of the experiences of shame. Like Lewis, he shows the close interaction of guilt and shame, and the complex defenses against either. He also assigns distinct functions and characteristics to shame, and others to guilt.[9]

These authors, building their theories in one way or another on psychoanalytic clinical data, differentiate shame and guilt from each other as separate affects. Tomkins, on the other hand, does not find (1963:118) shyness, shame, and guilt "distinguished from each other at the level of affect," although they are not "the same experience." This makes his comprehensive description of shame less useful for my differentiation of the depressed response from other affects.

The role of guilt in the development of identity

In addition to the messages about the desirability and undesirability of what we *are*, we also receive from infancy constant overt and covert directions about what we may *do*, must do, and must not do. If we are lucky, we are from early on surrounded by people who encourage our efforts to express ourselves and explore our surroundings. Aware of our limitations, they set sensitive and sensible limits to our adventures at the same time. The reward of successful adaptation to these directions is security in a varied social network and the pleasure of doing what we believe is right.[10] Here, too, we may be less lucky or very unlucky in our development due to the overt or covert demands, prohibitions, and punishments we meet as children and adolescents. Again, from our experience combined with our innate tendencies we develop conscious and unconscious standards of our obligations to others, how we must and how we must not treat them. The painful emotion aroused when we fail to meet this standard we call guilt feelings. Physiological components of guilt feelings are similar to those of fear: rigidity of posture, staring, feeling chilled. Symptomatically, shame and guilt are closely related to fear and anxiety, although for theoretical and clinical purposes it is useful to view them as separate because of the differences in the appraisal causing them and in their adaptive function.

The adaptive function of shame and guilt

Psychoanalysts have successfully studied many intrapsychic processes of guilt and, to a lesser degree, those of shame, although they often have included shame in what they called guilt. But although connecting guilt and shame increasingly with the development of interpersonal communication in significant relationships, they have – with a few exceptions like Erikson, Piers, and Stierlin – been less concerned with the connection of these affects with social roles in groups, with social function, or with cultural and biological heritage. They left this domain to other disciplines. Yet, the following questions must be raised more persistently than has been done so far: what is this good for? When does it yield personal or social advantages to react with some form of shame or guilt feelings? When does our reacting with excessive guilt or shame become destructive not only to ourselves but to our family or larger group? When does excessive shame lead to violence and war?[11]

It is likely that psychiatrists, psychologists, psychoanalysts, ethologists, anthropologists, and sociologists will have to share their knowledge and research before conclusive answers to these questions will become possible. The type of work Bowlby, Parkes, Weiss, and some others have presented concerning attachment behavior, grief, and loneliness needs to be done concerning comprehensive concepts of shame and of the normal interaction between guilt and shame. I agree with Stierlin (1974) that these two affective patterns of response are crucial for the maintenance of both small and large social groups. There is no life possible for humans outside of group relatedness – even if at times a person retains such relatedness only in fantasy. Even the hermit in the desert was intensely related to his images of God, Christ, and the saints, and to memories of human relations prior to his withdrawal.

At the present stage of our knowledge, I can propose a differentiation between the adaptive functions of the depressed response and of shame and guilt only in the form of a hypothesis about the latter emotions, to complement my hypothesis about the basic depressed response. To some extent, my hypothesis overlaps with the position of the authors to whom I have referred. Of necessity my presentation contains oversimplifications, but it can nevertheless be useful in clinical observation and in planning research.

I hold that despite frequent individual and social distortions, the affects of shame and guilt, tending to appear together like fraternal twins, have a vital function in human life. It is useful to examine these two possibly basic affects as essential to the emergence and cohesion of smaller human groups and entire societies. Cohesive social structures require leaders, followers, different ranks and roles, with a division of labor and responsibility. They require a variety of interpersonal relationships that ensure reasonable stability of leadership, spontaneous support of and submission to leadership by the rank and file, and the protection of both leaders and followers.[12]

Much learning, conscious and unconscious, is necessary for our fitting first into the structure of our family, nuclear or extended; then into peer groups, into the interaction between teachers and pupils at school, into the hierarchies of employment or military service; and, last but not least, into the division of labor in mating and parenthood. This requires of us that we develop an exceedingly complex system of interpreting multiple clues received from without and within about what to feel, think, be, and do in order to meet expectations – our own and those of others; expectations customary in our environment or idiosyncratic on our own or someone else's part.

The emotions of shame and guilt are indispensable guides in our selecting significant messages for attention among those we are receiving but may want to disregard; in our concluding what meaning they can have for us; and in controlling our spontaneous response before we engage in action. However swiftly the action occurs after a message is received, we must assume that selection, assessment, and interpretation of meaning has occurred even in the briefest interim. The sequence of selection and appraisal is accompanied by affect or emotion, as considered in Chapter 2. There, I showed briefly when we react with grief, when with anxiety, with anger, or with tenderness. The grief of mourning and the pleasure of feeling tenderness, often the experience of getting angry or anxious, are connected with our experiences of closeness. They guide our behavior in intimate relations with one person at a time. We feel deep shame or painful guilt in that context also, but shame and guilt are more prom- inent than basic grief or tenderness in our dealings with a group. While shame and guilt develop first in our relationships with individual members of our fam- ily, they later help us find our way in the complex patterns of participation in groups; in our assuming roles and responsibilities in different group situations.

Even in stable, relatively simple social environments with clear-cut roles it is inescapable that we can only learn by much trial and error how to strike an appropriate balance between opening ourselves to closeness with, and protect ourselves against intrusion by, others and their curiosity; and also a balance between showing interest in or touching others and keeping proper distance. In our multicultural, multiracial society with its many different economic, educational, and occupational layers it is even harder to learn how to fit into different group contexts with a measure of security and tact – tact meaning that we know how and when to touch what should be touched, but refrain from touching what should not be touched.

Provided we have grown up under conditions favorable to such learning, our capacity to react with shame and guilt is not a frequent source of distress but, rather, an important guide in becoming sensitive to our own vulnerability in social intercourse and to the vulnerability of others. Shame can alert us to what we *are* in contrast to what we would wish to be; and how we *appear* to others in contrast to how we would wish to be seen. This awareness can help us on one hand to learn and improve; and on the other to find a proper place for ourselves in a group, a place that we are able to hold, rather than seeking to attain the impossible or inappropriate. If shame guides us in this way it serves the personal aspect of its adaptive function. It also serves this aspect if it helps us maintain privacy for what in a given group or relationship should not be exposed, lest we risk ridicule, envy, contempt, or exploitation.[13] Our blushing, on the other hand, our embarrassed behavior or withdrawal can alert others to our vulnerability, so that they may become less intrusive or ridiculing. If so, the social aspect of the adaptive function of the affect is served. Furthermore, our own experiences of shame can help us become sensitive to what others might react to as embarrassing or as painful shame. In that case the social aspect of the function of shame is also served insofar as we profit from the respect and appreciation that such sensitivity earns us, cementing our security in social relations.

Guilt is the signal that tells us when we are breaking our inner rules of what we should do for, or not do to, others. The personal aspect of its adaptive function is mainly that its discomforts can guide us to behave in ways which allow us to like ourselves, to be sure of ourselves, and decisive in our actions. Also, if guilt feelings cause us to refrain much of the time from harming others, or to make amends or to change our ways after we have offended or harmed others, this tends to lead to our being forgiven for our mistakes and accepted into or kept in a group or an individual relationship. Or at least, we may be freed from punishment, or the punishment may be less severe. The social aspect of the function of guilt has been served.

Unfortunately, many children grow up in families and social circumstances that are not conducive to their developing the type of shame and guilt responses that provide them with effective guidelines within the society that surrounds them. They may develop too little, too much, or too rigid shame and guilt patterns. Too little shame and guilt may land them at the fringes of society or in prison; too much and too inflexible shame and guilt, and rigid defenses against them, tend to cause depression-proneness, anxiety-proneness, or other disorders. When we are ashamed or feel guilty, we may want to do something to relieve the anxiety aroused by these emotions; to remedy the external situation; or in other ways to overcome the consequences of how we are or of what we have done. If we attempt and fail at an unrealistic solution of the problem, including various defenses as a solution, this is likely to bring on the depressed response. If, instead, we can bear the pain of shame and guilt without unrealistic efforts to escape it, we will not become depressed.

Shame, guilt, anger, and anxiety compared with the depressed response

Comparing shame and guilt with the depressed response, we find that each of these three emotions contains a concern with some aspect of ourselves: the first with what we are; the second with what we do, mainly to others; the third with how effectively we function. But there are significant differences none the less between these emotions.

Normally, when we are ashamed we recognize what ails us: finding that some characteristics of our appearance, personality, endowment, race, nationality, or other background falls short of what we wish it were. We wish we could hide this shortcoming from ourselves and others. When, instead, we experience that it has been, or imagine that it might be, exposed and noted by others, or that we cannot hide it from ourselves, this causes a very intense and specific pain. When we are depressed, on the other hand, some function of our total organism or personality is not doing its usual job and we do not know why. Of course, the cause of our shame can be felt to be so humiliating that it has been repressed; or shame can have been instilled so early in childhood that it is a chronic disturbance we do not understand. In that case it will provoke the depressed response in addition, and on the surface the two become difficult to distinguish.[14] But the normal function of being depressed – facilitating improved information processing – is easily distinguished from the normal function of shame – protecting ourselves against damaging or painful intrusion and acquiring a sound appraisal and acceptance of our limitations (reasonable modesty).

Feeling guilty differs from being depressed in two ways: for one thing, we have a clear idea of what we should have or should not have done; for the other, what we have done or are about to do involves damage or injury to someone else, or to some good cause. It usually concerns interaction with the world outside the self. We feel that we deserve punishment. Being depressed, on the other hand, concerns something being amiss within ourselves, something we do not see clearly, or at all. It is a process exclusively involving parts of our self. No one else but we ourselves can fully appreciate what is amiss, although a therapist can, by identification, be instrumental in our discovering it. Feeling guilty can be aroused by what we believe others need or expect. Feeling depressed is aroused by a sense of inner deadlock of which at least some aspects remain uncomprehended until being depressed has facilitated successful information processing and the depression lifts.

As regards anger, little needs to be added to what I have said in Chapters 2 and 6 about its cause and function. Loss and major change, as well as circumstances leading to shame and guilt, can arouse anger: we do not want to suffer grief, humiliation, or remorse. We may react with protest: why does this have to happen to me, who can be blamed for this, other than myself? When someone else interferes with our strivings, we have an actual culprit to get angry at, to attack, or put in his or her place. In the case of bereavement and other painful loss (except in the case of desertion, where we do have a culprit), or in the case of shame and guilt, we may seek a culprit, and if necessary find one by projection or displacement. Anger, unsettling but not painful, can then be used as a substitute for the painful emotions of grief, shame, or guilt. Being angry suggests to us that we are not helpless but can act to remedy the situation. In our relations within a group, our anger orients ourselves and others to our needs, to the position to which we aspire, and the roles we reject.

Conclusion

In conclusion, I find that the major painful emotions can roughly be seen as serving our adaptation in the following way: fear and anger, each in its way, can help to preserve our life and protect us from recurrent harm. Basic grief can help us recognize, bear, and overcome painful and damaging results of loss and change. Shame, guilt, and anger can direct our behavior in ways that are useful in attaining and maintaining personal relationships and participation in group processes. Shame and envy can enhance constructive effort and learning. Anxiety alerts us to the risk of undesirable consequences of our own behavior or of the circumstances in which we find ourselves, while the depressed response alerts us to the fact of some hidden cognitive or emotional (or possibly physiological) dysfunction in ourselves.[15] It alerts us to the absence, for the time being, of the normal pleasure in functioning well that Bühler (1922) has called *"Funktionslust"* (pleasure in functioning) and that Mahler has described (1975) as the toddler's elation in the period of practice. Although emotions often substitute for one another for defensive purposes, only the genuine, original emotion serves its unique function effectively. Our emotions can help us adapt in these ways, but whether they do depends on many favorable developmental and environmental circumstances.

Chapter eight

Two examples of depression and treatment

Much psychopathology stems from "impressions, scenes and experiences" of childhood having, apparently, been forgotten yet continuing to influence thought, feeling and action.

Bowlby (1979:407)

... the human brain's unique capacity and insistence on making inferences from observed events is responsible for the two different constructions of creation theory and, finally, personal beliefs. Give the inference system orderly data ... and it generates an orderly universe. Give it disorderly data, and the inference system constructs a vastly more complex notion of creation – one that emphasises the helplessness of man.

Gazzaniga (1985:175)

In this chapter I shall present two case examples of more or less severe syndromes of depression and of recovery or remission with the help of different types of treatment. They are summarized from the autobiographical reports by McRae (1986) and Endler (1982). When referring to them as authors I use their last names, but referring to the personal experience they describe of being depressed I use their first names to fit into the pattern of my case examples, except that here the actual first names – Margaret (McRae) and Norman (Endler) – are used. Margaret received psychoanalytic psychotherapy during a period of fifteen months, first once, then twice a week; Norman received no exploratory psychotherapy, only the therapeutic effect of his psychiatrist's interest and support. He was treated with tranquilizers, antidepressants, electroconvulsive therapy (ECT), and Lithium. In this chapter, the two cases will be presented with only limited discussion, but in Chapters 9 and 10 I will take them up again for discussion, when they will be used to illustrate given topics.

Margaret: a self-report of severe depression and recovery

McRae published her autobiographic report, *A State of Depression* (1986), eighteen years after the termination of fifteen months of psychotherapy with Dr Goldblatt (to whom I shall refer as Dr G.), which saved her sanity and possibly her life. The report is based on the detailed notes she took after every therapy session except for the last four months, when she had become confident of recovery and fully trusted her therapist. Her motivation for these notes was at first her fear, her distrust, and a desire for self-protection, but later increasingly the conscious desire to retain what she herself saw as her learning from her therapist – and very likely a less conscious wish to feel close to him as an attachment figure during the difficult intervals between her sessions. For a long time these two motivations blended and alternated. Dr G., whose work load during the first eight months of the therapy did not permit more frequent sessions than one a week, points out in his introduction that some of the detail of McRae's description of sessions does not coincide with his recollections, but rather is colored by her deep anxieties and the nature of her defenses at the time, but he confirms that the total story with gradual insights, changes, and developments represents McRae's own experience and rings very true. It shows us a person of remarkable persistence, honesty, and courage. Since her recovery, she has taken a university degree, is a college lecturer, and married.

McRae's account of her life follows first the circumstances of her breakdown and then the content of therapeutic sessions and of her experiences between sessions. It takes its departure from the acute phase of trauma and disintegration before therapy, then weaves back and forth between the present and the past until a chronological picture of her fate is gradually put together, such as is typical for the course of a successful therapy. Here I shall not retrace the entire sequence of these developments, but start with giving a chronological summary of significant circumstances, influences, and events during her childhood and adolescence, that made her prone to react with inhibition of mourning and later, when her emotional balance was threatened by an accumulation of traumatic events, with severe depression.

Background history

Margaret was conceived early during the Second World War. Her parents were devout members of a Protestant sect which under threat of hell-fire set down for its congregation rigid rules of behavior with many prohibitions. Aside from full-time employment, her father spent Sundays and four nights a week away from home as a lay preacher of the Gospel. Her mother stayed at home to take care of the household and children. At the time of Margaret's birth, her two brothers were two and a half and five years old. Her mother was wishing for a girl, but at the same time felt very guilty about setting another child into a world of war. After Margaret was beyond early infancy, her mother had a severe inhibition of touching her. She never caressed her. Her farewell kiss later on, whenever Margaret left home for a trip, felt like a gesture of duty rather than tenderness. Father was more demonstrative, took her on his lap and embraced her, when he was at home. But since she was taught that one should love both parents alike, and her father's being demonstrative made her love him more, this filled Margaret with guilt and she avoided the contact, particularly in her mother's presence so as not to make her jealous. Whether Margaret's mother showed the same inhibition of touching her husband and sons does not become clear.[1]

Mother, who disapproved of any expression of emotion, expected of Margaret that she should be the conventional little girl in curls and pink clothes, who plays with dolls, never gets dirty, and doesn't fight. Margaret was a lively child who wanted to climb trees and play ball like her brothers. To get her mother's approval, she had to deny her genuine tendencies; to have fun and satisfaction in activity, she had to forsake her mother's approval. She was early taught rigid moral rules, and was under the threat of eternal hell-fire for transgressions. Margaret and the younger boy never got along and had many fights. Her major source of security and satisfaction was her older brother, Alan. He played with her, loved her, protected her, invented games for her, and they had fun together. To him she could come with her troubles to be comforted. Nonetheless, her mother's depressed mood, her guilt about Margaret's existence, and Margaret's failure to gain her mother's approval and be close to her, suggested to Margaret quite early that she was worthless and not really lovable.

Margaret was ten when she noticed a change in Alan. He withdrew from the family and did not take any notice of Margaret, who missed his companionship and worried about him. His facial expression became fearful, he would shout strange sentences, and developed peculiar eating habits. Two years later, in his first place of employment, he soon felt persecuted and refused to report to work.

After a brief and traumatic psychiatric examination, Alan was hospitalized for five months, which was an unhappy experience for him. He was treated with ECT and then with insulin shock, which he hated. Returning home he appeared improved and one could talk with him. He and Margaret were companions again, going on long walks together, confiding. But now Margaret was the one to protect and give comfort. She desperately wanted to help him. After a few months Alan refused to go on with his monotonous job at a plant nursery. After several failures to secure higher education, and after rejection from military service, Alan deteriorated rapidly. He was paranoid again, had frequent violent outbursts of temper, misconstrued what he was told, was restless, and stayed in his room or disappeared from time to time in anger. Margaret tried to identify with his ideas and feelings and fervently prayed to God for his recovery. Apparently this went on for years.

Margaret was eighteen when Alan one day expressed his despair to the family. Feeling that the family was being destroyed and trying to console Alan, Margaret pleaded that he should let them help him, promising that she would find a doctor for him who would understand. He flew into a rage and with angry accusations left the house. Three weeks later his body was found in the River Thames. Margaret felt that she had let him down, that she had not prayed enough to save him, and was guilty for his death. Her faith in God was shaken. No one took any notice of her anguish and the double loss of her brother and her trust in God.

Eight years later, Margaret is a nurse and midwife. She is about to complete a course to become a health visitor, when she and two young women, fellow students, go on a vacation abroad: "our three weeks' cycling trip became a symbol of hope and normality, like a life raft to a person drowning in an angry sea" (1986:3). A close friendship emerges, particularly with Pat, whose support, understanding, cheerfulness, and hospitality later comes to play a major part in Margaret's remarkable recovery from her severe depression.

By this time Margaret is a stable, self-controlled, and emotionally distant person, who represses and denies many feelings, who is unable to say spontaneously what she is thinking or aware of feeling, who feels constantly obliged to do what she thinks others expect of her, is considerate of others at her own expense, and has more negative expectations than she realizes. These are rather frequent personality patterns among persons prone to become and stay depressed. She has repressed much of her grief over her brother's fate and over her loss of him as a loving companion. She has no romantic or friendship relationships with men.

Precipitating circumstances and onset of disturbance

After her return from the cycling trip, at the beginning of a menstrual period, Margaret suffers a severe hemorrhage in class. She is terrified and feels faint when her new friends take her to her physician's office. He is on vacation and his partner examines her. She is told to return if, after a few periods, the symptom has not subsided. It keeps recurring unchanged, and when she later consults her own physician he is evasive and gives her a referral to the gynecological out-patient clinic. Alarmed by his unusual evasiveness, Margaret opens the referral letter and sees that aside from the fibroids he has mentioned, there is an additional suspicion of cancer of the uterus or ovaries. Having nursed women dying of such cancer, Margaret, twenty-six, is aware of the fact that at her age a cancer may develop rapidly.

During the following months Margaret is exposed to constant evasiveness and unavailability on the part of medical personnel. No one responds with interest or information to her questions and anxieties. Some weeks after referral, exploratory surgery is performed to remove and examine the fibroids.

Margaret is living with her parents, though not sharing their meals, but is unable to expose them to any information that might worry them. She has no one to confide in except a sympathetic older colleague on the job, Rita, and soon also Pat, who is now a health visitor in a village at some distance from London. Margaret is afraid of dying and misses her former trust in God's protection.

Late in November 1966, five anxious months after her first hemorrhage, Margaret is at last given a sympathetic and satisfactory consultation with her surgeon. He takes time to discuss with her all the implications of the situation: the fibroids are not malignant now, but of a type that tends to recur and suddenly may become malignant. Margaret sees no other way for her to cope than immediate hysterectomy. Her parents are shocked at the prospect of her becoming unable to bear children, but they are not told of the cancer risk, they ask no questions, and the subject is quickly dropped.

The hysterectomy is performed forty-eight hours later. It proves to have been a wise step, as since the exploratory surgery several new tumors have developed, though as yet they are benign. On the ward, Margaret is very tense and afraid of nursing errors. She continues to be terrified of the possibility of dying, uncertain as she is now about what would happen to her after death. She is still on the hospital ward, when she begins to realize that physically she will recover and regain her strength, but she begins to feel a loss of womanhood and a conviction that now no man will want her; that she would deprive a man of his right to children if she married him. There is no grief over her own loss of unborn children, but she feels more depressed than ever. Her father, noticing her distress, buys her a car, which pleases her.

Margaret worries about her state of mind. She becomes alarmed by her uncontrollable outbursts of inappropriate amusement at "the funny side of distressing situations" that other patients have to cope with. When she is discharged to a convalescent home, she goes for many walks, but always alone, avoiding contact with other guests, partly out of fear of behaving inappropriately. At Christmas-time she spends two weeks with Pat in her village. With Pat she is not afraid to reveal her genuine moods, which mostly show her listless, frightened, grieving, and depressed, but at times hilarious. Pat is concerned and takes Margaret to the local physician, who prescribes Librium.

Soon after her return to London, Margaret consults her own physician to check whether it is sound to continue taking Librium. On hearing her description of her state, he says that this does not sound like a reactive depression and advises Margaret to continue with Librium. His obvious concern about her avoidance of social contacts reminds Margaret of the fact that this was the first symptom of her brother's disturbance. After the consultation, she sits for hours in a park, flooded with recollections of the years of his illness. From then on she is consciously afraid that she might be developing schizophrenia.

Margaret is still on sick leave, but when her isolation and inactivity make her apprehensions unbearable she returns to work. There, Margaret finds herself seriously handicapped in performing her duties. She does well on Wednesdays, when she teaches classes for expectant mothers. She manages with great effort to visit and advise women who have recently become mothers and have requested counseling. But more often than not, she finds herself unable to enter the homes of mothers who have made no such requests but are to be visited routinely. What could she offer these women, without having the first-hand experience of what it is like to become a mother? For hours she sits at her desk, inactive and in despair. Clinic personnel are understanding and tolerant. Rita is like a helpful mother, listening to Margaret's outbursts of despair and self-criticism, and trying to reassure her unobtrusively.

Margaret begins to have nightmares and frightening spells of violent tremors at night, when she cannot move her limbs. Three weeks after Margaret's return to work, Rita suggests psychotherapy. She knows the name of a highly recommended psychoanalyst and psychiatrist, Dr G.. Rita calls him and, describing the seriousness of the situation, she obtains an appointment for Margaret during his lunch hour two days later.

Interrupting the summary here to compare these recent events with Margaret's earlier life history, one is struck by the repetition of specific traumatic experiences. During childhood and adolescence she suffered severe emotional deprivation because of her parents' incapacity to cope with their feelings and to communicate them unambiguously in words and behavior. She suffered from their inattention, lack of understanding, rigid religious beliefs, and preoccupation with their own difficulties, and from the lack of tender bodily contact with her mother. Now, Margaret's parents have failed her again. Moreover, in this crisis she is as dependent on medical personnel for her welfare and survival as children are on their parents, but with doctors and hospital nurses she encounters the same type of evasiveness and insensitivity to her need for unambiguous information and for consideration of her feelings. Even the surgeon whom she trusts first ignores her need. At the same time this situation repeats some of her unfortunate brother's experience with parents and professional authority. Unable to criticize authority, to protest effectively, and thereby feel more secure, Margaret increasingly identifies with Alan's experience, fearing his fate for herself. Furthermore, the earlier deterioration and loss of satisfaction in her companionship with Alan is now repeated in the loss of her psychobiological potential for fulfillment through biological motherhood.

As this massive repetition of former traumatic experience now increases the old accumulation of repressed painful emotions and of inhibited impulses, Margaret has no way of coping available to her, other than her usual means: repression, denial, projection, displacement, isolation, reversal, and inhibition.

These partly pathogenic defenses now have to be intensified in order to prevent forbidden emotions and impulses from breaking through, and make her vulnerable (Brown and Harris 1978). It becomes more difficult than ever for Margaret to live up to her ideal self: the stable, helpful, warm person on whom others can lean. This causes the depressed response to sound its alarm, but the work of depression is impeded by her excessive shame and guilt, by her defenses and inhibitions. Therefore, depression cannot become productive – as will be discussed in the next chapter. Her depressed response is a signal of inner dysfunction, while her anxiety alerts her to the internal and external consequences she fears, secretly still including hell-fire. The affect of grief is now profuse, but she cannot allow herself as yet to recognize its real causes. It is quite possible that, if Pat had not replaced Alan as a satisfactory companion, and if Rita had not served as a protective, understanding mother figure, Margaret could have developed a psychotic episode and would have needed much longer therapy.

The therapist's contribution to change and recovery

Aside from his brief comments in the introduction to the book, we see Dr G.'s contribution mainly through Margaret's eyes and through its reflection in her development, but we can conclude that during the initial consultation he recognizes in Margaret the strength, intelligence, and motivation she will need to utilize psychoanalytic psychotherapy despite the severe strain created for so distressed a patient, when such therapy is conducted with a week's interval between sessions. Gently but firmly, and without in any way implying that she is to blame, he works toward making Margaret aware of distortions becoming apparent in her images of self and others, and of human relations in general. Rather than working on these problems with the exclusive focus on current functioning inherent in the technique described by Beck (1967), Dr G. begins in the first therapy session to relate the anxiety Margaret experiences in the therapy relationship and set-up to the origin which her negative expectations can be assumed to have had in the dynamics of her family, particularly her mother's reactions since Margaret's birth. This is soon confirmed by the memories and new information Margaret reports.

During the first weeks of therapy, Dr G. concentrates his comments on Margaret's fear of dependence on others and her misconceptions of the consequences of letting herself be dependent as necessarily negative; on her unawareness of the necessity and advantages of interdependence of human beings at all ages. He succeeds quickly in arousing Margaret's curiosity as to whether his concepts are applicable, in stimulating her memory, and in motivating her to become observant of the difference between profitable and disadvantageous situations of dependence in her current life.

Soon Dr G. also begins to highlight Margaret's deep-seated, though rarely conscious, feelings of worthlessness, her pattern of always adapting her actions and feelings to what she conceives as the wishes of others, her unawareness that she could have any right to have her own feelings and needs, and that they could be healthy. He persists with these interpretations, although they arouse much pain and anxiety in Margaret. At first, he concentrates his description of these problems on their earliest roots in her mother's behavior and dissatisfactions. But when, in the twenty-first session, Margaret dares to take up her religious anxieties, he modifies his interpretation. He shows Margaret how the dictates and threats from her religious sect have reinforced the original conflict between her genuine, healthy desires and her severe, self-denying conscience.

Dr G. is not shaken in his approach by the increase, during the first six months of therapy, of symptoms hard to bear for Margaret. Although Margaret is alarmed by her avoidance of more superficial social contacts, Dr G. no doubt recognizes the value of Margaret's relationships of increasing trust in Pat and Rita. He remains firm, without being rigid, in resisting Margaret's efforts to have him give her specific advice, or present her with a diagnostic label to her difficulties. Except for two occasions, Dr G. proceeds with having her use the couch as long as only one source of her dismay is evident: her wish to adapt her behavior to what she might detect in his face about his possible approval or disapproval. But during the twenty-sixth session, the last before Dr G.'s summer vacation, another cause surfaces for Margaret's difficulty in revealing herself freely when lying on the couch: the prostrate position on the couch reminds her of the humiliating experience of the gynecological examinations at the hospital clinic, whereas sitting up talking to Dr G. is reminiscent of the respect and consideration her surgeon showed when she had to decide for or against hysterectomy. At this point both Margaret and Dr G. change their minds: she no longer needs to insist on sitting up in sessions, while he decides it may be helpful to her to do so.

Many more aspects of Dr G.'s verbal and non-verbal communications to Margaret could be cited to show that he not only provides her with new concepts she can use as tools to look at herself and others more realistically, but that he also creates a climate of experience between them in which she can discover how many reactions – as, for instance, anger and envy – that she formerly had to disown to avoid shame, guilt, and fear of rejection, are normal human responses which it is advisable to tolerate in oneself and express to the right person.

The contribution of others to Margaret's recovery

As was emphasized in Chapter 4, favorable or unfavorable circumstances play an important role in the outcome of a person's work of depression. That

Margaret cannot turn to her parents to share her anxieties and confusion contributes to the development of her syndrome. But the empathy and support she can count on in Pat and Rita make it possible for her to tolerate her severe symptoms and the increase of anxiety during her therapy. The presence of both women in Margaret's life makes it possible for Dr G. to proceed as rapidly as he does despite the long interval between sessions. Several times Margaret is close to breaking off treatment, a step her father would welcome, but due to Pat's and Rita's reassurance that she is in good professional hands, she is able to persist. When she despairs of ever changing with the help of therapy, both Rita and Pat succeed in showing her that she actually has begun to change. On another occasion, Margaret is reassured, when Rita happens to make a point that Dr G. has also made, namely, that Margaret never is satisfied with her own performance, unless it is perfect. Margaret's long letters to Pat about therapy sessions appear to constitute a part of her work of depression.

That Margaret has a familiar place of employment to go to regularly despite her reduced capacity to function professionally is an invaluable factor in her tolerating her symptoms and the emotional upheaval she experiences in therapy. Rita is instrumental in keeping her on the job and creating the accepting climate that Margaret needs.

A young man, Peter, also plays a supportive, and later a challenging role in Margaret's emergence from her social and emotional isolation. In mid-July 1967, when she has had some twenty sessions of therapy, he approaches her at church and invites her to have tea at his flat and to listen to some records. He makes it clear that he only wants a friendly association, no romantic involvement (nor sex relations). A friendship develops in which she can enjoy sharing interests and activities with him and his friends at a time when she has not yet been made aware of, and helped to overcome, the unconscious taboo on sexuality imposed by her upbringing. Also, Peter is willing to listen to her anxious complaints, when she needs to telephone someone in the middle of the night. A year later, she is ready to test his suitability for a deeper involvement and then becomes free to move on.

Last but not least, one cannot dismiss the possibility that Margaret's remarkable persistence in her struggle to help herself is in part due to her having learned as an adolescent, for her love and need of Alan, to tolerate terror without giving up; and that despite her difficulties, she carries buried in herself the memory of his early loving care as a model worth reviving in other relationships.

Margaret's development in therapy

Margaret is encouraged by her first contact with Dr G. on February 21, 1967: she feels understood and taken seriously; his accepting her for therapy suggests that he considers her disorder treatable, which is a relief. But she doubts that he would accept her if she disclosed her fear of being schizophrenic; and the idea of lying on the couch trying to associate freely without seeing his face makes her far more anxious than she can express in her feeble protest.

Arriving the next time, Margaret feels worthless, lost, and in danger. In the waiting room she is tempted to run off, but is held back by the thought that this is probably her last chance for recovery. For the first six months of therapy she remains prey to the intensely disturbing feelings aroused by her conflicting perceptions of Dr G.. She wishes and hopes to get helpful understanding and guidance, and soon she begins to recognize the usefulness of his comments and gradually becomes able to apply them. At the same time, she is frustrated by not getting advice, diagnostic and prognostic statements, words of comfort and sympathy; and by having to use the couch. All this she interprets as proof of callous indifference and cruelty. She expects him to reject her if she displeases him by her behavior. Although she becomes increasingly impressed by the pertinence of his observations and increasingly dependent on her sessions as the major anchor in her current life, some of her symptoms become more severe. After the fifth session, she begins to apply the new ideas she receives from Dr G. more and more systematically. New concepts lead to new insights and to some change in her behavior – as, for instance, grief about what she has missed as a child. Then she is overwhelmed by doubt, whether this change really is for the better.

The symptoms that frighten her most during these months are her constant nightmares and night terrors; suicidal thoughts; mood swings consisting of brief intervals of feeling hilarious, assertive, and boisterous for a few hours in between the prevalent mood of feeling anxious, frightened, worthless, useless, and confused; the resulting limitations in her functioning at work; a period of inability to decide what to buy or do at the grocery store, feeling confused to the point of fearing she might be caught in inadvertent shop-lifting.

After having become more accepting of her own dependence, she recognizes next how guilty she feels toward her parents and toward Alan; and that she has felt inferior long before her inability to bear children has given her an explanation for such feelings. As Dr G. becomes more insistent in showing that she believes she has no rights in life, no right to happiness or love, to freedom of choice, or even to her depression, and as he relates this to her background and the disregard by her elders of her needs as a child, Margaret reacts with such pain and heightened anxiety that on one occasion, disoriented, she first wanders, then runs the streets for a long time. When she finally returns home and prepares to take a bath, she quickly has to empty the bathtub down to two inches of water, so as not to carry out an impulse to drown herself. The next day she calls Dr G. during his lunch hour to report her panic. When he briefly explains that the current intensity of her symptoms is due to the content of their sessions, which are traumatic and frightening for her, she respects him for his composure but does not believe she will survive until the next session.

This session, the fourteenth on 25 May, becomes the first turning point in the therapy. Margaret tells Dr G. that she hates him when he says certain things. Then she admits her worries about being schizophrenic and not wanting to live if she is. Dr G. tells her that she is not only afraid of being ill but also of being well, and that she is afraid of the long road toward health. After leaving Dr G.'s office, Margaret gets very angry with him for what she experiences as his cruelty. In fantasy she shouts abuse at Dr G. while he lies on the couch; she tries to make him, an analyst, cringe on his own couch. Then she realizes with a start that he wouldn't cringe at hearing abuse, but would tell her he was pleased at her learning to express her feelings; that enjoying anger for the first time in her life, and not feeling guilty about her anger, means progress.

During the following session, Dr G. makes Margaret compare her own experiences of anger and its causes with Alan's responses of anger. She sees that there is a difference. While she still doesn't know whether her disorder should be called schizophrenic, she suddenly doesn't care about not knowing, because Dr G. will give her the help Alan didn't get. She feels more hopeful, but is none the less relieved the next day to hear Rita tell her that she is not schizophrenic.

From then on Margaret is observant of feelings aroused in her during the week, mostly anger, envy, and jealousy; and she takes them up in sessions with Dr G. Without telling him, she recognizes that she can bear to hate him, but not to love him. Once she is pleased that he makes an erroneous comment. She feels triumphant at having outwitted him, but then she sees that this is an unproductive attitude. Late in June, with Dr G.'s help, Margaret begins to recognize that the thought of never bearing a child causes her pain. When she begins to tremble uncontrollably on the couch, Dr G. comments that she is frightened about something within herself. This makes her realize that she will have to take up her religious background and doubts with him, although he is not Christian. After she has done so in the next session, Dr G. begins to emphasize the conflict between her desires and her conscience. Now Margaret keeps swaying between her growing trust in Dr G. and her self-accusation for trusting a man rather than God. Dr G. accepts her hating him for the anguish he causes her, but Margaret feels guilty about hating him and experiences a consuming hatred of herself as a result. She has a terrifying nightmare of having become two Siamese twins, a happy fat one, and a depressed lean one, who keep devouring each other. In June Margaret also becomes aware of her bitterness about her loss of Alan, and then she mourns him.

The next turning point comes late in August during the last session before Dr G.'s summer vacation. Margaret has mustered the courage to send him a letter about his failure, as she sees it, to respect some basic needs of hers, among them her need to face him. On arrival, she is very disappointed that Dr G., as I described earlier, requests that she first use the couch to examine the feelings this arouses. After she has discovered that the couch reawakens the humiliation suffered when she felt gynecologists treated her "like a lump of meat" rather than a person to be talked to, she remains on the couch to relate something she has never talked about before. For three years during nurses' training she had a close friendship with a fellow student who clung to her with homosexual feelings. Margaret enjoyed many aspects of their companionship but resented her friend's controlling possessiveness. She could not cut loose for fear that her friend would commit suicide like Alan. Margaret sees this as the origin of her avoidance of bodily contact, but Dr G. tells her that this avoidance is due to the taboo on both hetero- and homosexual contact she has grown up with in her family and Church.

Margaret has begun to try hard to combat her rigid conscience, but her first attempt to liberate herself from the prohibitions of her background takes an immature form. She decides to drink sherry in her room, at first when she needs comfort during a state of panic, later simply to enjoy it. Once, when in despair, she gets drunk in bed. Then, after Dr G. has left for his summer vacation, Peter, whom she has met in June, wants to take her out on her birthday to dine with two male friends of his. Margaret is not at all in a mood for this, but does not manage to decline. She gets herself heedlessly drunk, vomits, collapses on the floor, sings, shouts abuse, has to be put to bed by the young men. She thoroughly enjoys all of it. She has no regrets the next day, only a hangover. She decides never to drink for comfort again: she has no desire to become an alcoholic.

Following two satisfactory weeks with Pat, Margaret drives from the country to Dr G.'s office for the first session after his return. She allows several hours for the trip in order to think about therapy: whether it has changed her self-image, her emotions, and her conscience. She finds that there is change, but is uncertain whether this means being healthier. Then she looks at her symptoms for an answer to this question. She finds that while her symptoms remained practically unchanged until Dr G.'s departure, there has been gradual improvement ever since. While taking stock, Margaret experiences moments of panic, but she is calm when she arrives at Dr G.'s office.

Sitting and facing Dr G., Margaret finds that her thoughts come quickly and she speaks with ease as she reports her conclusions. But returning to work she finds the demands of the job incompatible with her current needs, and asks Dr G. whether she should not quit. He advises against dropping her job at that point and encourages her to be satisfied with a lower standard of performance instead. His trust in her ability to perform passably increases her confidence and she does better at work. From mid-October her symptoms decline. Dr G. can now see her twice a week. Margaret is happy for two weeks and then has a relapse into feeling anxious and unhappy. It turns out that, without having admitted this to herself, she is wishing she could move to an apartment of her own, where she could reciprocate social hospitality. She feels guilty toward her parents for such longings. From then on, when she feels unhappy or other symptoms increase, she concentrates her thoughts on these feelings and on the circumstances in which they arose. She discovers that usually she gets depressed when she feels unwanted, which happens easily. Slowly she learns not to adapt her behavior to such misgivings, unless she can find a very good reason to deem them valid.

Margaret's attitude to Dr G. is changed. She trusts him, finds the sessions helpful. They often focus on anger and its purpose in normal living. Her nightmares continue well into spring, but they frighten her less. She discovers how painful it is to see the happiness of other women, when they bear and then care for their babies, and she goes through a period of mourning the loss of her procreative ability. Then she begins to enjoy her work with mothers and babies. Gradually, Margaret becomes frustrated with the platonic character of her friendship with Peter. She discovers that part of her tie to him has been his heart condition: he would not want children and, consequently, she would not be in the position of depriving him of his right to children. She can now freely talk to Dr G. about her sexual longings, and learns from him that not all men would find biological paternity in a marriage more important than the companionship and love of a woman.

In May, Margaret begins to think in terms of making changes: she wants to move away from her parents and from Peter, who lives nearby; although she now enjoys work, she wants to change jobs and get away from the dependence on Rita and other staff members established during her disorder. She decides to leave health visiting and for the time being to return to midwifery. She applies in a community at some distance from London for a residential position in a home for pregnant, unmarried mothers. She terminates therapy late in August 1968 to enter that position. Her plans are thoroughly discussed in therapy sessions during the summer. She realizes that she still has a long way to go to inner security and healthy self-expression, but she believes that she can reach her goal without further assistance.

This development shows how in Margaret's case the capacity for productive work of depression, completely blocked to begin with, became liberated step by step in the course of psychotherapy.

Norman Endler: a self-report of severe depression and remissions

Endler completed writing his report two and a half years after affective symptoms had disappeared and twenty months after his heart attack. The report is written from memory. He gives us (1982) a day-by-day, often hour-by-hour, account of his suffering, within two years, two cycles of a disorder diagnosed first as severe unipolar affective disorder and later rediagnosed as bipolar. A year after the second remission from depression he had a minor heart attack. The description of his own experience, behavior, and treatment alternates with extensive didactic sections on bipolar affective disorder with its typical symptoms, on various psychopharmaca with their indication and hazards, and on electroconvulsive therapy. The content and manner of the presentation suggest a sincere, straightforward author. He was encouraged by his psychiatrist to publish this account. Medical treatment – first psychopharmaca, then electroshock, and finally Lithium – led to remarkable symptom relief or remissions from a severe acute disorder. The book was published too soon to know whether it is justified to speak of recovery. The report shows growth in self-awareness and a genuine striving to cope with the disorder in a constructive way. Nonetheless, one gets the impression that life experience, behavior patterns, and current social influences may, despite symptom relief or remissions, have interfered with a fully productive outcome of the work of depression in this case. One detects in the presentation an ambivalence: all symptoms that would be of interest to the reader who follows current views of organically oriented psychiatry are described in detail with remarkable courage and honesty. But many significant data of recent and past life history that would be of interest to the reader who wishes to consider whether, despite psychiatric opinion, dynamically pertinent causes for the breakdown could be established are left out. Only a few such clues are given, some of them in passing, as if inadvertently.

Background history

Norman grew up in a Canadian city as the second child of a Jewish couple who observed religious practices. As an adult he is apparently on friendly terms with his sister, a social worker, who lives with her family in another city. The difference in their age is not mentioned, nor are we given a developmental history. His father died on August 5, 1971, when Norman was forty. After this bereavement he grieved, was depressed, and slept poorly for some weeks or a few months, but in contrast to the current disturbance, there was no anxiety and agitation. This is the only recollection offered of symptoms of acute grief or depression earlier in life. We learn nothing about the father as a person, about their early and adult relationship, or the cause of his death. His mother is mentioned briefly only twice: first in connection with his expecting to meet her at the bar mizvah of his nephew, two days after the last treatment of the ECT series, which after the first episode of severe depression restores him to his normal functioning. His mother does not then or later know about his depression. The second time, she is mentioned in connection with her visiting Norman and his family for three days to celebrate the Seder in April 1978. His second episode of depression has just begun, but he manages to conceal his state of mind: "It would have been impossible to be with her had she known" (1982:94).

Norman attended primary and secondary schools with almost exclusively Jewish pupils, and then spent a year in Israel. Otherwise, we learn about his childhood and adolescence only the significant fact that in grade school he was second in class, that in high school he found it distressing not to be at the head of the class, as he had hoped, that he never felt "like a winner" until his doctorate, but not "like a loser" either (1982:24). He was married at twenty-four. His wife, an artist, is four years younger. They come from a similar background and share many interests and tastes. At the onset of his disturbance they have been married over twenty-one years, their son is nineteen, and their daughter fifteen. Norman is a successful professor of psychology, teaching at the doctoral level, serving as consultant, and is chairman of the largest university department of psychology in Canada. He has published widely on developmental psychology, anxiety, and other subjects.

Onset and preceding circumstances

From the description given one gathers that Norman, before the onset of his affective disorder, is a physically healthy, athletic, and ebullient man, feels successful and satisfied in his profession, is pleased with his marriage, and has a warm relationship with his children. He has many friends, particularly among his professional colleagues, about whom he tells us much more than about his closest relatives. He has many cultural interests and engages in sports, favoring tennis. He places the onset of the first, hypomanic, phase of his disorder in August 1976 during the interval between an exhilarating vacation trip with his wife, and two weeks of a trip with the whole family. During this interval he starts playing tennis with Ann, a woman his age. As he resumes the contact in September, an intense friendship develops. Although his wife does not play tennis, Ann is a good match for him on the tennis court, and tennis becomes almost a passion. In contrast to his wife's softer temperament, Ann has more of Norman's ebullience. They have long talks about the cultural background they share, about psychology, and other subjects. He sees her several times a week. He tells his wife every time he is to meet Ann, but there are no questions asked. Norman emphasizes that the relationship is platonic, but that he becomes more and more infatuated. During that fall and winter, in addition to his many professional functions, he becomes excessively active, practically day and night, both socially and in sports. He is never still for a moment and greatly enjoys everything he does. He discovers much later that by his family, his friends, and his colleagues his total behavior during the period from September 1976 through March 1977 was experienced as different from his usual responses, but he himself was unaware of being different.

What is described here appears quite typical of what I have referred to in Chapter 1 as avoided depression, when an unconscious perception of discrepancy between a significant striving and actual functioning is prevented by the diversions of hyperactivity from eliciting the depressed response that could direct attention to the deadlock.[2]

At the end of March 1977, Ann informs Norman that she wishes to cut down considerably on their contact, and from then on he finds her rather irritable and unfriendly toward him. Apparently, he takes her withdrawal as a rejection, without considering any other interpretation – for instance, that she could be threatened by feeling too attracted to a safely married man. At the same time, a research grant he has held for years is unexpectedly not renewed.

Now he rapidly develops the symptoms of a syndrome of depression. He becomes increasingly fatigued, listless, sleepless, anxious, agitated, and apprehensive. Within a week his sexual responses have disappeared. Within three months he has lost self-confidence to the point that he feels like a fake and incompetent, not deserving his position, his reputation, his degree, his marriage, anybody's love. He expects to be fired and to become destitute. He tends to get confused, cannot concentrate or organize his time, cannot make decisions. He becomes unable to drive his car and has to take sick leave from his work. He becomes afraid to go out alone, afraid of getting lost even when accompanied. He becomes extremely dependent on his wife, who shows unusual patience and steadiness. He becomes afraid of being deserted, very distrustful, feels that colleagues watch him to prove his incompetence. He believes that Dr Persad, to whom I shall refer as Dr P., a very busy chief psychiatrist, is keeping track of whether Norman is taking his medication: should Norman fail to do so, the dreadful consequence would be placement in a mental hospital. He is helpless, dependent, bizarre in some of his demands, and occasionally he almost cannot get out of bed. At the same time, he can usually receive the friends and colleagues who come to visit him, and enjoys the conversation. Except for the paranoid distortions of what he suspects of others, and the distortion of his self-image, he remains rational. There are no suicidal tendencies, no violent impulses. It should be added, that neither during the months preceding nor those following Endler's severe depression was there any outright manic behavior.

Developments under and after treatment

At the end of May, Norman, who has dismissed a friend's suggestion that he seek "deep psychotherapy," is persuaded by another friend and by his wife to seek psychiatric help. He decides to consult Dr P., chief psychiatrist in a psychiatric unit of the university, where Norman chairs the psychological department. He finds Dr P. friendly and understanding. He feels respected and treated as an equal. He appreciates that Dr P. interviews Norman's wife only in his presence. Somewhat later, he feels at times treated too much as a colleague by medical staff, rather than as a patient. During the first consultation some background data are discussed, but Norman mentions only the loss of his research grant as a possible precipitating factor. Ann is mentioned only some weeks later. Norman is given antidepressant medication, but within two weeks it has to be replaced because of severe inability to urinate, and as a result, great anxiety. Repeated changes in medication invariably lead to the same complication, before any antidepressant has been taken long enough to affect the depression.

In August Norman begins to consider going on disability pension. There is no improvement until, after two and a half months of chemotherapy, seven ECT treatments at the rate of three a week yield the dramatic result of apparent complete recovery. Norman returns to his work and normal social life.

During his depression, Norman has very mixed feelings about the treatment. To begin with he has, as he later sees it, too much of the psychologist's prejudice against psychiatric views and treatment. Rarely having needed to take pills, he hates taking any medication and doubts their efficacy. He is intensely opposed to ECT and expects it to cause lasting damage. Yet, he submits to Dr P.'s recommendations, it seems, without much strenuous protest, taking the medication "more out of paranoia, docility, compliance, and fear" (1982:51) than out of any belief in its efficacy. At the same time he hopes it might help after all. He is in despair about the lack of improvement when he accepts ECT. Dr P. has assured him that, as applied nowadays, ECT does not present any hazards to the patient.

But actually, although Norman appears to have escaped damage, Breggin's review (1979) of the medical literature "pertaining to severe and permanent brain damage caused by electroconvulsive therapy" (1979:ix) shows that the safety and advisability of ECT treatment is far more controversial than Dr P. suggested. On the other hand, Kendell takes the position (1983) that the risk of death for patients treated with ECT is considerably less than for patients not treated for their depression or treated by tricyclic antidepressants or psychotherapy.

It does not become clear at what point between the first psychiatric consultation and Norman's first remission as a result of ECT treatment he switches from his original speculations about psychological causes of his condition to his later view that this is a purely biochemical illness.

In his book, Endler actually recommends psychotherapy for manic depressives conjoint with organic treatments, but he does not at any time appear to have considered psychotherapy for himself. Dr P. does not appear to have proposed psychotherapy, and apparently Norman's wife is in agreement with this position.

Norman describes himself as hypomanic for more than two months following the disappearance on about September 1, 1977 of all symptoms of the syndrome of depression. At some time during this phase, Dr P. raises the question whether it would not be very valuable if Norman published his experience with depression. After some hesitation, and against the advice of some colleagues, Norman embraces the idea with enthusiasm. In mid-November he is back to his normal level of mood.

Toward the beginning of the year 1978, regular contacts with Dr P. are discontinued. In March, Norman is contacted by Dr P., who tells him he would like to interview him about his illness on an anonymous video-tape to be used strictly confidentially at a staff conference to be held on April 11 on the subject of depression. Norman agrees and the tape is made late in March. On April 11, Norman and his wife join Dr P. and a few other members of Dr P.'s staff with their wives for a pleasant dinner party, before all of them attend the conference. Listening, Norman is preoccupied with the question whether he can be recognized. He does not feel well, but blames this on a gum infection and the penicillin he is taking. The next morning he leaves for four days of lecturing in Texas, where he experiences a good deal of anxiety and insomnia. When he comes home, his depression has returned full force. This time he seeks Dr P.'s help immediately.

At the time, Norman expects to leave with his wife early in May 1978 for several weeks of a travel fellowship in England, where he is to lecture at several universities. Now he is in a panic that he may have to cancel. When increased medication does not help, he is given ECT treatments at the rate of five a week, rather than the earlier three a week. Although this does not remove all symptoms, it enables him to leave some ten days later than planned, but in time not to miss his first lecture in England. With a good deal of anxiety and insomnia he manages to perform well at all his lectures, and to enjoy some aspects of the trip.

Returning home, he is far from well. This time ECT is less effective than the first time and he does not fully recover until Lithium is added to his regimen. This causes some unpleasant side effects until the proper dosage is established, in combination with an antidepressant and a tranquilizer. From September 1978, however, all is well and remains well until Norman has a minor heart attack on August 5, 1979 – the anniversary of his father's death, as he calls to the attention of psychoanalytically oriented readers. This requires two weeks of hospital care and some time of recuperation until, early in November, he can depart for his sabbatical visit at Stanford University, where he stays until April 1980. There he writes, among other things, the first draft of *Holiday of Darkness* (1982). At the time Norman completes his final draft, in April 1981, he is taken off Lithium on a trial basis. He finds it reassuring that he can always return to Lithium, should this be necessary. From some of his closing discussion it seems that, more than his depressions, his heart attack has helped him see the advisability of reducing his pace of living and working.

This account raises many challenging questions, although material showing personal history prior to onset is too sparse to permit reliable conclusions. We saw that Endler switched in his attitude from the position that his depression must have psychological causes to the position that it was a purely biological dysfunction. But why could it not be both?

Mind, body, or both?

Organically and neurologically oriented psychiatrists tend to be trained in approaches to the interpretation and treatment of pathological behavior that are different from what psychotherapists learn in their training. Neither are given sufficient orientation in the research findings on which the various approaches are founded. This, unfortunately, tends to maintain the old mind–body dichotomy, although recent research should make it clear that the psychological and physiological aspects of behavior interact constantly, are dependent on each other, and can only in theoretical abstractions be separated. In the living organism they belong together in the initiation and course of all processes, behavioral and other, as Peterfreund emphasizes (1971).

There is no reason to question that the alternation of Norman's hypomanic and depressed behavior is in part caused by a neurophysiological, biochemical, perhaps genetically determined, disposition to overreact to certain stimuli with exaggerated mood swings – or, if you will, that he has a volatile temperament which, given specific and severe stress, can quickly go to extremes and then get hung up there. This position appears to be founded on reliable medical research. But does the existence of a person's genetic or other predisposition to overreact with mood swings rule out that the same person could have been exposed in early or late childhood to relationships and circumstances that make people depression-prone who have no such predisposition? Should one not explore that possibility in each case, as was done by Fromm-Reichmann and colleagues (1954) and by Leff et al. (1970)?

Where is the evidence to prove that in this instance the severe specific stress was purely biochemical and had no roots in life experience and personality development? What the difficult precipitating intrapsychic stress was in Norman's case, we do not know. Finding likely external precipitating factors, let alone the *meaning* attributed to them by the depressed person, tends to take many months of careful examination, as Leff et al. demonstrate (1970). But with regard to the second depressed episode, one cannot help wondering about the role which Dr P.'s behavior may have played when he first suggested that Norman publish a book about his experience, and later encouraged Norman to let himself be interviewed on a videotape to be shown to colleagues and, as it turned out, to their wives. Conflicts in the relationship to a needed parent figure could have been revived that were unacceptable to Norman and therefore deeply repressed.

Furthermore, what biochemical explanation are we given for why the outbreak of the disorder did not come before the age of forty-five; why both depressed episodes started early in April; why each depressed episode came to an end late in August; why many months of hypomanic behavior preceded the first depression, but none the second one, although Norman was not yet taking Lithium? Was the precipitating experience in 1978 too powerful to be controlled for a while by hypomanic behavior? Was the heart attack mainly precipitated by accumulated years of overactivity; or by the stressful side effect of trying diverse medication for the control of the disorder? Or could it be that, when excessive control of depressed reactions by psychopharmaca and ECT removed the useful alarm signals of the depressed response and thereby prevented the work of depression concerning a hidden problem, the marvellous human capacity for adaptation instead resorted to a heart attack to sound a forceful alarm, followed by enforced rest and introspection? Did the heart attack serve as the change in the environment that can remove cause for the depressed response so that the work of depression is no longer needed? Did it remove significant pressures on Norman, or alter his appraisal of his circumstances?

Endler points out that his behavior was typical for the affective disorders. Yes, indeed, but it is important to remember that only the *affective* components of depression or anxiety are mainly physiological in nature: loss of appetite, disturbance of sleep and sexual responsiveness, fatigue, and so on. But a given person's *ideation* during depression is part of that personality and a result of interaction between that person's native disposition and life experience. Norman's distressing ideas during the depressed phases form a much too cohesive pattern to be caused by a purely physiological process. That they resemble the ideas of a good many other people during periods of being depressed – whatever the diagnosis – is due to the fact that many of them have had similar traumatic childhood experiences which, never recognized and emotionally expressed, continue to be virulent. The ideas they share tell us about a person's having felt lost; not having been seen for what he or she was, but ignored, used for an adult's purposes; having had to perform to get love and attention. The capacity to function normally and function well most of the time despite these hidden scars is usually due to defenses adequate under benign circumstances, combined with luck in one's life situation. But these defenses can collapse under specific stress to which a person has remained vulnerable.

Endler mentions the paper by Leff *et al.* (1970), and yet, he does not object to Dr P.'s failure to consider in what way psychological exploration or therapy, conjoint with medical treatment, might be indicated.[3]

Inasmuch as it has no doubt been very important to Endler to leave out most anamnestic data that might facilitate a conclusive psychological interpretation of early influences, it would seem unfair to present speculations concerning the few but significant clues his report does contain. Therefore, I shall only suggest that, at very high cost to himself, he appears, like so many depression-prone persons, to be very protective of attachment and authority figures.

Chapter nine

Handicaps promoting unproductive depression

Apparently, first it's necessary to find someone who feels as ambivalent and destructive towards me as Danny or my mother; then I search my soul to discover what there is in me to provoke such feelings. I concentrate on my faults to explain away the hatred and also to maintain hope. . . . It was a child's dream – you'll see, I'll be good, I'll be very good, and then you'll love me.

From the journal of Bloch's patient, Norma (1978:148)

Introduction

If, in order to become able to help, one wants to empathize with the misery of repetitive or chronic states of being depressed, one must bear in mind the combined frustration of two basic needs which is implicit in my definition of what causes us to get depressed. I mean our need to experience joy in the give and take of an increasingly secure relationship, and Bühler's *"Funktionslust"* (1922): the joy of feeling that we are using our faculties well. Depression due to frustration in sex relations, for instance, is an example of how the combined frustration of both needs causes trouble.

Whenever we dimly perceive that we are failing in any striving in our relating to ourselves and to others, and in the use of those faculties that should serve our purpose, becoming depressed can help us overcome this impasse by potentially facilitating our grasping and resolving our own contribution to the impasse, so that we become better able to influence the contributions made to it by others. If one wants to discover when and why the equipment of the basic depressed response fails to serve this adaptive function, one has to ask oneself two questions: first, what in depression-prone people – possibly including ourselves – gives them so frequent and persistent cause to get depressed; and second, what causes the process of their depression to run an unproductive course?

I have proposed that the basic depressed response serves our adaptation to frustration and change by facilitating our readiness for the type of information processing that might resolve an inner deadlock in our execution of a significant, often largely unconscious, effort to attain, perform, create, or cope. If the work of depression proceeds well, we are going to discover what has gone wrong – or is impossible – and how we can reach a satisfactory resolution of the deadlock. Usually, reaching such a resolution requires a measure of strength, flexibility, and the courage to face unexpected and possibly unpleasant insights. As I have pointed out in Chapter 4, it may also require benign interpersonal and social conditions. Information processing adequate in this context can, of course, be interfered with by a variety of factors, such as immaturity, unavailability of necessary data, external threat, exhaustion, starvation, or a disease process. In some people, it can also happen that due to some physiological state or disposition, depressed reactions and related affective responses quickly acquire dimensions that for some time defeat rather than facilitate relevant and intensified information processing, as, for instance, in manic-depressive conditions. But more often than not, when being depressed fails to run a productive course, this is not primarily due to physiological causes or external interference. In most instances of prolonged or recurrent depression, mild or severe, we find that the depressed person is handicapped by attitudes that distort or inhibit his or her thinking and feeling, particularly his or her image of self and others; or by the use of symbols in communication that are too idiosyncratic to be understood by others. If we can take the time for the necessary exploration, we find that these patterns have developed in the context of specific early interpersonal relations and social circumstances.

These patterns are handicapping in two ways. When one examines cognitive and emotional handicaps that interfere with flexible, effective information processing that should help us resolve a given cause for our being depressed, one realizes that the handicapping patterns, often due to early or current terror and to developmental arrest, are the very conditions for failure to develop and maintain satisfactory relationships with others, good feelings about ourselves, and a basic trust in our capacity to function to our satisfaction. In other words, the same patterns that first cause our getting depressed then prevent our understanding and overcoming our cause for being depressed. This is the vicious circle that can make psychotherapy of chronic or recurring depression so arduous a task.

Alternatively, there may be patterns of avoiding depressed feelings and avoiding other depressed reactions, either by socially acceptable avoidance patterns of overwork, flight into illness, or dependence on medication; or by socially unacceptable patterns, such as addiction to alcohol or drugs, or antisocial behavior. This creates the same vicious circle: the unawareness of our basic strivings and our motivation for avoidance behavior sooner or later leads to inner contradictions that unconsciously are interpreted in ways provoking the basic depressed response. This in turn requires further avoidance behavior leading to an accelerating vicious circle, as can frequently be observed in alcoholics. When for the first time a person who, rather than becoming depressed, has for years in drinking bouts acted out the hidden grief, shame, and rage accumulated since early childhood, clearly assesses the disastrous state of his or her human and business affairs and stays in bed, very depressed but without having bought liquor or wanting to drink, this is a major triumph for the patient and his or her therapist. Now one can begin to explore what really ails him or her and what may be done about it.

The propensity to become and stay depressed for the reasons I suggest is symptomatic for most diagnostic categories of personality disorders, symptom neuroses, and psychoses. After presenting two more case examples, I will describe and examine a number of personality patterns that tend to make people depression-prone. Any of these patterns can appear in more than one diagnostic category, whether these are formulated on psychoanalytic or other grounds. A good many further depressogenic patterns characteristic for one specific clinical picture could have been chosen as well to illustrate my point. For instance, some attitudes and defenses frequent in narcissistic personality disorders as described by Kohut (1977,1984), or in schizophrenia as described by Karon and Vandenbos (1981), clearly must lead to getting and staying depressed, but this might have taken us too far afield. My aim is to facilitate empathic understanding of the adaptive function of one affect only, of its failures, and of its fate in our society. How this approach differs from the aim of diagnostic differentiation of various types of disturbed personality will be taken up in the next chapter. Each approach makes its own necessary contribution to therapy and prevention.

Intrapsychic processes, interpersonal relations, social events, the meaning the depression-prone person ascribes to them, the emotions these meanings arouse, and the defenses against meaning and emotion are intimately connected, although the limitations of our thinking and vocabulary often cause us to examine them as if they were separate. Any of these factors in human behavior can lead to getting depressed and then interfere with pertinent information processing and satisfactory outcome of being depressed. I shall take up only a few types of handicapping psychological patterns in order to clarify my view of being depressed as a process that, depending on circumstances, becomes productive or must fail to do so.

The frequent complexity of handicaps is illustrated by Bloch's case (1978:141ff.), Norma, who has many characteristics in common with depressed patients with whom I have worked. Bloch's inclusion of passages from Norma's own journal of the thoughts stimulated by her therapy sessions brings Norma's plight very much to life. In order to avoid confusion with Endler's self-report, Norman, I shall in my summary of the case refer to Norma as Olga.

Bloch takes the position that much psychopathology has its roots in a childhood fear of being killed by a parent, or at times by an older sibling. Not infrequently this fear has arisen from actual threats, or from a perception of wishes or impulses on the part of the parent or sibling to do away with the child. Bloch shows in her cases that children tend to develop elaborate fantasies built on denial and repression of the frightening perceptions; on distorted and wish-fulfilling interpretation of the meaning of what is or was perceived; and on reversal of roles and responsibilities. If a child's fantasies defending against fear of infanticide are not treated and resolved during childhood they will, usually elaborated further during adolescence and then deeply repressed, persist in the adult. They will control the adult's images of self and others, the perception of causal connections, as well as many other aspects of behavior. These distortions prevent the flexible, curious, realistic examination of our outer and inner situation that would be necessary to understand and resolve a frustrating discrepancy between our intentions and the measures taken to carry them out.

Two examples of handicapped personality

Olga: complex handicaps in information processing

Olga underwent an earlier analysis in her twenties when severe depression with suicidal impulses followed after her husband had left her and their infant daughter. When Olga is referred to Bloch at the age of thirty-seven, she is worried by the homosexual overtones in her close friendship with a woman, Ada, and upset about Ada's hostility. Olga is a good-looking woman, totally unaware of her own charm and talents. She is the youngest of her parents' four surviving children. In the course of therapy it becomes apparent that her older sisters have always been hostile to her and that her brother, Danny, four years her senior, has terrorized her as a child and still influences her negatively. Before Olga was five a baby brother died in infancy of meningitis. She thought that it was her fault and she felt like a murderer. Olga was aware of her mother's miscarriages and stillbirths. Olga's father worked long hours, but when he came home the children were lined up to be kissed by him and he was particularly demonstrative toward Olga. His kissing and being demonstrative ended after Olga was about four, when his wife's aggressive irony discouraged him. A sketch of the mother's childhood history in Chapter 13 will show why she was jealous of her children and particularly of Olga. Mother was at home and keeping house but apparently severely and chronically depressed. She never caressed her children, had almost no social contacts beside husband and children, hardly spoke, and ignored Danny's cruelty toward Olga. She arranged for her children to get an education without ever showing an interest in any child's school performance. The family legend is that she was a martyr to the family. The family were Jewish and held to the tradition that only sons are important for the family. The mother has been dead for some years when Olga begins her second analysis, but she holds the center of the stage in Olga's thinking and feeling.

Olga has a dramatic "investment in feeling worthless" (1978:142) and in seeing her mother as a noble martyr who loves Olga but cannot show it because Olga is so worthless. "The more noble I make her, the more understandable is it that she couldn't love me" (p.141). Olga feels that she has no identity, that something is basically wrong with her, although she doesn't know what. She wants analysis to discover what it is, at the same time as she secretly wishes it to discover that nothing is wrong with her. All her energies are set on winning her mother's love, even after her death. This means that she must not, under any circumstances, discover that her mother was unable to love her and actually hated her. As long as being unloved is due to Olga's own badness, there is hope of changing things by ceasing to be bad. Actually, Olga hates her mother, but this must not be discovered, because on closer inspection it could then become evident that she hates her mother in response to her mother's hateful rejection and neglect of Olga (see Chapter 13), rather than the other way round. This would excuse Olga, but deprive her of the hope for love that helps her survive.

If anyone is critical of her, Olga flies into a rage, because this confirms her badness and threatens the hope for winning her mother. But if one expresses any approval, she gets equally disturbed, because this threatens to collapse the illusion that only her worthlessness, which she might overcome, is the cause of her mother's not showing love. It implies that something may be wrong with her mother. Then there is no hope and Olga must end her life. As a result of this dilemma, Olga cannot allow herself to discover her intellectual and artistic potential, let alone enjoy it. Expectation of failure because of one or another kind of worthlessness causes her to fail in any venture, including intimate relationships.

After some years of her analysis, when accurate and well-timed interpretations gradually have deprived her of one distortion of her reality after another, she gradually considers the possibility that her analyst could be right rather than tricky and destructive in telling her (1978:151), "The only thing wrong with you is your determination to believe that everything is wrong." She also recognizes that she has made herself totally dependent because, having known maternal bodily care only as a helpless infant, she believes love can only be had if one is helpless. As she allows herself to recognize formerly ignored clues to her mother's resentment of having children and to her many attempts to end her pregnancies by abortion, probably also the pregnancy with Olga, the idealization of mother turns into its opposite of seeing her as evil, without any effort to understand what made her mother become the person she was.

As Olga begins to know who she is and some self-confidence develops; as she recognizes how the self-defeating drama of seeking her mother's unattainable love is repeated in her relationships with men and with Ada, whom she has chosen in her mother's image, Olga becomes secure enough for crucial repressions to lift; she remembers episodes at the age of four to five that caused her to fear that Danny was planning to push her off the high roof of the apartment house, and that mother would approve of this; she remembers the self-protective fantasies she developed to cope with this terror, as the beginning of the later complex structure of her defenses. Only then does she become interested in family history explaining the climate in which all this could develop.

Even under more favorable life circumstances, depression-proneness can develop due to limitations of information processing and cause unhappiness not only for the depressed person, but also for the members of his or her family. My description of the following case is, with only minor changes, taken from an earlier paper (Gut 1985:102ff.).

Fanny: recurring but milder depression

Fanny was five years older than her brother. Her father, a successful artist, and her mother, an energetic housewife without intellectual leanings, were devoted to each other. The birth of Fanny's brother deprived her not only of her mother's undivided attention, but he later became her mother's favorite. Fanny always conveyed that she had been her father's favorite, that he enjoyed and encouraged her drawings, her vivid imagination, and her tendency to dramatize her fantasies in play and song. Apparently, he encouraged what he saw as the talents of an exuberant child, while her mother would get exasperated with Fanny's pretenses and fanciful tales and, at times, even call her a fake.

When Fanny was ten her father became ill. He died two years later and left the family in limited economic circumstances, which meant considerable change in their style of social life. Her mother, who had lost her own mother at eight and her father at fifteen years of age, was deeply depressed during the first year of mourning, leaving Fanny to her own devices in coping with bereavement and social change.

Through a grant, Fanny received more advanced secondary education than was usual for girls at that time. Very active social life with peers, a dramatic involvement with a married colleague and former friend of her father's, and doubts about her capacity to pass examinations are likely to have combined to make her receptive for an infectious illness at the time of written final exams, so that she did not graduate. All her life she felt ashamed of this failure, which she covered up, but she never tried to make up for it. Shortly thereafter she married a young physician and had two children in quick succession. The marriage ended in divorce after a decade of mutual deceit. By then, Fanny had begun to devote a good deal of her time to art work and did well at it despite very little formal training.

Fanny idealized the memory of her father whom she recalled as sensitive, spiritual, and educated. She was deeply identified with his interests and pursuits. Originality and command of public acclaim were values that guided her demands on herself and on those dear to her. As an adolescent she had dreams of becoming a singer, but her mother, who later approved of her son becoming a moderately successful musician, discouraged Fanny's dream. To satisfy her hunger for excellence and recognition Fanny later tended to get involved with talented and successful men. Her second husband was just such a man, and old enough to be her father.

Unconsciously, Fanny was longing for her undemonstrative mother's understanding and support. Consciously, Fanny reacted to her with a blend of condescension and genuine respect. The hidden admiration could only be detected in Fanny's emphasis on the values of honesty and reliability which she tried to instill in her children and pretended to possess herself, and in the importance of lasting friendships with women of both her own and her mother's generation who, in addition to having talent and intellectual interests, were honest and reliable.

As an adolescent, Fanny began to feel the need to compensate with an exaggerated display of charm, wit, and artistic know-how for not being male like her mother's favorites – father, brother, and a maternal uncle – and for her inferior economic status. During Fanny's youth women of her social background were, unless they remained old maids, viewed as belonging to one of two categories: the chaste and faithful monogamous mother and housewife; or the passionate lover. The latter was expected to bear the burden of secrecy, deceit, and shame for giving herself to free or clandestine love. Yearning to outdo her mother, who had been a respected representative of the first category, and knowing that she could never compete with her on those terms, Fanny was attracted to the image of the passionate lover. In the role of artistic and brilliant *femme fatale*, she might outshine her more stable women friends. Wishing also in some respect to outdo the idealized creative men in her life, she needed to emphasize her capacity to bear children and be an exceptionally good mother.

No wonder that these conflicting ambitions to compensate for her sense of inadequacy caused Fanny to engage in many impulsive and exploitive actions which resulted in a mounting burden of guilt and shame. Despite her conscious attempts to see herself as sufficiently exceptional to warrant digression from accepted norms, her unconscious moral code remained traditional. This code made a web of lies and distortions necessary that required further denial and burdened her with shame. A loving wife in her second marriage, a passionate lover none the less with other men, a creative artist devoting much time and energy to establishing herself as equal to men, an excellent hostess and manager of a large household: she did not have enough inner resources left to meet the emotional needs of her children in the way to which she aspired. Recurring episodes of at times disabling depression with considerable anxiety, grief, guilt, and somatic symptoms were the inescapable result of her contradictory strivings. These depressions appeared primarily at the anticipation of, or following, painful separations and loss, such as the end of a love affair. It is not known to me whether repressed early fantasies about the causes of her father's untimely death could have contributed to these depressions.

Fanny's sense of guilt was largely conscious, and so was her exaggerated sense of inadequacy and of being a "fake," although she would rarely reveal them to others. On the other hand, just as her longing for closeness to the mother of her early childhood was completely barred from consciousness, so was any resentment or criticism of her father, or any sense of having been abandoned by him when he disappeared into illness and death. Thus, she was ill-prepared to defend herself effectively against neglect by her idealized male partners. Instead, she tried to escape such frustration through flight into unfaithfulness, unconscious of punishing both her neglectful partner and herself. She could not recognize that emotionally she had been abandoned by both parents. This would have caused a rage and despair as unacceptable and incomprehensible to herself as it would have to her parents, well-meaning as they were. Her helpless protest could find its outward expression only in the repetition compulsion of engaging in love relationships invariably involving adultery on the part of one, at times of both partners, and bound to end in disaster. When unconscious efforts, reminiscent of her responses to the original traumata, failed to stave off disaster, the depressed response was elicited.

Despite Fanny's intelligence, her capacity to be realistic in appraising her circumstances and anticipating the long-term consequences of her behavior was hampered by her cognitive bias: she idealized significant others and saw herself as inferior unless she competed successfully with idealized men and women. This bias, her conflict of goals and of social standards, her repressions, denials, and idealizations interfered with the type of information processing that would have been necessary to make choices between her equally attractive but mutually exclusive goals. This made her depression-prone. Nevertheless, being endowed with many talents and having experienced affection and adequate stimulation in childhood, Fanny was able to develop many relationships and skills that gave her pleasure. Despite her suffering, she had a rich life.

Personality patterns causing depression, then defeating its function

Unattainable aspirations maintained by cognitive bias

What we know about Margaret, Norman, Olga, and Fanny demonstrates how, for reasons they do not grasp at the time, their urgent strivings cannot reach their goal, so that they have cause for getting depressed. Their cognitive and emotional handicaps, reinforced by social circumstances, further defeat their goal and then interfere with a productive outcome of their being depressed. The nature of their defenses against the pain of realistic appraisal of their chances is the reason why the withdrawal enforced by their depressed responses must fail to lead to a clarification and modification of what is wrong with their goal, their methods to reach it, or both. Thus, their depression cannot be resolved.

More or less disabling depression tends to involve not only a single incident of failing to attain a significant goal of the moment. Rather, there is an accumulation of frustrated efforts to overcome past failure either by repetition of unsuccessful measures, or by the substitution of compensatory plans, to be carried out by equally ineffective means.

In Margaret's experience, we see that she started out by seeking to get loving acceptance of her spontaneous responses and natural disposition from a mother who after her child's earliest infancy was incapable of accepting and loving her for what she was. Like all children, Margaret drew the conclusion that her mother's distance and disapproval was due to Margaret's own inadequacy, not her mother's. This left her early with the vulnerability to feeling worthless, unlovable, rejected, or deserted. She found some limited compensation during early childhood in her father's tenderness – when he was at home – and during later childhood in her brother, Alan's, affection and companionship. But Margaret's vulnerability to feeling rejected, worthless, and guilty was increased when through her brother's illness and death she lost the limited acceptance she had attained for her spontaneous, genuine self.

In Olga's experience, except for the bodily contact and physical care received from her mother during earliest infancy as a symbol of closeness and intimacy, and the short-lived bodily tenderness of her father, the child's natural need of affection, of protection against attack, and of being reflected as an acceptable self in an attachment figure's view of her, was totally frustrated. Olga started out not only with a hopeless effort to attain love, but also with a struggle for safety beyond her power to secure.

Although incomparably more fortunate in her background, Fanny shared with Olga the hazards of being dislodged by the birth of another child from the position as the youngest, or the only one; and being replaced by a boy in social circumstances where a son's status is higher. To this misfortune, from the child's point of view, was added the fact that Fanny's mother, her original and major attachment figure, happened to be so different in temperament, disposition, talents, and later also in education, that she could not empathize with her daughter, while the father, who apparently could, disappeared into death during Fanny's vulnerable age of pre-adolescence. Thus, she developed early in life the goal of becoming something very special that would make her desirable and earn her acclaim, despite her secret doubts about her worth.

We know least about Norman. His few comments about his goals in school and about his mother, as well as his fears of failure and rejection during the acute depressed phase of his disorder, suggest that, despite his successful functioning at other times, a similar vulnerability to rejection or failure could have been established in childhood, promoting an accentuated goal of winning love and approval by high standards of performance and successful competition. But we do not know enough to explain why a hidden discrepancy between his desires and his chances or capacity to satisfy them appears to have remained a potential concern despite his adult successes, and although his circumstances were more benign than those of the three women, particularly Olga and Fanny: as a boy and young man he had the opportunity to develop his interests and skills, an opportunity that culture and economic circumstances denied the girls. These opportunities may have contributed to the fact that his defenses held the fort until age forty-five. We do not know the facts that would explain why, nonetheless, panic emerged at the height of his depressed phase that (junior) colleagues would kick him out and he would become destitute. Nor do we know whether the loss of his father made him more vulnerable.

There are considerable differences, although not specified in my case descriptions, between these four people in social, national, religious, and socio-economic background and in the time of their birth. Nonetheless, a stubborn cognitive bias is outstanding in the behavior patterns they share with one another and with many depression-prone persons: they valiantly resist recognition that their strivings for a very high standard of social behavior and academic or occupational performance as a prerequisite for deserving love are unnecessary and futile. In part, their perfectionism is imposed by cultural patterns and by family demands (compare with Fromm-Reichmann's research, 1954), as I shall discuss further in Chapters 13 and 14; in part it serves as a defense against the terror that the parental approval they long for might be unattainable.

As indicated in my paper (Gut 1985:102), the concept of cognitive bias is borrowed from Bowlby (1980:ch.13). It implies the tendency to interpret the meaning of an observation with a set of habitual conclusions, optimistic or pessimistic. These stereotyped interpretations of events may stem from happy or unhappy personal experiences, from accepting the view of others, from clinging to a compromise between conflicting data or strivings, or from other sources. Whatever the origin of our habitual interpretations, we can speak of cognitive bias when we are disinclined to question our interpretation, to test its validity, or to modify it; and when an attempt to do so is "not only arduous but painful and perhaps frightening as well" (1980:231). Obviously, cognitive bias will interfere with the work of depression and can also defeat us in our relationships.

The pattern described above is by no means the only cognitive bias typical for depression-proneness. The belief that we are responsible even for events totally beyond our control – as, for instance, the death of a sibling in Margaret's and Olga's cases; that people or circumstances are either good or bad, right or wrong, white or black; that disturbances in our relationships are exclusively due to our own short-comings, or conversely, always due to someone else's attitude and behavior; that it is our duty to protect others, while we have no right to expect or demand corresponding care, are other variants among many. The latter, by Bowlby referred to (1980:156) as "compulsive care-giving," is very frequent among members of the mental health professions. Such stereotyped thinking tends to defeat the information-processing work necessary to emerge from being depressed with productive results.

Disabling lack of self-confidence instilled by attachment figures

We saw to what extent children absorb the negative feelings that their elders experience toward them: Margaret discovered that whatever she might try to do, she was not desirable in her mother's eyes; Olga found that her being alive was a hateful burden to her mother; Fanny discovered first that a child of the opposite sex and of different temperament was far more attractive to her mother than Fanny herself, and later, that her father did not stay healthy and alive for her sake. What form of rejection was Norman's early experience we do not know, but his ideation and anxieties during his acute depression (and perhaps the opposite content of his hypomanic behavior) suggest that, despite his adult sense of being "a winner," there was some period in his early life when the pattern of feeling "a loser" was established that reappeared during the depressed phase of his disorder.

A child's fantasies and speculations to make sense out of damaging and contradictory adult behavior usually include the idea "I am no good." That hurts. A child's behavior, in fantasy and action, to overcome the distress of not getting encouraging responses tends to lead to defeat: more often than not, the child's behavior is not understood by the attachment figure it is aimed at, who does not understand himself or herself either, and rejects this child even more for being experienced as incomprehensible. The child's inner protest, despair, and anger leads to all sorts of defensive maneuvers that deprive the child of its genuine charm and further compound a bad situation. Increasing confusion, shame, and guilt create further conviction of being undesirable.

I recall a patient, Kitty, an only child whose mother was almost her only companion. Her mother needed Kitty in the ways described by A. Miller (1980). Kitty's being made to seem clumsy and wrong was to give her mother a sense of adequacy, at the same time as her mother flattered Kitty in some ways to tie her to herself. Blaming her own social failures on the child, her mother expected at the same time that Kitty should provide compensation for her mother's lifelong frustrations. It became evident only late in this therapy that Kitty never had a chance to remedy the situation by her own efforts, inasmuch as to mother she was forever wrong because she was the daughter of the wrong man: her mother kept complaining that in Kitty's father she had from two prospects chosen the wrong husband.

Another only child I recall, Leila, had among many other impossible expectations and demands of her parents no chance to be accepted by her parents such as she naturally was, because she was of the wrong sex. By her father this was denied with the odd statement, "I wanted a boy, but a little girl is even better because she can be both a boy and a girl for me," which actually deprived Leila of any normal gender, while her mother never mentioned the subject of Leila's sex, but often complained of the burden of being a wòman.

By the time such children have grown up, they don't have to face *one* failure in functioning but, because of their helpless efforts to do the impossible, layer on layer of multiple failures to achieve their most significant aims. Thus, there is an endless chain of causes to be depressed. Yet, lack of self-confidence, and often the lack of a clear identity, make it impossible to grasp and straighten out the recurring, defeating circumstances: hopeless aspirations, mistaken interpretation of events, inappropriate means to change matters. No confidence has developed in the validity of their own observations, their own memories, their own thinking, their own feelings; no confidence in the meaning and significance of their symptoms. The details of McRae's recollections (1986) and of the excerpts from Olga's (Norma's) journal (Bloch 1978) show this beautifully. Unfortunately, if the work of depression is to produce a solution of the riddle of dysfunction in ourselves, we need to rely on our emotional and cognitive resources as trustworthy and as adequate to helping us. We need the same to minimize situations that give us cause for getting depressed.

Thus, the sudden drop in conscious self-esteem noted by Bibring (1953) and by Leff *et al.* (1970) as accompanying the onset of acute depression, is usually due to a fresh perception of dysfunction having reactivated a repressed sense of deficiency of long standing – a vulnerability to failure. This is also emphasized by Bemporad (1983).

Without self-confidence and self-respect it is difficult to overcome the deep loneliness that often accompanies severe depression-proneness. Kitty told me late in her therapy: "Now that I respect my right to accept or reject on my own terms what others give me, I suddenly am aware of and can respect, even if I don't like it, what reasons others may have for their behavior. Before, I never gave that a thought. Now it's easier to cope." Margaret also observed at what point of her development in therapy she began to notice when other staff members looked distressed.

Inhibitions maintained by denial, projection, identification, repression

Early terrors that leave a mark in the form of defensive behavior of depression-prone personality tend to stem not only from actual experiences of frightening separation or rejection, but also from experiences of overstimulation that create a deep-seated avoidance of relationships of closeness. In fear of intimacy, there has frequently been both separation or other neglect alternating with overstimulation.

115

Somewhat later in childhood than these earliest fears, many circumstances can make it necessary for a child to ward off the overwhelming emotions of fear, anxiety, and rage. There may be the separation anxiety aroused by actual loss, by actual threat of abandonment, by the perception of parental depression or physical illness, the perception of a parent's suicidal impulses – let alone completed suicide. There may be disquieting perceptions of a parent or other family member hating and wanting to get rid of this child, as in Olga's case, or of a sibling; there may be frightening perceptions of violence, including sexual violence, in the family; or of alcohol or drug abuse; of sexual infidelity and deceit; and various other behaviors that provoke not only fear and protest in a child, but also shame and humiliation. In addition, there are the frightening fantasies of a child who is too young to understand the causes and meaning of adult behavior. A child interprets such events either on the basis of his or her projections of own turmoil, or with the help of symbols and events contained in fairy tales about witches, giants, sorcerers, and so forth.

Aside from the effort to avoid and deny the fearful perceptions themselves, the intense emotions stimulated in the child become a threat to defend against by various types of behavior, particularly if there is no chance to have these emotions and accompanying thoughts understood and accepted by an adult, if they were expressed; if the child instead has suffered at the hands of attachment figures or other significant adults – or seen siblings exposed to – severe physical punishment, verbal abuse, ridicule, contempt, or punitive silence. If parents or other adults overtly or covertly demand that the child deny and repress ever having seen the frightening behavior, the intense emotions and self-doubt aroused by adult disavowal of the child's perceptions become a danger in themselves to defend against at all cost.

The severe inhibition of anger and assertiveness in depression-prone personalities has been extensively described and discussed in the literature on depression. Often this inhibition is reinforced by projection of the accumulated unconscious rage. As a result, when the inhibition diminishes during therapy and the feeling of anger becomes conscious, its expression may at first be prevented by a deep fear of the person causing the anger, as if retaliation for anger were inescapable. Not only anger, but also shame, contempt, curiosity, and sexual interest and stimulation may have to be prevented by shutting out all perceptions that might stimulate such emotions. Therapists are familiar with the skill with which depression-prone patients may manage to ignore details and changes in the therapist's office or home. That a couch one has stretched out on for some years has changed from dark red upholstery to green may not be noticed, unless the patient is prepared for change in advance. A dress the therapist has been wearing for years may some day be experienced by the patient as new. In the patient's mind sharing tastes with the therapist may carry the risk of being engulfed and losing one's tiny sense of self; disliking the taste of the therapist, or showing the least bit of curiosity, may carry the risk of meeting hate, contempt, rejection, abandonment. Better not think about the few details one can't help noticing and keep silent about it so as not to risk that thoughts get started after all.

Shame about a physical handicap, about some limitation in looks and endowment, about one's sex, as in Fanny's and Leila's situation, about national, racial, and religious origin may, if it has been handled poorly in the family, also be so painful that it must be denied and defended with patterns that prevent genuine responsiveness in personal relations and become the soil for depression.

I have found the inhibition of independent thinking more prevalent in depression-prone persons than is apparent in the literature, except where inhibition of cognition is described as an inherent part of depression, while I see it as a separate defensive pattern that tends to give cause for getting depressed and then to interfere with productive outcome. Particularly in highly intelligent and gifted patients who were exposed to one or both parents' jealousy of their talents and educational opportunities – although the child's using such opportunities is often insisted on by the same parent – I have noticed a severe inhibition of thinking independently and creatively. Such people, at least the kind who have the capacity to persist in extended therapy, may be sufficiently gifted to go through a full course of academic training to a master's or doctoral degree and hold a professional position to the satisfaction of others, though not their own. They remain haunted by the hidden perception that they are performing far below their potential, disguised on the conscious level by nagging doubt about their capacity to perform adequately. Due to their remarkable capacity to adapt and conform to the thinking and wishes of colleagues, teachers, and superiors, they pass their examinations, write the thesis expected of them, and manage to defend it publicly despite their hidden deep disagreement with its content, and at the cost of great anxiety and often of many somatic symptoms. When they cannot accept a theory presented to them by authority, they do not experience disagreement, but rather feel too stupid to comprehend it. In therapy, they are so quick to adopt the therapist's views and to present associations, dreams, and "interesting" material that they sense the therapist expects, that they may graduate from analysis or other therapy without patient or therapist having become aware of the patient's inability to have a thought truly his or her own. When there is no clue to what the therapist thinks or expects, such a patient's mind goes blank and the patient feels empty. We saw Margaret struggling with this problem, although only for a matter of a few months. Between sessions, such a patient, after an interpretation by the therapist has been welcomed with acclaim, is unable to take this discovery a single step further. Next time, the interpretation may have been forgotten, rather than being contradicted.

A milder form of this inhibition may be that a person remains – or through therapy becomes – able to discuss his or her views to an accepting, perhaps admiring audience but suddenly has no more thought and "nothing to say" if hostility is perceived, rightly or wrongly, in a questioning authority figure. The mind goes suddenly blank and may feel like a piece of dead wood, as one patient put it.

In Olga, we saw another variant of selective inhibition of thinking. Although very able to contradict her therapist with opinions of her own, tailored aptly to the needs of the moment, she was unable to follow certain lines of thought if they threatened to unsettle a vitally needed defensive fantasy.

Stopping a gifted, potentially inventive mind selectively from operating is in itself no mean feat. It probably takes a very intelligent child to learn this in such a way that acceptable academic and some other learning remains possible, albeit at a high cost of anxiety and frustration. Learned early, this inhibition is difficult to overcome.

As far as inhibition of emotions is concerned, anger and self-assertion are by no means the only affective responses that may have to be inhibited as a result of frightening events and/or the child's frightening interpretation of events. The dangers may be exaggerated and distorted in the child's mind, but I have found – as did Bowlby (1969,1973,1980) and A. Miller (1980), among others – that in contrast to the picture given until quite recently in case histories by many authors, patients entering therapy often idealize rather than denigrate their parents. Olga presents a vivid example of the kind.

Many children learn to inhibit attachment behavior, demonstrating aloofness and independence instead. They may inhibit envy and become excessively generous and self-sacrificing instead. Shame as well as its opposite, contempt, are quite often inhibited, and all awareness of such feelings in the past, and their causes, are repressed or at least denied. When shame or contempt are stimulated, they may reach the surface only in the transformed shape of guilt and self-accusation, which, being active rather than helpless like shame, is more bearable, while at the same time guilt is socially acceptable, which contempt is not.

One could go on describing the role of defensive identification with an aggressor or with anyone believed to be indispensable for safety and survival; the role of projection in coping with the terror of the past which, never having been fully expressed, remains active under the surface; but I believe that what I have sketched here suffices to demonstrate my point: cognitive bias; lack of self-confidence and self-respect; inhibition of perception, thinking, and feeling; and many other pathological personality patterns are bound to prevent a person from establishing satisfactory, flexible communication with self and others about self and others; prevent a person from establishing, maintaining, and relying on secure and pleasing relationships in private life and work; and interfere with optimal enjoyable work performance. Such short-comings interfere with the realization of common human goals. Time and again the basic depressed response will be elicited but prevented from serving its adaptive function. These features are illustrated by the cases of Potok's character Rivkeh Lev, Jacobson's case Mr V., McRae's description of Margaret, Bloch's case (Norma) Olga, my descriptions of Carola and Fanny; and by Endler's description of Norman during his acute breakdown, and in Chapter 17 by Doris, George, and Mrs D.

Amnesia and a multitude of other cognitive and emotional disturbances is at times the result of exposure during the formative years to incest or other sexual abuse, particularly if this exposure is ignored or denied by attachment figures. The origin of these patterns being hidden creates powerful cause for overt chronic depression or for any variety of avoided depression (compare Poston and Lison 1989).

Multiple current pressures

It should be repeated here that depression-proneness, created by personality factors developed under pressures of earlier life experience, is often reinforced by pressures from current relationships and circumstances that may have a cumulative effect. Patterns in family relations, as in Margaret's case; the structure of a marriage – for instance, one built on a wife's dependence and the husband's superiority; employment conditions, or a therapist's emotional needs, can make it inadvisable to become aware of one's true feelings and wishes. Ill-health in the family – or one's own – crowded housing, and other socio-economic difficulties can interfere with coping efforts.

The interaction of various factors predisposing a person to getting and staying depressed at any given time has been thoroughly examined in the research conducted for more than a decade in English urban communities by Brown and his colleagues (Brown and Harris 1978; Brown 1987). They used large samples of working-class women in the general population, who on first contact were either under psychiatric care for acute depression, or not under care, or not depressed. First, research was focused primarily on negative environmental factors – such as early loss of mother – that under sufficient past and current environmental pressures might predispose a person to respond with depression to a new traumatic life event. But later, intrapsychic developmental factors were also given attention as threads in the complex web of psychosocial features in a given person's past and current life that may promote depression or relieve depression at any point of time.

Despite the difference in purpose, method of exploration, concepts, and terminology between the work of these scholars and my own, I consider their findings in keeping with mine. Where our findings are not the same, they are complementary. I cannot present data based on the observation of large-scale samples, but I can present intimate observations of why and how a given person's intrapsychic processes succeed or fail in response to factors of the kind Brown can identify as significant mainly on the basis of their frequent appearance in the circumstances of different subjects showing similar responses.

Chapter ten

Diagnostic perspectives

The disease model of any functional psychiatric syndrome is most
obviously deficient, however, at the point where evidence is most needed;
that is, at the point where a link has to be made between the
psychological characteristics which clinicians recognise as a syndrome
and the underlying hypothetical biological process.

Wing *et al.* (1974:4)

What constitutes a depressive illness is itself subject to dispute and
disagreement; the boundaries between depression and sadness, between
depressive illness and anxiety states, between affective psychosis and
schizophrenia and between recurrent depression and personality disorder
are all arbitrary and ill defined.

Kendell (1977:5)

Potential contribution of a model of normal depression

In the preceding nine chapters I have developed my central themes: the diffuse
awareness of some inner deadlock that arouses the symptomatic reactions of
the basic depressed response; the adaptive function that getting depressed can
normally serve; the multitude of factors that may prevent the process of
depression from serving its adaptive function; and the importance of clearly
differentiating the depressed response from other distressing affects that often
appear in close connection with it.

Early in this discussion I pointed out that my terms "productive" and
"unproductive" depression are not to be understood as diagnostic terms in the
sense of describing disease entities, but only as characterizing the outcome of
a given person's given depressed episode. But what about diagnoses? one might
rightly ask. The symptom of being depressed unproductively is prolific among
patients who seek, or are referred, to receive professional help from hospitals,
clinics, and private practitioners. It is prolific in all syndromes named

"depression" of one type or another, and also in many conditions considered to be different disorders. How can my hypothesis of a potentially adaptive depressed affect and its vicissitudes help us find among the many existing and more or less controversial approaches one that will provide us with a satisfactory differentiation and classification of syndromes? How can it help us to find the right criteria to sort out from one another the many types of depressed patients so that we may know what to expect in a given patient, what treatment to give, or how to design further research?

As Kendell points out (1977:3), "During the last fifty years, and particularly the last twenty, innumerable different classifications of depressive illness have been proposed, and several disputes are smouldering away between the protagonists of rival schools." There are the classical Freudian views of depression still adhered to by many psychoanalysts, be they psychiatrists or psychologists; there are the ego-psychological views adopted by other essentially Freudian psychoanalysts; and there are many further schools of thought within the psychodynamic approach to human behavior. In psychiatry, there is a wide range of approaches, from psychodynamic with a classical Freudian view to a completely organic orientation ruling out any significance of psychological processes in the origin and course of a syndrome of depression. As both Wing et al. (1974) and Kendell (1977) point out, all this is in flux, and in various areas, with the help of increasingly sophisticated and controlled research, different issues are being clarified, slowly, step by step. In what way can my hypothesis contribute to a gradual revision of views?

The major themes of my hypothesis are the outcome of doing intensive individual psychotherapy, mostly though not exclusively in private practice, and of supervising psychotherapists in a variety of settings. But individual psychotherapy as a significant aid to outgrowing depression-proneness is far from available to all who are handicapped by extended and excessive depression; and it is far from being suited or acceptable to all of them.

The lessons my experience has taught me may be most applicable in extended, deep psychotherapy, but this does not mean that they have no value in the different context of clinic and hospital treatment, or in dealing with patients who personally or socially are inaccessible for intensive psychotherapy. Awareness of a normal model of being depressed, of its adaptive function, and of how personality patterns or social influences can interfere with its function, can be helpful in any diagnostic and therapeutic approach to depressed patients. This needs to be illustrated in two ways. In Chapter 8, I took up what an awareness similar to mine on the part of Endler's psychiatrist might have contributed to the treatment of his severe depression reported in 1982. Here, I shall select a few theoretical positions that overlap with my views and briefly indicate why my views cause me to differ in some respects despite many similar conclusions or observations.

Some schedules of diagnostic criteria in psychiatry

DSM-III (1980) is a complex guide to psychiatrists as to how, on the basis of widely accepted criteria and established methods of documenting the reasons for one's diagnostic conclusions, to arrive at a clinical diagnosis meeting standards for professional communication and research. It gives detailed instructions and is from time to time revised in keeping with new considerations and research. The diagnostic criteria are mainly descriptive of mood, behavior, and affective symptoms. All other observations and conclusions of significance are to be reported in different, hierarchically ordered columns or "axes." The clinical picture during the time of hospitalization is of major importance in determining the diagnosis, but "psychosocial stressors" in recent life and "level of adaptive functioning" (1981:27,28) are also to be considered. "Predisposing factors" are stated in terms of "Characteristics of an individual that can be identified before the development of the disorder and that place him or her at greater risk for developing the disorder. Not included in this section are general societal or environmental conditions (such as poverty) that may predispose all individuals exposed to these conditions to develop the disorder" (1980:31). Nor are early relationships mentioned as significant in strengthening or weakening a child's secure development.

Various syndromes of depression are organized under the classification of Affective Disorders, which are divided into four major classes: Bipolar Disorders (including the subclasses of Manic Episodes and of Major Depressive Episode); Major Depression (including Major Depression, Single Episode, and Major Depression, Recurrent); Other Specific Affective Disorders (including Cyclothymic Disorder and Dysthymic Disorder or Depressive Neurosis); Atypical Affective Disorders (including Atypical Bipolar Disorder and Atypical Depression). The diagnostic criteria for each sub-class are given in terms of duration of current symptoms and in terms of a sufficient number from a list of carefully described possible symptoms being apparent.

Decades, if not centuries, of psychiatric clinical experience are abstracted into this impressive document. Any experienced clinician will find the described behavior and affective symptoms of depressed patients familiar. The same holds for the list of possible current psychosocial stressors, and also of the list of significant adaptive functioning preceding onset. The limitations of what can be determined and evaluated in the short time allowed a psychiatrist to reach an initial diagnosis in a clinic or hospital setting makes it inadvisable to burden him or her with too many further considerations. And yet, if there were some awareness implicit in the comments of the manual concerning a model of *normal* depression – awareness of how being depressed can be adaptive or when it may be doomed to fail – this could nevertheless serve to alert the diagnostician, especially if he or she is inexperienced.

For instance, one might add some comments to qualify the significance of the duration of symptoms of depression as somewhat relative. Duration depends by no means only on the depressed patient's competence to cope, but also on the social circumstances and their personal significance to the patient. In a woman with children, with no income of her own, no occupational training, no supportive family of her own, who is living in a disastrous marriage, being depressed for two years need not indicate the presence of Dysthymic Disorder but be the expression of a realistically hopeless conflict between a wish for self-preservation and a wish to care for her children, a conflict calling for social support. In another case, two months of exactly the same symptoms could be due to developmental pathology of personality.

Alertness to the role of early family experience and its often damaging though hidden deprivations is another factor that does not seem to be encouraged by DSM-III. At the time of having to make a diagnosis in order to institute treatment, there may be no opportunity to establish the complex dynamics resulting from early life events and relationships and their effect on the development of depression-proneness and on the impact, which a repetition of such events can have in provoking the current episode. But without considering such a possibility it is difficult to evaluate a patient's basic strength and the potential for a recovery without medical intervention other than psychotherapy and/or social intervention. McRae's experience (1986), presented in Chapter 8 as the case of Margaret, is an example of remarkable capacity for recovery and new development despite unusually severe depressed reactions following a hysterectomy. Without consideration of her total life experience, her prognosis would have seemed much more negative than it was. Such a negative evaluation might have led to the kind of medical intervention that to Margaret would have confirmed rather than counteracted her negative self-image. This might even have enhanced her suicidal tendencies.

So much for some of the detail. Another issue is more important. At the present stage of development in our knowledge of human functioning it is natural to devise diagnostic classifications that are partly derived from groupings of typical symptom pictures, and of late partly from the discovery that persons showing similar clusters of symptoms tend to react in a similar positive or negative way to specific medication. But is this really proof enough to take for granted that we are dealing with phenomena deserving the description of disease in the medical sense? Does it prove that a biochemical process fitting the concept of *disease* causes the behavioral and affective symptoms we observe, rather than being just a normal part of the constant interaction between physiological and psychological aspects of human responses? Is it proven beyond a doubt that the stresses leading to an inner deadlock and the resulting basic depressed response do not affect the body chemistry in normal ways to provoke the symptoms we note and at the same time the biochemical responsiveness to or reaction against a given drug? In other words, could such a "link" (Wing et al. 1974:4) be the reason why persons, who because of their interpretation of the stress to which they are exposed suffer from particular depressed reactions and moods, react similarly to particular drugs? This is a crude way to raise the question, somewhat like asking what comes first, the chicken or the egg. But by professionals better qualified than I to formulate it, the question needs none the less to be pursued. And this concerns not only DSM-III but the diagnostic approach to "depressive illness" in general, although, as Kendell (1977) and Wing *et al.* (1974) point out, at the present time existing diagnoses are still indispensable.

The diagnostic criteria for use in psychiatric research presented by Feighner *et al.* (1972) differ from DSM-III in a number of ways. First, rather than being largely based on clinical judgment and experience and on differentiation from other disorders, they are also based on laboratory studies, studies of prevalence of the disorder in the patient's family, and follow-up studies. As in DSM-III, the Feighner criteria are descriptive of mood, behavior, and affective symptoms; duration and number of symptoms of a given category determine whether a diagnosis of a certain pathology is made. They do not focus on typical developmental disturbances, emotional conflicts, or attitudes. The authors differentiate Primary Affective Disorders (Depression, Mania) from Secondary Affective Disorders (which are defined in the same way as the primary ones, but occur with either a pre-existing, non-affective psychiatric illness or with a life-threatening or incapacitating medical illness which precedes and parallels the symptoms of depression). Second, the aim is organization of patient groups suitable for psychiatric research, while DSM-III clearly is aimed at reaching a diagnosis to determine treatment and care. Third, they do not consider their list of illnesses complete, reporting only what they consider well-established.

The research diagnostic criteria developed by Spitzer *et al.* (1978) have as their major purpose "to enable investigators to select relatively homogeneous groups of subjects who meet specific diagnostic criteria" (1978:774). Diagnoses are judged as either not present, probable, or definite. Again, the *number* of characteristic symptoms determine whether a diagnosis is made, and if so, the diagnosis is qualified as probable or definite. In contrast to fifteen diagnoses in the Feighner criteria, there are twenty-five here.

In both these instances, the diagnostic criteria seem highly suitable for research where these diagnoses apply, but hardly for research in psychotherapy with a psychodynamic orientation. Having read only the two papers by these authors mentioned here, I have no opinion as to whether their acceptance of my hypothesis could contribute anything of value to their work.

Finally, a word about Wing *et al.* (1974) describing their PSE (Present State Examination) and Catego programs. The authors have in the course of several years devised and improved a standard interview to interrogate patients about any psychiatric symptoms having appeared in them during the preceding month. The interview follows a rating schedule including 140 possible symptoms. With the help of the Catego computer program, the symptoms found present are then combined into thirty-eight possible symptom clusters (here referred to as "syndromes" although they do not yet represent a diagnostic classification). If desired, the syndromes found present can be further combined to show a particular diagnostic classification on the list of the International Classification of Diseases (ICD-8). They see two parts in an investigation like theirs: first, "we need to know whether there are clinically recognisable syndromes which all psychiatrists can agree upon and label in the same way. . . . The second step can then be taken, which is to test the various explanatory theories" (1974:2–3). Their book

> is mainly devoted to two questions connected with the first step. First, whether certain psychological and behavioural phenomena which have generally been thought by psychiatrists to be "symptoms" of mental illness can be reliably recognised and described, irrespective of the language and culture of the doctor or patient, secondly, whether rules of classification can be specified with such precision that an individual with a given pattern of symptoms will always be allocated to the same clinical grouping. If these two conditions could be fulfilled we should be in a position to proceed to the second stage of investigation, that is, to test individual disease theories. We can do nothing, however, if the first stage proves unsuccessful.
>
> (1974:3)

The categories used are descriptive. To my mind, the authors reach their stated purposes. They discuss all aspects of their program – its complexities, its applications, and its limitations – with impressive consistency and clarity. My approach to the dynamic understanding of partly unconscious productive and unproductive *processes* of being depressed is not relevant to a research program organizing *descriptive* diagnostic categories of observable and consciously communicated symptoms. But to clinicians making use of PSE confirmation of their descriptive clinical diagnoses, my view may offer a complementary dimension.

A divergence from Klerman's view

Klerman identifies (1974:132) four adaptive functions of affects: (1) social communication; (2) physiological arousal; (3) subjective awareness; and (4) psychodynamic defense. As an affect, he finds that depression serves a signal function in the infant: "It alerts the mother and/or other members of the social group that one of its helpless members, the infant, is in potential danger." In the course of discussing his research, Klerman emphasizes that depression is independent from hostility and other affects, and that it has a signal function. Also, "The capacity to become depressed is almost universal and not restricted to any personality type," although "the clinical depressive state is comprised of multiple affective components, including anxiety, guilt, hostility, and irritability" (p.136). He finds that

(1) loss and separation are not universal in all depression, (2) not all individuals who experience loss and separation will develop depressions, and (3) loss and separation are not specific to clinical depression but rather may serve as precipitating events for a wide variety of clinical conditions that are not only psychiatric, but also general medical (Holmes and Rahe 1967).

(1974:139)

But then, looking at clinical depression and the vulnerability of the depressed patient Klerman comes to the conclusion that, although adaptive in the infant, depression is maladaptive in the adult. Later, Klerman identifies (1975:1,004) the same four functions in the discussion of normal depression.

Although I have reached my conclusions on a road different from Klerman's extensive research, they are in many respects very similar to his, except for my concept of the normal function of the depressed response to initiate an adaptive process toward problem solving in the adult. In Chapter 11 it will become apparent that I see the function of adult depressed reactions as developing through maturation of the infant's response. In the patient suffering from "clinical depression" I see some of this development as having been arrested.[1]

My line of thought, then, is mainly set apart from these various diagnostic approaches by my focus on the normal and adaptive aspects of the depressed response and on the effect of early interpersonal experiences on personality development in ways that will foster or obstruct productive work of depression.

Diagnostic perspectives for psychotherapy

So far we have only looked at psychiatric diagnoses and found that at present psychiatrists, even within the same country or cultural area, hold many divergent views of depression. To my knowledge, there is no diagnostic view generally accepted among cognitive or behaviorist psychologists, either. As far as psychoanalysts are concerned, Mendelson has presented (1974) a thorough survey and discussion of the development of psychoanalytic concepts of depression, mainly among members of the psychoanalytic movement represented by the International Psychoanalytic Association (IPA). He deals with pathological states of depression, not with the function or process of the normal affect. In closing (1974:317), he expresses the belief "that the psychoanalytic task of understanding depression has been largely completed, although there will undoubtedly continue to be revisions and refinements of theory." He also believes "that the significant focus of new work on depression will continue to shift in a neurophysiological and psychopharmacological direction." In addition to the contributions covered by Mendelson, there are the implications for concepts of depression in Kohut's, Kernberg's, and Masterson's views of narcissistic and borderline disorders; the views of authors in the Washington

School of Psychiatry, and of various other so-called neo-Freudian groups.

Even among psychoanalytic practitioners who consider themselves adhering to the tenets of the classical psychoanalytic movement, there are great differences in diagnostic views and therapeutic approaches, dependent on which theory from Abraham and Freud to recent developments in ego psychology they embrace. Thus, I cannot refer to a generally accepted diagnostic view of the depressed patient in dynamic psychotherapy. But although the last part of this book will deal with aid to the work of depression, psychotherapeutic and other, I shall close this chapter and Part I with a brief sketch of my own approach, illustrating it with Asher Lev's crisis described in the beginning of Chapter 1.

If we go back to the diagnostic questions raised there, it is evident that psychiatric opinions would differ as to whether he should be diagnosed as suffering from one or another milder form of depressive illness, or whether he had only gone through a severe developmental crisis necessitated by realistically difficult family and cultural relations. But what if a close friend of Asher's or of his family came to me to ask me for my opinion on whether Asher – or a live man like Potok's character in a similar situation – needed therapy and whether he should be encouraged to seek it? Let us assume the totally unlikely situation that I would get to know much about what I have described about Asher so far, and in addition also a good deal about his childhood disorder and circumstances to be described in Chapter 12. What would I consider before deciding what to say?

I would try to consider the reality factors now and in his childhood and adolescence, including strengthening as well as damaging influences, and try to assess the capacity he has demonstrated to adapt and develop under these circumstances. This includes looking at the positive relationships he has experienced and been able – or has had an opportunity – to develop and maintain; and at his ability to develop new meaningful relationships, be that with a therapist or outside therapy. I would consider his opportunity to express himself and work through various problems by intellectual, artistic, employment, or other activities. I would inquire: does he *want* help at this time from a person who is not an artist, does he seem to seek an opportunity to confide? I think I would come to the conclusion that at that moment – unless he were to grasp at a reference to a trustworthy therapist – perhaps the parents or other concerned person needed some support and explanations more than Asher. If Asher, with the same emotional struggle, were in a socially, economically, or occupationally pressed situation, my decision could be different. But in contrast to Norman, whose career and capacity to support his family is at stake so that quick measures are called for, Asher – quite aside from being less disabled – has a life situation where he can take his time: he is his own boss, he seems economically secure, has no responsibilities for dependants, and has a social network he can resort to as he sees fit. He can afford to work through his conflicts at his own pace with the help of his art, and to test to what extent he now can cope without dependence on any parent figures. At another time, under different circumstances, a man like Asher might profit from psychotherapy, if he desired it, but this is not the time.

Whether and when psychotherapy is helpful does not only depend on a person's personality and a therapist's competence, but on the total web of the person's past and current life situation and on the future to be expected. A diagnostic label in terms of disease does not necessarily illuminate this evaluation. At times, even a technically sound diagnostic label can be a hindrance to an empathic and flexible approach, unless the therapist is quite secure and experienced.

Part II

Development of the work of depression

Chapter eleven

Development of the function of getting depressed

Across people and, by implication, across development, there seems to be an organized aspect of inner life that can experience and resonate with depressive feelings. This universal pattern of experience is presumably rooted both in biology and in the human condition. However, it also seems true that depressive feelings change with development. The meaning, the dynamics, and the cognitive context for experiencing depressive feelings increase in complexity as the child develops.

Emde *et al.* (1986:140)

Infancy and early childhood

The cause for the depressed response

So far I have illustrated my view of the basic depressed response with its cause and function (as described in Chapter 3) only with episodes in the lives of adults. But how and when during the first two decades of life do we begin to experience what later can be called cause for the depressed response? How and when can the social and personal functions of the depressed response be thought as emerging? When can we begin to speak of a work of depression and when are we justified in seeing it as succeeding or failing?

Until very recently, the literature on depression in children and adolescents focused mainly on the nature and prevalence of "clinical depression." In recent years a great deal of research in child psychiatry and child psychology has been published concerning "childhood depression," but usually, as Rutter *et al.* point out (1986) in their preface, "depressive feelings" are not being differentiated in the literature from "depressive disorder."[1] Emde *et al.*, on the other hand, present (1986) in the same volume a discussion of children who are depressed. Whereas these authors are mainly dealing with the important interactional aspects of a child's getting depressed and ceasing to be depressed, my focus in this section is mainly on the development in children of the capacity to get depressed and on the outcome of their being depressed.

I shall not attempt to review the rapidly increasing literature on the behavior of children and adolescents that deserves either the description of being depressed or the diagnosis of a syndrome of depression.[2] I shall restrict myself to what I find pertinent to the developmental questions I raise here.

As far as infancy is concerned, we have to find our way without verbal expression or confirmation from the infant. The detailed observations of infant behavior in a research project can yield a stimulating image of a process, nonetheless. This I find in Spitz's paper "Anaclitic depression" (1946), which was preceded by his paper "Hospitalism" (1945). Even if some of his research methods, findings, or conclusions may be questioned,[3] his description of the circumstances to which the infants reacted is very suggestive.

Spitz examined 139 infants in two institutions during their first year of life. In the first paper he compared the total development of these infants with the development of infants in two types of family settings – professional families in a city and the families of poor fishermen in an isolated village. Significant findings, forming the background for his discussion of severe depression in the second paper, were the following.

Health and optimal development were found to be primarily dependent on a continuous and intensely emotional relationship between the infant and his or her mother (or mother substitute). Poverty or affluence in the family or the high standard of hygiene in both institutions were not significant factors in the child's physical and psychological development. From the beginning, however, the opportunity for stimulation and social contact and, as soon as any form of locomotion began to develop, *the opportunity to move about freely*, made a significant difference in the baby's general development and the capacity to cope with distress.

In one of the institutions, Nursery, which was attached to a penal institution for delinquent girls, the babies, although placed in glassed-in cubicles, were healthy and developed well – as well, in fact, as the babies in either type of family setting. Their cubicles during the first six months of life allowed for a free view of the corridor between cubicles where there was lively traffic of the young mothers, often with their babies. Moreover, the ward had windows toward the garden on both sides of the rows of cubicles so that the babies had a view of the garden. They had toys to play with. During the first six months of their life, these babies were cared for by their mothers who were inmates of the penitentiary and most of them teenagers. For these girls the full-time care of their infant provided the only satisfaction of their need for body contact and emotional closeness, for self-respect, for activity and stimulation, and for competition with other girls. Thus, the babies received a great deal of attention. There was ample evidence that the infant's potentials developed best and most rapidly in response to an intense interaction with a continuously available, responsive, even though not necessarily mature mother.

At the age of six months each baby was moved into a nursery for five to six infants. There, the babies were allowed to move about freely on the floor and were cared for by well-trained nurses in sufficient numbers to give them considerable individual attention. They were in excellent health and mortality was low.

In the other institution, Foundling House, the babies of socially deprived women were not admitted at birth but cared for by their mothers at home until the mother could or would no longer take care of them. After their third month they were cared for by nurses with one nurse to eight infants. The glassed cubicles were constructed in such a way that the infants could not look out. They were kept in their cots even at an age when children normally begin to crawl and walk. They had no toys. Despite excellent hygiene, these babies were in poor health and mortality was high. They did not learn to sit, crawl, walk, or control their elimination at a normal age, if at all.

In both institutions some babies developed a striking condition. At first, babies who had been smiling and sociable began to weep silently and show an increasingly sad facial expression, resistance to contact with adults and other babies, increasing fear of people, and desperate clinging if contact could be established. Gradually all this increased, the baby might scream in terror if efforts were made to establish contact. The babies lost their appetite, would not play with their toys, could not sleep, and tended to lie on the mattress with their face turned toward the wall. Some, though not all, of these babies began to play with their feces, often under intense genital masturbation, although masturbation is rare during the first year of life.

Spitz found that all babies who developed this condition had been separated from their mother and that, at the time a change in the baby became noticeable, the separation had lasted for at least two weeks. Thus, the condition did not start or become evident immediately after separation, but if there was no satisfactory substitute replacing her it appeared gradually after upwards of two weeks and became increasingly severe if the mother did not return or a substitute replace her. The condition disappeared immediately upon return of the mother, or when the infant had accepted a substitute. Often the loss of development was overcome with amazing speed after the reunion, but at times this improvement could be maintained only partially. The babies who had the best and most intense interaction with their mother before separation developed the most severe anaclitic depression, while the babies who had no mother did not develop this type of depression, although their general development was severely retarded all along.

As Spitz points out, during the second half of the first year a baby becomes active in seeking out such a substitute contact by using his or her increasing ability to move about: crawling, shuffling, walking. In his study he found that babies allowed to move about on the floor after the separation from their mother developed less severe symptoms of depression than those kept in their cot. Spitz saw the crawling of the less disturbed babies as the infant's attempt to compensate for the damage done by the separation from the mother or other attachment figure: moving about not only helped the baby to make contact with a substitute, but locomotion also expressed some of the anger caused by the separation and thus lessened its intensity. Today we know, thanks to the research of C. M. Parkes (1972:39), that the impulse to search is an integral part of the mourning response also in adults.

That anaclitic depression is a response of distress upon prolonged separation from a satisfactory mother without an adequate substitute is convincingly demonstrated by Spitz's observations and reasoning. I agree with Rutter (1986:19) that this is a natural response that should not he considered a disorder. When part of this response with its cognitive and emotional features has fully developed in adolescents and adults, we call it grief and pining. But at this age it is unlikely that distress has begun to be differentiated into what in later childhood and in the adult are the distinct responses of grief, anxiety, anger, and depressed response.[4]

It appears, however, that rudimentary features of what later deserves to be called the depressed response may also be evident in the situation and the response of these babies. As Spitz emphasizes, the infants develop their locomotion in response to the mother's cooing and calling, to her stretched-out arms. Provided, moreover, that the mother or other attachment figure is there to return to at any moment, infants with a secure attachment develop their locomotion also out of their impulse to explore the environment. The satisfaction of this impulse is blended with the satisfaction that goes with the development of skills. How vivid this is in infants only a few months older than the babies described by Spitz is conveyed in the description (1975:65ff.) by Mahler *et al.* of the toddler's exuberance during the developmental stage she has called the "subphase of practice" in the "separation-individuation phase." This could represent an initial stage of what later develops into our striving to apply our resources in order to reach a significant goal. Throughout life we derive joy from functioning adequately and from sharing with a significant other. To interference with our functioning we later react negatively with anger, shame, or the depressed response, depending on our appraisal of the situation.

During the second half of its first year there is in the baby a tremendous push toward trying out and learning: by handling, mouthing, and exploring objects, by moving away from, returning to, and following mother or another attach- ment figure. If the person who offers the security, stimulation, and model indispensable for this learning and its satisfactions suddenly becomes inaccessible, this appears to mobilize distress that sooner or later will become differentiated into the discrete affects of fear, the grief of painful longing, and anger[5] at the frustration of the impulse to move toward mother and attract her attention. Perhaps, there is an additional quality of turmoil, an early form of what I describe in the adult as perplexity. When the necessary participation of the mother ceases, this turmoil would be created by the sudden and unfamiliar frustration of the baby's capacity to move about securely, to explore, to share the experience with mother, and continue learning. This hypothesis seems to get support from the observation that the anaclitic depression became more severe in those babies who had no chance to move about on the floor and seek adult response.

The limited function of the depressed response in early infancy

It is important to remember here that I am speaking only of the early affective response of distress in the baby and not of the complex emotional disturbances that can develop during later childhood, adolescence, and after. Quite often in psychiatric, psychological, and psychoanalytic literature, these complex conditions are referred to simply as "depression." Consequently, it has been widely held by psychoanalysts that "depression" cannot occur in early childhood, and this has been based on the following arguments: until children have developed a superego they cannot feel guilt; they lack the self-awareness and other cognitive development necessary to suffer loss of self-esteem; they are not sufficiently mature to defend with self-destructive impulses against their destructive impulses toward attachment and authority figures. I agree that these and other depressive patterns discussed in Chapter 9 have not yet developed in infants and young children. If our concept of "depression" embraces the activation of such patterns, infants and young children should not be described as suffering from depression. We can only say that their current distress contains the roots from which the basic depressed response will develop as an affective and psychological pattern of response.

Aspects of what elicits the infant's distress seem on the surface to correspond to what in the adult mobilizes the depressed response. Lacking the adult capacity for complex information processing, however, the circumstances promoting frustration of an infant's intent to be active in a specific way can neither be appraised nor changed by the infant. A response that gradually matures into the experience of anger is likely to be a child's first reaction to the frustration of its efforts, but when severe frustration continues for any length of time despite the expression of distress, a response that later will mature into the depressed response appears to take over (see the description of phases three and four in Chapter 3). Thus, the *work* of depression cannot operate as yet. The *personal function* of the depressed response cannot be served. Alert adults have to respond to the infant's signals of distress and intervene to change the distressing circumstances. Often they do. Thus, the *social function* of the depressed response can be served successfully from infancy.

Of course, even anxiety in the young child can only serve the social function of motivating adults to reassure and protect the child. The child has not yet developed the faculty required for the personal function of anxiety, which serves to find and apply protective measures against anticipated increase of danger.

Individual illustrations

Now we turn to some descriptions of individual infants and young children considered acutely depressed.

Emde *et al.* (1986:141) give a description of anaclitic depression in a seven-month-old who had a satisfying, stimulating relationship with an excellent foster mother with whom he had been placed when two weeks old. Then, due to life circumstances, the foster mother developed an acute depression. As she became emotionally less available, the baby lost his appetite, became immobile, his face was sad, and he wept inconsolably when approached. On the rare occasions when the baby was able to respond to the mother's attempts at interaction, the mother's depression kept her from responding in the way she would have done before. "Often in irritation and out of touch with her infant's needs, she would push the child away, generating a cycle of frustration and distress. With sensitive intervention and slow resolution of the mother's depression, the depressive response of the infant also resolved" (142).

The authors point out that a "depressive response" can result not only from physical loss of the attachment figure but also from loss of the mothering function. In an older child, such a change would elicit a grief reaction, anger, and anxiety. I do not know, whether in a seven-month-old these affects have begun to be differentiated into distinct experiential components of the distress. But the baby's developmental push which required the foster mother's participation was now unexpectedly and uncontrollably frustrated. So was the baby's effort at satisfactory communication: instead of alerting the foster mother as usual, his signals of distress – weeping, screaming, withdrawal – were now adding to her own distress and, thus, promoting her withdrawal and rejecting behavior. We can, perhaps, see in this baby's behavior when he failed to elicit response from its foster mother, some rudiments of the patterns shown by adults in the depressed response.

Emde and his colleagues give (1986:142) another example of a young child considered acutely depressed and, like the baby, unable to alert adults to his distress.

A three-year-old was hospitalized with severe burns on his legs. His parents were unable to visit regularly. His "apathy and withdrawn behavior initially were interpreted by the hospital staff as cooperative behavior." He was quiet when alone, but irritable and demanding when someone was with him. Consequently, he was left alone for long periods. For some time it was not understood that he was becoming increasingly depressed and that his protestations were "an attempt to engage the environment." After a child psychiatric consultation he received not only psychiatric attention but was assigned a "primary care nurse and a consistent foster grandmother." The latter alerted staff to the shame demonstrated by the child when his burnt legs were uncovered. Gradually it became apparent that he was deeply humiliated by the necessity to wear diapers. He had recently mastered toilet training but the burns precluded his using a toilet. Then the staff helped him understand this temporary need for diapers as a protection of his burns. "As a result of these interventions, his depressed mood improved" (143).

The authors state (1986:143) that "depressed children can drive away those who are attempting to respond to their depression . . . irritable behavior may appear to signal that efforts are 'making the child worse' when, in fact, the child is trying to interact." They go on to say that by "two years of age, the children have developed a sense of self-awareness" and have "more than previously recognized . . . a sense of adult standards for what is 'right and wrong.'" In terms of the clinician's view of depression they find the pre-school age "an important period because of the appearance of shame" which "appears to play a major role in the feeling of depression at this age . . ."

In other words, the social and personal functions of shame and guilt appear only when cognitive functions are more advanced and the stimulus of group interaction (see Chapter 7) is more prominent than at the age when grief, anxiety, anger, and the depressed response begin to differentiate from pervasive distress.

Indeed, in the total emotional state of this three-year-old, shame about ugly legs and dirty diapers appears to have played a major role. At that age there may even have been a sense of shame aroused by being unable to awaken more satisfying caretaking responses. It may be justified to speculate, however, whether an early form of what I call the " basic depressed response" was not active as an emotional response separate from – though not unrelated to – the feelings of shame. Here was a child who in all likelihood had become able, at home, to communicate and perform much of the time in keeping with his own and his parents' expectations and with his sense of what they thought was right. Suddenly he was not only suffering great pain and a shocking change in his appearance, as well as the humiliation of dirty diapers, but he was in an unfamiliar environment. He was probably uncertain of what would be considered right and wrong behavior. He was deprived of the familiar ways of communication with his parents. His attempts to convey his feelings and his need for support, for explanations, and for liberation from shame were unsuccessful. At his age it was impossible for him to understand what he was trying to accomplish, let alone why he was failing in his efforts. Is this not rather similar to what I have described as setting the depressed response in motion in the adult? Is the plausibility of the same reaction in a child not borne out by the effective relief the authors describe? This child certainly had cause in his inner life for the basic depressed response. At his age, the personal function of the depressed response could not be served by any work of depression. This becomes possible only in later phases of cognitive and emotional development. But the social function was finally served, indeed, through the effect that the child's behavior had on the child psychiatrist and the foster grandmother.

Fully developed, the personal aspect of the function of depression is aided by a sense of identity, an awareness of intentions and purpose, a capacity to grasp change in the self and the environment. It requires the capacity to see some causality and to reason, to experience and recognize various emotions within ourselves without too much defensive distortion. Without these characteristics the basic depressed response can neither initiate nor facilitate a process leading to the resolution of an acute inner deadlock. Infants and young children have not developed these means to understand and modify the cause of a depressed response or of its precursor. They are dependent on help from others. Their depressed behavior serves to alert those who might help, without the child realizing that it is sending out alarm signals.

Many observers have found that in young children a typical depressed mood tends to be of relatively short duration. Generally, this has been explained as showing that young children cannot tolerate the discomfort of depressed feelings for any length of time and, therefore, defend against it with denial and diversion. This is a very plausible explanation. But there could be an additional cause: with only the social function of the depressed response ready for operation, it does not seem entirely impossible that once the alarm signals have been sent out to the environment, the symptoms subside if the provoking cause is not disastrous. Even anger and crying can subside relatively quickly in children, without the environment having changed a great deal. One can wonder whether this could be an economic response to lack of power, a response we often see even in adults. Again, this is speculation but it deserves further exploration.

To summarize: the baby's behavior that resembles parts of the depressed response in the adult – withdrawal from human contact, sad expression, crying, fearfulness, insomnia, loss of appetite – tends to alert the most responsive adults: the mother or mother substitute and other special persons. When such an adult is available, the response serves its social function. A personal function of this behavior, however, cannot be served until the work of depression has become possible. This requires emotional and cognitive processes on a more mature level. Because of the child's dependence on others for its distress to be understood and met, we cannot differentiate in a young child between productive and unproductive outcome of the process as we can in adult depression. "Productive" outcome implies the ability to take care of oneself. The term "unproductive" implies the failure of this potential.

Middle childhood through adolescence

Primary process in the work of depression

In earlier chapters, my illustrations and discussion of the work of depression have emphasized the role of features that belong to "secondary process," a term introduced (1915) by Freud for the psychological processes I have stressed so far: the organization and integration of experience by comparison of memories, perceptions, and other information, conscious and unconscious, and of the conclusions we draw from these data. I have spoken of self-awareness and reasoning; of recognition and insight. Such components of the work of depression are easiest to communicate in words, easiest to observe in our patients, and easiest to recognize introspectively in ourselves. Freud considered (1915) these processes a later development in the child's integration and expression of experience than what he called "primary process": the expression of experience through the language of the dream, of fantasy and imagery, through symbols, opposites, allusions, similes, reversal, condensation, and body language. He also saw primary process as the expressions of the unconscious and as related to the id, but secondary process as belonging to the ego. Even if one does not structure psychological observations in terms of id and ego, the terms "primary" and "secondary process" are very useful.

What, then, can we see as the role of primary process in the resolution of an acute episode of depression or in its prevention? Earlier I have indicated that in some persons or instances a depression may end in a new burst of meaningful activity without hitherto unconscious emotions or thoughts having reached awareness. Often in such instances there is no awareness of a connection between the disappearance of the depressed mood and the fresh activity following it. Particularly in creative activity this may be the case.[6] In other words, integration of old and new information during the work of depression and the working through of an acute difficulty need not follow the path of secondary process. Integration and reorientation can also follow the path of primary process. This is particularly typical of children. Unless their use of fantasy has become inhibited, they can integrate many difficult experiences through their play. How helpful this is to children in acutely trying circumstances has been apparent, when opportunity to play has been available to children not only in psychotherapy but during treatment on pediatric wards.

Another example can be found in artistically highly gifted children. Even if they have become inhibited in some of their affective or cognitive responses, they may still have an opportunity to use their gift as a means for expressing affection, longing, protest, or fear by story-telling, music, or visual arts. As long as their artistic expression is not interfered with or prohibited, the ability to cope to some extent independently with depressing inner experience may develop in such children much earlier than in other children. This will be illustrated in the next chapter.

Cytryn and McKnew (1974) have described "depressive process" in children as manifesting itself in three different ways: (1) in fantasy material as demonstrated in the children's dreams, spontaneous play, and in projective psychological tests; (2) in verbal expression of hopelessness, helplessness, guilt, being unattractive, worthless, and unloved, and in suicidal preoccupation; and (3) in mood and behavior, including "manifestations of depressive affect that can be noticed by an observer without the need of verbal exchange" – including retardation, evidence of sadness in posture and facial expression, crying, disturbance in appetite and sleep, and "such signs of masked depression as hyperactivity, aggressiveness, school failure, delinquency, and psychosomatic symptoms" (879–80). Particularly in points 2 and 3 we see the beginnings of those personality patterns I described in Chapter 9 as promoting frequent, persistent cause for the depressed response and as preventing productive outcome.

Cytryn and McKnew found, further, that "depressive fantasy" is present "almost all the time in the children diagnosed as having depressive reaction"; that verbal expression is less frequent in children; and depressed mood and behavior "the least frequent and least stable finding." As the child's depressed episode subsides, "depressive mood and behavior" disappear first while the fantasy material disappears last, "usually only after the resolution of the depressive conflict" (1974:880). Unfortunately they did not exemplify the content of these fantasies, nor give the age of these children. But in a further paper (1980) they give short cases of children who are six, seven, and twelve years old, respectively. The term "depressive fantasy" is suggestive of ideas not reflecting reality. It is likely, however, that depressed children are, as described in detail by Bloch (1978), occupied with depressing thoughts and fantasies of action that are stimulated by the reality of their situation, and represent an effort to cope with it by means of primary process elaboration.

Other authors have emphasized that children tend to defend against depressed reactions with hyperactivity and temper outbursts; that they deny the frustration that normally elicits a depressed response. But Cytryn and McKnew abandoned (1980) from their categories of depression the term "masked depression" for hyperactivity, aggressiveness, school failure, delinquency, and psychosomatic symptoms in children who for other reasons were diagnosed as "having depressive reaction." They found "masked depression" a "difficult and controversial clinical entity" and replaced it with the term "conduct disturbance with depressive features" (1980:23). Yet behavior called "masked depression" corresponds to what in adults I call "avoided depression." Such terms imply that there is an effort made to cope in special, defensive ways with those internal difficulties to which others tend to react with the basic depressed response. In masked or avoided depression the perception of internal failure is not only warded off but the source of the discomfort connected with the denied perception is sought in, or attributed to, external factors. The necessary search within tends to be replaced by responses toward the environment if it is not replaced by psychosomatic difficulties. The following is an example.

During the International Symposium on Death, Dying and Bereavement held in Stockholm, Lamers (1982:107) described a six-year-old boy who was referred to him because he had suddenly become a behavior problem in class and aggressive toward the other children. Neither the parents nor the school psychologist nor the pediatrician could find an explanation for this sudden change. Within the first few minutes of the interview with Lamers, the boy replied to the question of what was bothering him and had caused the change in his behavior: "I just wanted to see my Grandpa not breathing." It turned out that his grandfather had been a frequent babysitter for the boy and his younger sister, but then he had become ill and recently he had died. The boy had wanted to attend the funeral but been told that he was too young. He had imagined that at the funeral he could see his grandfather in his coffin and see whether he was or wasn't breathing. He and Grandpa used to make lunch for and feed each other. Grandpa was "buried down under the ground in the cemetery now. And if he's breathing he's hungry... and I have to feed him." Lamers explained to the child why it was not possible that his grandfather was breathing and hungry. After the interview Lamers explained to the parents that their child needed the opportunity to talk with them about Grandpa, his illness, and his death. As a result, the boy became his usual self again in class.

Lamers presented this case as an example of the variety of reactions by which grief upon bereavement can be expressed. I prefer the term "mourning" rather than "grief" in this context. In the case of this boy's mourning there was not only what I would call grief – the painful longing for Grandpa – but also a depressed response masked or avoided by hyperactivity and a resentful reaction toward the frustrating parents. This response was apparently displaced on to his teacher and on to his peers in class. The reason why I suspect that a depressed response had been activated but avoided is this: this child had an impulse not only to continue his relationship with his grandfather, but within it specifically to care for his grandfather's need for food, if Grandpa were alive and breathing. He had an impulse to check whether Grandpa was breathing. He wanted to mobilize adult help with this, but did not succeed. He was too immature to comprehend his own frustration anger in this situation and consequently unable to cope with it in a more effective way than by being explosive in school. Most of this disturbance was not caused by his loss of his grandfather in itself but rather by the unresponsive behavior of live members of his world and by his inability to influence them according to his intentions. When he received the necessary information from Dr Lamers and a new responsiveness from his parents, his behavior was promptly restored to normal, although his grandfather remained lost and no continuing substitute relationship with Dr Lamers replaced it. This boy was not suffering from a behavior disorder, although, without Dr Lamers' intervention, there was risk of a development in that direction, provoked by his environment.

Emerging social and self-awareness

In keeping with libido theory, psychoanalysts have long held that between the crises of the oedipal phase, before seven, and the crises of puberty and adolescence, after eleven, children have a relatively calm period of development. This is seen as due to a latency of the sexual drive.

In a Swedish study (1986) by Cederblad and Höök, however, of emotional disturbance in 345 children from city and rural areas, at ages three, seven, nine, twelve, and fifteen, the emergence of new symptoms was found to be highest at the age of nine. In Stockholm's child guidance clinics and pediatric clinics, staff members also found, as reported by Högberg et al. (1986), that the rate of referrals tends to be particularly high at the age of nine. In child guidance it was found, quite in keeping with Piaget and Inhelder's description (1969), that the children between eight and ten had begun to comprehend and be preoccupied with parental tensions and separations, as well as other stresses in the family. They react with emotional disturbance, expressed by the boys mainly in aggressive behavior and learning difficulties, leading to child guidance referral; in girls by somatic symptoms, withdrawal, and other signs of depression leading to medical referral. But in the American and English literature there is no consensus on such observations as yet, and further research is needed to confirm them.[7]

That many children are emotionally more unbalanced at the age of nine, or at least at some point between eight and ten, than they are at some other periods, has been noticeable in the Habilitation Center for Handicapped Children at a county hospital in the Stockholm area (Lagerheim 1983, 1986, and personal communication 1984). Note that while in other countries the term "rehabilitation" is used in the work with handicapped adults and children alike, in Sweden the term "habilitation" is substituted where children are served.

At this center the children receive medical, physiotherapeutic, child-guidance, and educational services. Child-guidance services include intensive work with the parents, particularly as they go through phases of mourning in their adjustment to having a handicapped child. This handicap may be one of locomotion, mental retardation, or other disabilities.

The first people to alert the center's child psychiatric staff to a frequent problem at about age nine were the classroom teachers. They reported a change in these children's attitude toward themselves appearing between age eight and ten. At the same age, it was noticed by center staff, these handicapped children who earlier had co-operated well with all aspects of the program began to show an increasing denial of their special needs. They began to refuse participation in special gymnastics and no longer wanted to attend special classes or to use special transportation.

As a research project was undertaken, the following observations were made. Of a group of 209 children, 140 boys and 69 girls (including 52 mentally retarded children), 80 per cent showed some change in their behavior and symptoms between age eight and ten. The children in the special classes for the mentally retarded reacted most strongly, although later than the children attending regular classes. Their symptoms of a disturbance began and reached a peak at least one year after those of the other children. The symptoms to appear first among the 157 children able to follow a regular school curriculum were nonverbal. Motor hyperactivity or aggressiveness began to show at eight. Close to nine the children tended to withdraw into themselves, and almost 10 per cent developed somatic symptoms like stomach- or headaches, or even convulsions. These symptoms reached their peak before age ten. Between nine and ten the children began to react verbally by raising questions and expressing unhappiness about their not being like other children. In individual work with the children and their parents, the following problems became apparent.

At about nine, these children have become capable of recognizing that they are not only different from other children, but also that their parents are not able to change this. Earlier, the children cooperated in all measures of the Habilitation Center in the belief that this would have a far more curative effect than it does. The parents who have overcome an earlier phase of mourning their having a handicapped child are often thrown back into a new crisis when the child begins to ask questions and to react with distress. They tend to deny and evade their child's anxiety by minimizing the hardship and comforting too readily. Other adults react in a similar way. This leaves these children very much alone with their major problem of the moment: social isolation among peers. It is difficult for handicapped children to be accepted into other children's activities and groups, or to compete successfully with healthy children for a best friend. About one out of four children were bullied at that age by the normal children. Yet, to understand why this should be so and why efforts to be accepted are ignored, rebuffed, or ridiculed, a nine-year-old is too young. The situation was most difficult for the less handicapped children. Being tied to a wheelchair is more tangible than subtler differences from the normal child. Individual work with the parents and the child, helping the youngster to express feelings that were until then bottled up, and helping him or her to understand the situation better and get adult support, led to a reduction of distress and a resolution of the somatic and behavioral symptoms. Much emphasis was placed on helping the parents to accept the child's handicap, because parental acceptance becomes the foremost model for the child's own acceptance.

Confirmation of my impressions about the development of the work of depression has to await conclusive research findings. In the meantime, the material discussed in this chapter and clinical observation have led me to the following hypothesis. The work of depression which serves the personal function of the depressed response and improves communication about distress is most effective when both primary and secondary processes operate freely. It begins to develop as the child

(a)   becomes able to express itself with some independence – that is, creatively – in fantasy and play, storytelling, poetry, drawing, painting, acting, dancing, or music; and

(b)   develops language, memory, self-awareness, and some sense of separateness from its attachment figures, particularly in thinking and reasoning.

Adolescence in different cultural settings

In keeping with Freud's theory (1905) of sexual development from infancy, and beginning with the pioneering work of Jones (1922), Aichhorn (1925), Bernfeld (1938), and A. Freud (1936, 1958), there is an extensive psychoanalytic literature available on preadolescent and adolescent personality development. Without adopting all aspects of psychoanalytic metapsychology myself, I find this literature indispensable for an understanding of the many-sided emotional experiences of the second decade of life.[8] For an understanding of the development of our cognitive equipment during this period, Piaget's work (1969) is helpful. Here, only a sketch is given of those aspects of the adolescent's internal and external situation that are relevant to the frequency of normal as well as abnormal causes for getting depressed during that stage of development.

The second decade of life is a period of many changes. Our body changes rapidly in its proportions, its forms, its strength, and in its male or female characteristics. In addition to emotional upheaval, the hormonal changes connected with sexual maturation during puberty may affect our moods and interests. (By "puberty" I mean the physiological maturation of our reproductive organs, by "adolescence" the psychological transition from childhood to adulthood.) The development of our intellect – such as abstract thinking and a new awareness of the passage of time – leads to a new orientation in life: the capacity and need to plan for the future. The combination of sexual development with growing imagination about the future leads to a gradually increasing urge to explore sexual partnerships, which requires some ease in gender identity. This is enhanced by the impulse to compete with peers. It requires revisions of behavior that may cause conflict, anxiety, and guilt. At the same time, the world around us changes in its attitudes toward us and in its demands. What formerly was permitted or encouraged becomes forbidden or is met with ridicule, if not contempt. What formerly was forbidden may now become permitted and encouraged. We become exposed to aspects of adult life from which formerly we were shielded. The combination of these inner and outer changes is promising, confusing, and at times frightening. Our identity – that is, our view of ourselves – changes often, in forward and backward fluctuations. So does our view of those around us. What seems admirable one day may seem ridiculous the next. What is trustworthy one day may seem dubious the next. There is much trial and error. There is wavering between wanting to belong, to cling, to be a dependent follower, and wanting to be independent, separate, different, and a leader. There are phases of forward thrust in development and phases of retreat. There is instability in the choices of where to belong, on whom to lean, whom to emulate, whom to admire, from whom to be different and distant. Various phases in this development lead to surprising and satisfying successes. Others lead to the painful failure of premature or otherwise unrealistic aspirations and choices.

All major changes in life involve separation from or loss of attachments. They involve loss of expectations and identifications, of familiar environments and routines – as when we change schools or domicile. Consequently, we experience a blend of happy expectations, of eagerness to experiment and take on new responsibilities, with sadness or grief when the familiar disintegrates, with guilt at deserting the familiar, fear of the unfamiliar, anger at the discomfort that all this causes. We react with the depressed response to our bewilderment when we try in vain to be effective in carrying out our intentions. There are moments of triumph and moments of despair. Consequently, during the changes of teenage we experience much ambivalence which, in turn, tends to arouse ambivalence toward us in our elders, or fuels their existing ambivalence.

Mass media and the rapid change of socio-economic conditions and technology in the cities of western industrial civilization impose greater adaptive tasks on our youth than do more stable societies. In western metropolises, and probably in rapidly changing communities of the developing countries as well, rapid change of values and social conditions makes communication between the generations difficult. There, we find cultural diversity of the population, dissolution of the extended family, occupation of both parents outside the home, an increasing variety of educational avenues, and often uncertainty of future employment opportunities. There are many avenues for social, cultural, and political associations and recreational activities open to the young, their economic and educational circumstances permitting. These circumstances and the necessity for making choices may create confusion, indecision, or premature decisions. For these reasons we find so many episodes of short or prolonged depression during this phase of life. In the well-developed and secure teenage personality and under favorable social circumstances, the episodes of depression are likely to be brief and increasingly productive. Under relatively benign circumstances, gifted adolescents are likely to resort to artistic, intellectual, technical, political, or sports activities to master their changing emotions, including the depressed response. Some of these involvements are solitary, some are shared with a close friend, others with a group. Using one's talents to the hilt is a way of surviving the impact of rapid and extensive change. Some of these preoccupations aid the intensive information processing that is necessary to make an episode of depression productive.

On entering this phase of development a youngster is not yet able fully to deal with depressing circumstances by means of productive work of depression, although some intellectual and cognitive prerequisites for mature information processing have begun to make their appearance. If all goes well, however, the challenges and stresses of this period force the adolescent to integrate and utilize both primary and secondary processes, and to mature emotionally, in such a way that truly productive work of depression has become possible when he or she enters adulthood. In this success, the adolescent's parents or parent substitutes play a crucial role. Bowlby abstracts (1973:328ff.) several studies, notably those by Grinker (1962) and by Offer (1969) describing the type of parental attitudes and behavior toward their children that foster favorable development during adolescence even in our complex culture.

Other teenagers do not have secure social circumstances and stabilizing activities to resort to when under duress. Members of their social network may neither understand nor encourage their leanings. Deeper conflicts and pathological defenses established earlier may now lead to severe emotional disturbances, such as unproductive depression, schizophrenia, social violence, other forms of delinquency, or addictions.

It appears that in other cultural settings puberty and adolescence are not as hazardous and turbulent a phase of life as in ours nor as demanding of individual parental competence. In other cultures and in some of our subcultures, the work of adult family members does not proceed in isolation from the family's children and adolescents. These can identify with the work of their elders as they observe it or responsibly participate in it. Where the extended family still is close at hand, a teenager may withdraw from dependence on his parents and still have a supportive confidant with familiar standards available. Also, where there are fewer educational avenues available outside the home, and social change proceeds slowly, the potential for exceptional individual development is more limited but so is the risk of personality disintegration. Intimate sharing between the generations not only in daily work but also in religious devotion may assist the young in establishing an early vision of their future. It gives them a reassuring identity. At least, this was found by Eaton (1964) in a study of the Hutterites in North Dakota. They are a religious sect maintaining an early ninteenth-century communal way of life in a rural area. There is little opportunity for their young to be exposed to and tempted by other ways of life. They appear to be calm and stable adolescents who, by following existing models, manage to enter adulthood at the time and in the manner expected of them. One may assume that the social rewards, restrictions, and taboos of such a setting maintain a balance on the surface, but that the balance is achieved at the price of more fully developed emotional and cognitive flexibility. This sacrifice may be a necessary adaptation for secure belonging in one cultural group, yet pathological in another.

Factors promoting unproductive depression

During the second decade of life, then, we may become increasingly ready to respond with some of the emotional and cognitive flexibility that is needed if the work of depression is to become productive. When this flexibility does not develop at this age, then there are no intrapsychic remedies available for the modification of a depressing experience. Then the observer is justified in speaking of unproductive depression. In preadolescence and adolescence, unproductive depression is usually due to a combination of factors. First, because unfavorable family or other social influences, illness, or handicap have interfered with favorable personality development, there is now a lack of relative flexibility and maturity. Second, current social circumstances or family attitudes interfere with successful adaptation.

The professional literature on depression in adolescents deals largely with unproductive depression. We owe to psychoanalysts and other psychotherapists many case descriptions of teenagers with personality patterns of the kind I described in Chapter 9; patterns that interfere with the productive outcome of the work of depression. These youths are inhibited in experiencing and expressing certain emotions. They are inhibited in their cognitive capacities and given to stereotyped conclusions inappropriate for their age. They are constricted by conflicts. They are excessively dependent on their parents or other authority, or blindly rebellious. They suffer from excessive guilt, shame, fear, and anxiety. A major problem for psychotherapy in such cases is the complex pattern of personality disturbance. Of this, their persistent or recurrent depression is only a consequence, not the core problem. A further difficulty is the unfavorable influence of the home environment. Among others, Sandler and Joffe (1965), Anthony (1975a and b), and Arieti and Bemporad (1978) have made important contributions to the subject of pathological depression in childhood and adolescence.

Chapter twelve

Development of the work of depression, an illustration

Our task ... is to show that depression is also an existential component of existence, different from yet interrelated with anxiety, and that it is not necessarily pathological.

Anthony and Benedek (1975: xviii)

The issue of balance between favorable and unfavorable circumstances

The literature on disorders with depression as a significant symptom emphasizes the frequency in the patient's life history of early loss of an attachment figure through separation from, or change in the behavior of, the significant other. Yet, it has also frequently been pointed out that not all children who have suffered such losses suffer as adults from unproductive depression or related pathology. In fact, some outstanding figures in cultural and political history have been orphaned or suffered other hardships in childhood. It stands to reason to assume that other nurturing figures or circumstances were available to them; and also that innate resilience may vary from child to child. Furthermore, it is not the total absence of stress that makes for a child's optimal development of its potential, but a balance between required effort and adequate support. On the other hand, in our clinical acquaintance with chronically depressed adults, we frequently find that they had depressed parents – perhaps also similarly disadvantaged grandparents – who, having suffered early deprivation, were unable as adults to meet the emotional needs of their children. This is so common that in psychiatry the disposition for depression is often deemed biologically more than socially transmitted within families.

Unfortunately, we do not have conclusive longitudinal research findings as yet on the further development of persons who as children became acutely and overtly depressed. What native temperament, sensitivities, and endowment; and what social influences in their lives will cause them to be depression-prone in adolescence and adult life; and which factors will instead help them develop the capacity to tolerate and productively overcome their getting depressed?

I am acquainted with only one longitudinal study, by Poznanski *et al.* (1976). Cicchetti and Schneider-Rosen (1986) refer to this as the only longitudinal study published. I agree with the latter authors in that the sample in this study, two girls and eight boys, is far too small, and that there are other methodological flaws in the procedures preventing us from considering the findings conclusive evidence. None the less, what Poznanski and colleagues report is very much in keeping with the life histories that clinicians hear from their depression-prone adult patients.

The authors wished to explore how significant the home environment is in the development of depression-prone children and adolescents. They undertook their longitudinal study to explore how children who before puberty had been diagnosed "overtly depressed" would fare as adolescents.

During the original contact the eight boys and two girls, who were later examined in the follow-up, saw themselves as "dumb," "mean," and "no good"(1976:491); they were withdrawn and cried excessively; they were preoccupied with death; they had "serious problems with aggression" and problems with peers. Their families showed considerable pathology, including "a high incidence of depression," difficulties in handling aggression, and overt rejection of the children. At the time of the initial contact, all the families later seen in the follow-up had been advised to obtain psychiatric treatment, but with one exception such treatment had not been sought (p.492).

At an average of six and a half years later (the interval ranging from four to eleven years), clinical interviews were conducted with the ten subjects of the follow-up study and with their parents. The girls were by then sixteen and twenty-three, while three of the boys were sixteen, and the other boys twelve, fifteen, seventeen, nineteen, and twenty. Five of the ten, including both girls, were found to be "overtly depressed" and to be "following a stable depressive style" (p.495). The younger girl was psychotic. The other five were viewed as currently not depressed, but they recalled having had depressed episodes in the interim. None of the ten was free from psychopathology. None was overtly aggressive any longer, but they had become more dependent. They had poor school or work records, and inadequate peer relationships.

Five of the ten families were headed by one parent, the mother. Where there was a father in the home, the relationship with the father was very poor and, at follow-up, two of these five fathers were depressed. With one exception all relationships with the mother were also bad. One mother was psychotic and most of the time incoherent. The only boy who had a reasonably good relationship with his mother was in the acutely depressed group, but he was the only one whose school performance had improved dramatically since the earlier contact. The others had no parent to whom they could relate.

Without being conclusive evidence, this material suggests the following: sufficiently unfavorable family patterns and early traumatic events (such as the father disappearing due to death or divorce) tend to foster in children those personality patterns that create unsolvable problems which typically promote the depressed response and later on keep depression unproductive. In families where children have earlier been exposed to adverse influences, home conditions during their adolescence are rarely improved to the point of counteracting the earlier unfavorable development. On the contrary, current home conditions are likely to reinforce the negative self-image, the poor capacity to relate to peers and elders, the inhibitions of affect, and so forth.

The cases I have cited in the preceding chapter, on the other hand, suggest that despite an early disaster, children may recover the capacity for favorable development if sufficient support from their human environment counteracts the earlier traumatic exposure. But until we have reliable findings available concerning the balance between traumatic and healing experiences in the lives of those who become capable to cope with incomprehensible distress, to what features should we be alert as potentially destructive and as potentially healing, respectively?

I find that Potok's novel touches many readers deeply and causes them to identify with its characters as if they were real people. This is not only because of the author's use of vivid language, but because of the comprehensive presentation of a developing child's innate endowment and sensitivity, combined with his exposure to deprivation and neglect during family disaster which, despite his favorable initial development, brings him to the brink of psychotic breakdown at the age of ten; while due to sufficient supportive components in his social environment he is helped in the course of adolescent development to compensate for the earlier developmental disruption. Therefore I use this story as if its characters were live persons.[1] I use it to alert clinicians and researchers to the multitude of influences that can contribute to making a person depression-prone, and to alert them at the same time to the many circumstances that may counteract the effect of the damaging experiences.

Illustration of the role of primary process

Potok's description of his hero, Asher Lev, is a vivid illustration of the service rendered to a child by the use of his talent. It also shows what happens when one deprives such a child of this means of integrating and expressing his own experience of his situation.

Family constellations and mental breakdowns similar to Asher's appear in other novels by Potok. In view of the poignancy of all his descriptions of emotional turmoil we are justified in assuming that Potok has built his characters on personal experience and intimate observation.

In the history of Asher's mother, Rivkeh, related in Chapter 4, reference was made to Asher's interest in drawing and painting; how important a part it played in helping him to cope with frightening changes in his environment is illustrated below.

During the first years of his life, Asher enjoys the steady, attentive, and cheerful company of his mother, Rivkeh. His father, Aryeh, is affectionate and deeply involved in Asher's welfare. In addition, he becomes early an important figure for Asher inasmuch as he conducts the religious devotions of the family that mark certain times of the day, of the week, and of the year in a reliable rhythm. The warm and trusting relationship between his parents adds to Asher's early security. But Aryeh is away from home during working hours. At times he is away on travel for some days. Except for his maternal uncle, Yaakov, and to a lesser degree his paternal uncle, Yitzchok, there are no other adults to whom Asher can form warm relationships. Nor does he have playmates. In this closely knit, exclusive family structure, Asher develops into an affectionate, alert child, eager to learn and discover. At the same time, the lack of further relationships to fall back on makes him highly vulnerable to disruptions in the emotional balance of his parents.

Asher begins to draw and color unusually early. No play with age-mates diverts him from this interest. The activities that he and his mother share become the major subject of his drawing. His mother's pleasure in what he is doing encourages him

Asher has just turned six when news of his uncle Yaakov's accidental death throws the household into a turmoil. For hours, while the apartment is filling with hysterical adults, Asher remains forgotten in his room. His mother's screaming fills him with terror, and when she is suddenly silent he is convinced that she is dead. Then he is left in a neighbor's apartment, still without explanation. Only the next morning he learns that his mother is not dead, but that she is lying in bed and he cannot see her. He sees her only briefly a week later on her return from the hospital. Her appearance is so changed that he does not immediately recognize her. He is not only left without her emotional responses to him, but also without his major source of information.

During the following weeks, Asher is left to his own devices a great deal. He sees his mother only when she emerges from her bedroom from time to time and sits in the living room in a stupor. He is very observant of her changed appearance and behavior. To his questions his father tells him that his mother is ill. This suggests to Asher that she will get well again in time, but no one can tell him just when and how. He has little contact with the newly hired housekeeper. During his father's working hours he wanders about the apartment or looks out the window watching people passing by. But mostly he busies himself with drawing and coloring, waiting for his mother to become her old self again. Asher is relieved when Rivkeh, in a moment of awareness, asks him to draw pretty things, but becomes bewildered again when she does not respond to his giving her the picture he then draws for her.

One afternoon, when his mother is sleeping in a living room chair, with a full ashtray beside her, Asher spends hours trying to portray his mother's emaciated face with hollow cheeks and deep shadows under her eyes. At first, he is dissatisfied with what he can accomplish with pencil shadings. He discovers that using her cigarette butts gives a softer shade. He is so engrossed in his activity that he does not immediately notice his father's arrival. But then he realizes that his father is not pleased with him.

After Yaakov's death, Asher's father no longer travels but works in a small room in the office building of the congregation, spending most of his working day at the telephone. Recognizing that the housekeeper is inadequate company for the boy, Aryeh begins to take him along to the office every day. Now, Asher wanders about the office building, visiting friendly employees, watching his father at work, but mostly he draws pictures, usually of his father: at home; in the office, talking on the phone with an angry face upon hearing of current persecutions of Jews in Russia; and in the temple, praying or engaging in various rituals. Asher keeps asking questions of his father. Aryeh tries to answer him, particularly when Asher wonders about his mother. Yet, Aryeh tires quickly of the child's many questions and cuts the conversation short. He often frowns uneasily at Asher's pictures and calls his drawing childish foolishness. Asher continues to draw his father and much of what he observes on their street, but he stops showing his drawings to his father. It is disquieting for him to find his father disapproving of a skill his mother has enjoyed and encouraged.

One evening, when his paternal uncle, Yitzchok, is talking to Aryeh about Rivkeh's condition, Asher is sent to his room. He is fond of his uncle and busies himself with painting pictures of him. He makes him as stout as he is, but instead of the dark blue suits his uncle always wears, Asher makes the suit light blue because, as he later recalls, uncle did not "feel dark blue to him." Then the men enter the room. When the uncle, father of four, responds to these drawings with calling the child a new Chagall, and asks for a picture to keep, Aryeh interferes and shows his disapproval of such encouragement.

At this point, Asher has become preoccupied with the arrival in the neighborhood, thanks to the efforts of Aryeh Lev, of a Russian Jew, Yudel Krinsky, who lost his wife and children during the war and has spent eleven years as a prisoner in Siberia. Becoming aware of his father's anxieties and preoccupations, Asher asks many questions about Siberia of his father and the housekeeper. He begins to have fantasies about living in snow, ice, and darkness. He puzzles how he might paint snow, ice, darkness, and a street crying in the rain. A few weeks later, upon the news that when he enters school in the fall, Rivkeh will enter college, and his father resume traveling, Asher, in a state of panic, abruptly stops drawing. He suddenly becomes identified with his father's view that drawing is childishness to be grown out of. From then on he becomes an anxious and increasingly depressed child.

Asher has been suffering from severe emotional deprivations for several months before he stops drawing. He has ample cause for grief, although he cried, alone in his room, only when he believed his mother to be dead. He has also ample cause for anxiety. Being told that she is ill, he clings to the hope that she will get well – perhaps with the help of his drawing pretty things for her. But he is frightened by the change in his mother, and later also by the atmosphere of anger at and fear of persecution radiating from his father and members of the congregation. Asher senses his father's sincere desire to take good care of him. Yet, his father is not one to listen to and validate a child's expression of grief, protest, and anxiety. Nor is there anyone else to give support. This leads inescapably to the gradual repression of grief and anger which produces anxiety and guilt in its wake. These must also be repressed. One of the complex patterns is established that tend to give cause for the depressed response and, in patients older than Asher, can be said to interfere with its becoming productive. It should be stressed again that in such complex patterns the depressed response is only one component. In Asher's case, the depressed response is actually slow in appearing. For some months we have no signals suggesting an overt depressed reaction, nor indications that he is warding off a depressed response. He is active but no more so than he was when his mother still gave him her full attention. He remains alert to events in his environment. His curiosity and self-confidence appear unbroken. He tolerates a remarkable amount of frustration, and can wait a long time for a return to his former satisfactions before his hope collapses and his functioning becomes impaired. The security of his life prior to the catastrophe of uncle Yaakov's death would make most children confident and tolerant of some delay during a painful change. But the unusual development of primary process in Asher adds further strength.

Many incidents in Potok's description illustrate how this helps Asher to integrate his painful experiences of danger, loss, and neglect. It gives him a sense of coping which prevents his becoming depressed. He is pleased with what he accomplishes. When he discovers that the ashes of his mother's cigarette butts can be used to give softness to the shadows in her face, this keeps him emotionally and physically close to her person and her suffering. He tries to take her into himself despite her unresponsiveness. When he spends his days in Aryeh's office, observing his father's irritation and fears, he is well aware that he is in the way. He manages again to integrate this difficult experience by trying to identify with his father's many activities and moods as he portrays them. When he is sent to his room, away from the presence of an uncle who shows concern about Rivkeh's condition and understands drawings better than his father, Asher expresses his affection by coloring his uncle's suit in a light blue.

Despite these efforts, Asher's deprivations become increasingly threatening. Avidly he collects information about the horrors of Siberia. Ice and snow become symbols of potential dangers, of emotional isolation, and panic. Rain becomes a symbol of grief. He wants to cope with ice, snow, and rain by painting it, an effort beyond his skill. If he could have done it, it would have expressed his experience of the initial emotional separation from his mother, his disappointment in her failing to return to him emotionally when she could function again, and his awareness of his father's discontent. But here, his gift lets him down. Asher's genuine pleasure in drawing has gradually turned into a compulsive defense against anxiety and depression. The fantasies of snow, ice, and darkness are the depressive thoughts that Cytryn and McKnew (1974) have noted.

This turn to a slowly but steadily developing depression is rooted in Asher's discovery that his mother's behavior cannot be influenced by his drawing even when she begins to return to more normal functioning; and that she recovers this functioning not in response to what Asher offers and what he needs, but by identifying with her brother. Having been a pleasure to her in the past, Asher has now become a burden. His confidence in his drawing and in himself has been rooted in the relationship with his mother and in the meaning his drawing has had for her. Now, her response to his drawing has become superficial and is overshadowed by more urgent concerns. Under these circumstances, Asher does what might establish greater closeness to his father: he stops drawing, not quite seven years old. Probably, he also feels let down by the limitations of his skill in drawing and rejects it. At any rate, Asher surrenders the only deep satisfaction left to him: the use and development of his gift; his only means to express powerful feelings and disturbing thoughts.

A child who is able to work through and express his experience in his drawings, though rarely in words and affect, can for quite some time cope with depriving and frightening changes in his environment, provided that the joys of significant learning and self-expressive skills are preserved. Only when he loses confidence in the rescuing powers of his skill and represses his interest in exercising it his total development becomes depressive. He cannot comprehend the consequences to himself of this surrender. Being emotionally deserted by his mother as she recovers from her "illness" destroys the meaning this skill has had for him until now. In Asher's world, a child cannot turn instead to protesting and making angry demands. Without his art, Asher becomes helpless to integrate the changes in the family's way of life until, in despair, he resumes drawing at the age of ten.

Productive outcome of a severe depression in a ten-year-old

By identifying with her brother's mission in life Rivkeh has found a way to go on living, but this precludes her relating to her child quite as she did before. Absorbed by the demands of her studies she has very little time for Asher, although he continues to mean much to her. It is the housekeeper, a rigidly religious widow in late middle age, who has to attend to Asher's physical needs. His emotional needs and his need for stimulation are not receiving much attention. During weekdays, Rivkeh is at college. After dinner, if Aryeh is out of town, and that is often, she studies until late at night. Her deep fear that Aryeh and Asher will meet the same fate as her parents and her brother by getting killed in a traffic accident makes her irritable, often withdrawn. This, in turn, makes Asher anxious.

In his school, the Yeshiva, the curriculum contains both secular and religious subjects. In each classroom there is a large photograph of the Rebbe. After a while this picture begins to appear in Asher's dreams. As an adult he remembers little else of his first school years, although he liked his gentle teachers and the contact with peers. Compared with the vivid recollections of other periods this suggests an increasing withdrawal and a decrease in initiative and curiosity. Only during the summer, when the family rent a bungalow in a Hasidic colony on the shore of a lake, is there opportunity for a more relaxed contact between mother and child.

During Asher's first three years at school his father travels a great deal within the USA. Gradually he is given increasing responsibility. He is radiant. Through his services more and more immigrants from his native country, Russia, arrive in the neighborhood. When Asher is nine, Aryeh becomes deeply disturbed by the treatment of Jewish writers and physicians who are imprisoned and executed in Russia. Now, Asher begins to understand that his father is yearning to work in Europe where he could more effectively rescue Jews. Asher also grasps that this thought frightens his mother. Stalin becomes a demon to him.

Asher becomes increasingly vulnerable to the tensions in each parent. Often Asher cannot sleep. Increasingly he forgets to study for tests. He begins to fail his tests. His father learns of this, gets upset and reproachful.

Asher is ten years old when Stalin dies. On television, Asher sees Stalin in his coffin. Aryeh expects increased persecution of Jews in Russia but at the same time expresses the hope that it may become easier now to get into Russia and help Jews. Asher fears his father will go to Russia and be sent to Siberia or be killed. After school he begins to stop at the stationery store where Yudel Krinsky is in charge. Asher asks questions about Siberia, about Stalin, about Jews in Europe. He no longer solicits all important information from his parents but rather from Mr Krinsky or the housekeeper. He grows fond of Yudel Krinsky. Occasionally, he comes home quite late after school, although this upsets his mother.

Only a few weeks after Stalin's death in March, Asher's parents begin to talk about the possibility of moving to Vienna, Austria. The Rebbe may ask Aryeh to develop new Hasidic congregations in Europe. Cautiously Asher is asked about his reaction. He does not want to move. He becomes ill with a low grade infection, but for a week he runs a high fever and fantasizes. The thought of a strange city and people talking a foreign language and perhaps hating Jews terrifies Asher. He wants to go on living on his street with the buildings and people he knows so well.

There is continuing talk about moving to Vienna, and Asher's emotional state deteriorates rapidly. He is afraid to go on a bus or subway, terrified at the thought of taking an airplane. Then the date for the move is set for October. In despair, Asher pleads with his uncle Yitzchok to keep him. His uncle declines with facile reassurances. Asher begins to have nightmares about a mythical ancestor and dreams again about the Rebbe. Asher is afraid he is sick and should be taken to a doctor, but he does not mention it.

At the Yeshiva, the "mashpia," a kind and soft-spoken man, is responsible for religious teaching and watching over the boys' spiritual development. One morning, as the mashpia talks in class, Asher, unaware of what he is doing, draws a picture in his Hebrew notebook. Later he is shocked to discover that he has drawn Stalin, dead in his coffin. Then he cannot stop himself from drawing Stalin in all his notebooks. He draws him, "empty and hollow," "swollen and bloated," with distorted face, "a horror" in front of "a mountain of flowers." When Aryeh finds Asher's room strewn with such drawings he gets very angry and talks about Asher's poor school work. But Asher goes on drawing.

When a date is set to apply for passports, Asher pleads with his uncle again to keep him. The latter reports this to Aryeh, who gets very angry and talks about childish foolishness. At bedtime, when Rivkeh tells Asher that he is hurting his father, Asher bursts out, "I don't want to lose it again," meaning the ability to draw, and that he doesn't "care about anyone." He refuses to go to the passport office and application is postponed. Two days later, Asher makes a drawing of his mother while she is studying. He doesn't hear that she is trying to talk to him, which is a new symptom. Later, admitting that this is a beautiful drawing, his father expresses his uncertainty whether Asher's gift comes from heaven or from hell. Then, in order to explain the necessity for moving to Vienna, Aryeh tries to describe his faith and his responsibility to all Jewish lives. In the evening Asher says to his mother: "I'm also a Jewish life ... does someone have a responsibility to me?" He adds that something inside him tells him not to go to Vienna. But under the pressure of the entire adult world he is unable to keep up his resistance much longer. Soon he goes with his parents to the passport office.

Then, Asher begins to draw things burning – the office building of the congregation burning, piles of books burning. His mother takes him to the family doctor, who finds him healthy. Asher is taken to an eye doctor. His eyes are fine. He is taken to a young psychiatrist without being told about the man's specialization. There Asher draws a cat he has seen being struck by a car and severely injured. Asher notices that the doctor looks very serious and that on the way home, his mother is very quiet.

During a religious lesson on the next day, Asher, completely unconscious of what he is doing, draws a man's head across the printed page of a sacred text. It is the Rebbe's head as it appears on the photograph. The swelling whispering of the boys sitting near Asher alerts the teacher, who is shocked and angry. Only then Asher sees what he has done. That he could do this without even knowing it frightens him.

Asher's father is notified by the school. Asher is to come to the mashpia's office the next morning. At breakfast, Aryeh reproaches Asher severely for drawing instead of studying. He attacks his drawing as foolishness. For the first time Asher protests – eloquently, succinctly. He asks his father never again to call his drawing foolishness.

The mashpia is friendly when Asher arrives, gentle and sympathetic. But Asher is unable to listen to what the mashpia is saying and asking. His mind drifts off to watching the rain beating against the window, and to the problems of painting a street crying. Finally, by raising his voice, the mashpia succeeds in catching Asher's attention for a while.

They talk about Asher not being aware of what he was doing when he drew the Rebbe in the sacred book. They talk about his parents' plan to take Asher to Vienna. Asher says that, of course, he is going to Vienna. "How can an eleven-year-old boy live alone in Brooklyn?" He is going to Vienna. Then he bursts into tears of despair for a long while and his mind drifts off again. The mashpia puts a new sketchbook and a pencil on the desk. Before leaving Asher alone in the room, he instructs Asher to do some drawing and then leave it on the desk.

Asher feels a resistance at first. Then he draws page after page, his mother, his street, the people he knows, many of the subjects he has often drawn. Finally he puts down the sketchbook, leaves the room, leaves the building, drifts through the streets until he finds himself inside a big building, Brooklyn Museum. He is diverted and excited by what he sees there and stays until closing time late in the afternoon. On the way home he realizes that he has not drawn a single picture of his father for the mashpia. Why not, he wonders, why? The mashpia will notice. By the time he comes home his parents have become very anxious. His father is angry and prohibits his ever going to the museum again without permission. From then on, Asher comes home from school promptly whenever his father is in town but goes to the museum when his father is out of town.

In May, having received the notebook with Asher's drawings from the mashpia and heard his report, the Rebbe tells the Levs that Asher must be kept in Brooklyn, but Asher is not told about this until August. In October Aryeh departs for Europe alone, while Asher continues at his Yeshiva, and Rivkeh starts graduate work. Asher misses his father very much the first winter. At times he wants to say that he is willing to move to Vienna, but then he cannot bring himself to do so.

Precisely when Asher, in the eyes of his father and many others, is rapidly getting crazier, the largely unconscious information processing that is facilitated by his insomnia, his tiredness, withdrawal, and preoccupation is beginning to become effective. We must not overlook that Asher's emotional turmoil is not only due to deep conflicts, but also to a large extent to realistically disastrous circumstances bound to arouse anxiety and protest. The core of his personality and his deepest needs are ignored and violated by those to whom he is most deeply attached and on whom he is dependent, those to whom he is dearest. His growing capacity to question some of his father's values, and to object verbally to some of his father's behavior, is lost on the latter, though not entirely on his mother. How is he to get help? The fleeting hope that he might get support from a physician has, to Asher's knowledge, been a false hope. His kind and sympathetic friend, Yudel Krinsky, is powerless.

Thus, it should not be seen as an accident but rather as a result of an unconscious necessity that his most reliable means of communication, pictorial art, breaks through the barrier of repression while the mashpia is present in his classroom. His drawing of the dead Stalin conveys the unconscious meaning: I also am being persecuted and my life is being threatened by a tyrant who gets acclaim for what he is doing. But Asher's tyrant is neither dead nor buried. Nor would he want him dead. Asher is in a deep conflict. The mashpia would understand, but Asher cannot consciously betray his father. He needs to find another road toward rescue. Thus, it is no accident that Asher paints his father's and the Rebbe's offices in flames. The Rebbe has initiated the impending move to Vienna. Only he could change it. Asher's drawing a bleeding cat pulling its mangled hindlegs into a corner with the help of its forelegs tells the psychiatrist: look at what is happening to me; they are crippling and destroying me. It is no accident that he draws the Rebbe's head into a sacred text in a situation where this action will be publicized and reach the Rebbe's attention. The message of which he is unaware is: toward me, no one is living up to these teachings of our religion, not even the Rebbe. It shows that Asher has a clear, though forbidden and therefore repressed, understanding of his social situation and of his own needs. The total omission of his father's image in the sketchbook for the mashpia suggests Asher's hidden conflict of loyalty in his need to be liberated from his father's demands. Finally, it is no accident that his despair breaks through and that he cries in the mashpia's office rather than in the presence of his mother. Asher has found a way to be saved from emotional disintegration: he has succeeded in alerting the only two people who can help him: the mashpia and the Rebbe.

This success is not only due to an unusual capacity to use primary process for communication. It is also due to the fact that Asher has clearly begun to feel himself as separate from his parents and is conscious of having a talent they lack and cannot fully appreciate, a talent his father dislikes as something alien. Asher is beginning to recognize what his emotional needs are and how his identity is being threatened. He is consciously trying to defend himself. He is beginning to protest and resist verbally, though without any show, or even awareness, of anger. He defends against anger with despair, a defense that easily creates cause for the depressed response.

After Asher has learned that the Rebbe is preventing his being taken out of his environment, the deterioration of his social and academic functioning comes to a halt. Very slowly he becomes more stable, although at first there is little improvement academically. As we shall see, one more intervention by the Rebbe is necessary two and a half years later, before the consequences of that intervention help Asher to move into a remarkably stable adolescence.

Reading my description and evaluation of Asher's increasingly disturbed behavior during the period from age six through ten, clinicians may raise the question whether this should be diagnosed as a depression or rather an anxiety state in a child. But here we are not concerned with differential diagnosis but with the fate in Asher's development of a specific affective response. In his case, circumstances were of a kind that normally would activate both anxious and angry responses. The angry responses could not be expressed overtly and, when they could not be expressed pictorially, required neurotic defenses to remain repressed. The anxious responses remained very apparent but failed to elicit the kind of adult responses necessary at this age for the function of anxiety to be fulfilled (see Chapters 6 and 11). Furthermore, Asher's efforts by as much compliance as he could muster to recapture the satisfactory family interaction of his early years were frustrated. His natural way of coping with frustration, drawing and painting, he had sacrificed to no avail. As a result, getting depressed in addition to being anxious, was the natural, inescapable response. Whether his anxiety, or his depressed response to the deadlock in information processing caused by his defenses as well as environmental prohibitions, are to be considered dominant in his total response pattern is not the issue here. Our focus is on the fate of Asher's capacity to utilize his depressed reactions productively in overcoming his self-destructive defenses.

Beneficial separation

During the autumn months following Aryeh's departure Asher is very busy, in reality and in fantasy, drawing his father "in all the places where I had not drawn him earlier." This may serve the purpose of adapting to the separation; it may represent an effort to understand and feel close to his father. Asher also draws his mother very often. Aware of the hardship the separation is for her, his drawings of her may well include an attempt at restitution. He goes to the museum very often and pleads with his mother to explain some of the paintings to him that he cannot understand. Although he will not be able until he is a young adult to formulate this for himself in words, it seems that at eleven Asher already feels the need to become an outstanding artist in order to justify the heart-ache he cannot help causing his parents. He has no time, interest, or strength left to do his school work, although the entire adult world around him insists that a boy his age, particularly the son of his father, "should be studying Torah."

Rivkeh tries to strike a balance between Asher's needs and Aryeh's convictions. Since at the peak of his recent crisis Asher once stole oil colors from Yudel Krinsky's store, she gives him a present of the necessary equipment for painting in oils. She once accompanies him to the museum. Although she is appalled to find him intrigued not only by abstract paintings but mainly by nudes and by crucifixions, she tries, to her limited ability, to explain them. But she stresses that paintings of nudes and of Jesus are highly objectionable according to the family's religious beliefs. Nonetheless, Asher continues to fill his notebooks with copies of nudes and crucifixions. He explains to his mother that he cannot find on other faces the expression he sees on the crucified Jesus.

Only in his adult crisis, when Asher is driven to paint his mother as crucified between Asher and Aryeh, does Asher's fascination with the symbol of crucifixion become transparent: the suffering in Jesus's face must have expressed for Asher the torment of his mother's conflicts; his own torment in yearning for his father's accepting love while he wanted to be liberated from the same father's unreasonable demands; and it may have aroused his guilt over repressed wishes for revenge.

After six months, when Aryeh returns for two weeks, he learns from Rivkeh about the money spent on painting equipment, the sketchbooks filled with Jesus and nudes, and the poor school work. The entire two weeks he is in a rage, accusing Asher of becoming a goy, and of desecrating his father's home and work. If Asher does not study, Aryeh will force him next year to move to Vienna, even if that should make him "a little crazy."

Early in childhood Aryeh became a poor orphan when his father, in his urge to help other Hasids, forgot that a Russian Jew was not safe on the street during the Christian Easter holidays and was killed by a drunken Christian peasant. Apparently unaware of the parallel, Aryeh now takes chances of orphaning his son, but seems to transfer his repressed resentment about his father's desertion on to Asher, who with equal persistence pursues a passion that to Aryeh is a Christian characteristic.

Worst of all for Asher is hearing his parents quarreling in the bedroom. To his question why they must quarrel, his mother explains that his father becomes upset when she refuses to promise measures that she knows cannot succeed, such as keeping him from going to the museum. But she is not sure that his father is not right.

After these two weeks, Asher is not unhappy to see his father depart for Vienna. Nor is he as helpless as he was earlier. For the first time he feels angry about his lack of power. He decides to study the two subjects that "concern" his father most: "Talmud and Bible." He reads and memorizes. By not drawing quite as much, by not going to the museum quite as often, he manages to study just enough to get satisfactory reports in these subjects. He has understood that he must not give his father valid cause to take him to Vienna. It is no longer only a hostile foreign world Asher is afraid of. Since his father has set himself up as an adversary, Asher is afraid of him.

The next two years pass calmly. Asher and his mother spend the first summer at the bungalow colony as usual. Asher draws, paints, and studies Talmud. His mother puts the last touches on her master's dissertation. They row on the lake and walk together. Aryeh arrives in Brooklyn in September to spend the High Holidays with his family and congregation. Asher's school work is good now, but Aryeh does not mention it. Asher suspects that his father may regret the improvement. The next year, Rivkeh spends the summer with Aryeh in Europe, while Asher lives with his uncle's family. He paints, draws, and runs errands for his uncle and for Yudel Krinsky in whose store he spends much of his time. In the fall, Rivkeh begins her studies for the doctorate.

A calm adolescence

When Asher is thirteen, his entering manhood is to be celebrated by the religious rites and social festivities of bar mizvah. To prepare himself under the guidance of the mashpia for the customary meeting with the Rebbe, Asher spends weeks studying sacred texts and their interpretation. But instead of the expected examination, the Rebbe, in a friendly interview, guardedly conveys his awareness of Aryeh's limitations in understanding Asher and appreciating his talent. He terminates the brief meeting with some advice about how Asher should conduct his religious life.

Following this interview, Asher meets an internationally famous Jewish painter and sculptor with whom the Rebbe has made arrangements for Asher's education as an artist. An old man, Jacob Kahn no longer takes students, but upon seeing the sketchbook Asher has filled for the mashpia three years earlier, Kahn agrees to take on Asher as a student. Kahn grew up in Europe in a devout Jewish family but is not religious any longer. He greatly admires the Rebbe as a person and visits him from time to time. He warns Asher forcefully of the conflicts and difficulties he is likely to get himself into as a devout Jew, if he seriously involves himself in becoming an artist. Then he tells Asher how to prepare himself for their first meeting several weeks later. Asher has seen Kahn's work at the museum.

Aryeh is in town for the bar mizvah. When Asher comes home and excitedly tells his parents what has taken place, he finds that the Rebbe has talked to them earlier of his intentions. His mother seems tense and his father is very upset. Although it is the Rebbe's decision, Aryeh repeats over and over again, on that occasion and later, that he cannot reconcile himself to it.

Kahn is a stern teacher. He has high standards not only for an artist's skills but for honesty, genuineness, and incorruptibility in the artist's production. To him, "painting is a religion" which "has its fanatics and its rebels." He demands indefatigable effort and practice from Asher in learning to master the traditional techniques and art forms of western painting before he will be allowed to go beyond them. He projects five years of teaching Asher, and although he is in his seventies he carries it through. He introduces Asher immediately to his agent, a gentile woman, Anna. Seeing Asher's sketchbooks she is willing to exhibit his work whenever Kahn tells her. Kahn treats Asher's religious practices and beliefs with respect and tolerance except when they interfere with his development as an artist. The Rebbe has told Kahn that Asher should not paint nudes, but Kahn chooses to disregard this prohibition. It is too important an art form. Asher spends his Sunday afternoons at Kahn's studio and soon also some weekday hours after school. After the first few months Kahn makes arrangements with a young model who is to pose in the nude for Asher. Asher is shocked and anxious the first few times but then he overcomes his resistance. Also against the Rebbe's instructions, Asher is told to study crucifixions as an important art form. At times, Kahn attacks Asher for being sentimental in his painting, for telling a story instead of creating a painting. Asher understands and accepts the criticism. Kahn tells Asher that as an artist he is not responsible to anyone but to his art. On the whole, he treats Asher as a young adult.

While things move along smoothly in Asher's work with Jacob Kahn, from time to time there is still turmoil at home and at school. At the time when his apprenticeship begins, some weeks pass without any news from Aryeh. No one knows where he is and the Rebbe does not disclose it, if he knows. Rivkeh and Asher fear that he is in Russia. Asher reacts with terror and nightmares. Then news arrives that Aryeh is safe in Vienna. When he comes for a visit in the fall, he does not disclose where he has been. He is pleased with what he is accomplishing in Europe, but he has lost weight and looks gaunt and tired. He finds Asher looking well and happy, but he continues to resent what Asher is doing. During the following months Rivkeh asks Asher several times whether he would be willing to live with his uncle next year if she were to move to Europe after the completion of her doctorate. Asher protests. But Rivkeh's increasing suffering at not being with Aryeh upsets Asher. One night he cannot sleep at all. The next morning he falls asleep in class while a sacred text is being studied, and the teacher's threatening remarks amuse the class. A few days later, Asher finds a provocative poem in his book that ridicules him as an artist who will go to hell. A few days later he finds a similar poem. There is snickering and whispering in the class. That evening he gets into a rage and draws a copy of Michelangelo's *Last Judgement* giving all the faces of the damned the contorted features of the boy he knows to be his tormentor. He slips the sketch into the boy's book. This puts an end to the provocations. Asher's ability to defend himself continues to improve.

In the spring, a year after Asher became Kahn's pupil, Rivkeh decides that Aryeh now needs her more than Asher does, despite his protest. At the end of June, subtenants take over the family's apartment, Asher moves into his uncle's house, and Rivkeh joins her husband in Europe. Kahn and his wife take the fourteen-year-old Asher with them to their cottage on Cape Cod for the entire summer. Kahn sculpts, Asher paints, they swim and walk together. Asher prepares and eats his kosher meals in his room. On Saturdays he does not sketch or paint, but reads sacred texts and prays. A warm though undemonstrative friendship develops between Kahn and the boy. Both in the New York studio and on Cape Cod many artists come to visit Kahn. Asher profits from their discussions of art. From time to time Kahn stays in his room for a few days in a deep depression. When he reemerges he works intensively. Mourning and bitterness seem to be part of these episodes. Not only was much of his work destroyed during the German occupation of Paris, but it was also a severe disappointment to Kahn that prior to the occupation all his students abandoned him. Except for Asher, he has never again taken on students.

Asher spends the following summers with Kahn on Cape Cod until, at the age of eighteen, he has his first exhibition and Kahn stops teaching him. Asher has completed high school. On entering it he was surprised that, on the Rebbe's orders, French was to be included among his subjects. It turns out to have been a wise move.

Kahn and Anna, the agent, consider it important that in his first exhibition all aspects of Asher's capacity be presented and they insist that some paintings of nudes be included. Asher is deeply anxious about this but accepts their decision. The exhibition is a success but, as Asher has foreseen, the pictures of nudes prove a shock to the many members of his congregation who come to the opening, and most of all to his parents who have by then returned to live in Brooklyn. This leads to the first real rift with his father. The Rebbe advises Asher to go to Europe for further studies in painting; this will give his family and his friends some time to get over the worst of the blow.

The role of benign circumstances

Looking back on the beginning of Asher's teenage development, we see that at the age of ten he shows many depressed reactions. His mood is low and discouraged. He sleeps poorly and has nightmares about a threatening, powerful ancestor of his father. He cannot concentrate on his school work or on what people tell him. He is exceedingly preoccupied with his anxieties and fears, and with fantasies of how he might cope. More and more, he is afraid he will not be able to cope. But aside from repressing anger, Asher does not show the character traits that are prominent in the depressed children described by Cytryn and McKnew (1974), and by Poznanski *et al.* (1976). He does not show their low self-image, does not feel dumb, bad, mean, or sinful. He is not preoccupied with death. For a few years he accepts his father's view that drawing is a childishness to be grown out of, but then, without adult help, he overcomes this negative view. This can be seen as one productive result of his continuing depression. Asher's being different from those depression-prone children is not surprising when we consider that he has grown up in an affectionate home with parents who deeply care about each other and about their child. There is closeness and much sharing in the family, particularly in regular religious practices. A son is a very important member of a family in this world. Asher has self-respect.

In Chapter 11 we saw that from six months of age infants who have had a good relationship and intense interaction with their mother figure may, on prolonged separation from her, develop symptoms of distress similar to what we later call symptoms of depression. Precisely because Asher's relationship with his mother has been so intense and satisfying, he is hit very hard, first by her withdrawal into the reactions to her bereavement, and then by her preoccupation with her studies and with her anguish about her husband's traveling. Precisely because his father has been so affectionate and responsible toward him, it becomes traumatic when the same father cannot understand and tolerate Asher's urge to exercise his talent. Precisely because his parents are so close and so loyal to each other, it becomes threatening to Asher when they begin to quarrel about him. But the groundwork of strength and stability laid in this child during the first six years of his life, though shaken by the time he is ten, has not been destroyed when the mashpia and the Rebbe take action to prevent disastrous consequences of Asher's panic.

The Hasidic community in which Asher grows up is closely knit. Although in Asher's family there are no grandparents for him to turn to, when the relationship with his parents is out of harmony, the community offers other resources. There is the kindly interest in Asher's art work of the Russian Jewish refugee, Yudel Krinsky. The mashpia not only inspires respect for authority; he also shows and inspires affection. The Rebbe does not only arouse awe; he also arouses trust. On a child like Asher, his father's approval or disapproval has a deep effect. But in his life there are also powerful factors to counteract the impact of his father's growing resentment and protest.

For one thing, his mother, though understanding and respecting her husband's feelings, also understands her child's needs. She does not conspire with either against the other. Asher can trust her without guilt toward his father. For another, while his father is an important figure in the hierarchy of the congregation, the mashpia's and the Rebbe's authority are superior to his. When these two men support, protect, and encourage Asher's drawing and painting as something worthwhile, he can pursue this activity without guilt or shame.

Finally, although Asher's talent and interest are alien to his parents' talents and interests, his intensity in applying himself to them is by no means alien to family patterns. His father and his mother are as obstinately and passionately devoted to their pursuits as Asher is to his. There is a deep kinship between them.

All this explains why, when freed from his father's daily protestations and from constant exposure to his resentment, Asher can begin to recover without psychotherapy. It explains why, at the age of prepuberty, he has the strength and independence to turn to doing his school work in order to protect his artistic needs; why he can choose not to paint compulsively when staying in Brooklyn is at stake. But is this enough to account for a calm and undramatically progressive adolescence after so much turmoil? I am inclined to believe that for the latter the unusually satisfactory match with Jacob Kahn as a new father figure is necessary.

Although the content of their thinking and commitments is so different, Jacob Kahn and Aryeh Lev have a great deal in common. Both are Jews whose personality is marked by a family history of violent persecution. Both are immigrants to the USA. Both are passionately and uncompromisingly devoted to their respective calling. Both have a stable marriage. Kahn has also had one child, but his daughter died in childhood. Both admire the Rebbe.

Thus, Asher finds a father substitute who shares many important values and attitudes with his parents. In this relationship, Asher can preserve many of his parents' values and yet become independent from them in a world of his own. The power of his talent causes him to know very early what his major pursuit in life will be. The authority of the Rebbe and of his teacher confirms him in his own early choice of a profession. He is not confronted with the many social and occupational choices that cause confusion and false moves in many adolescents so that they feel inadequate to their efforts and become depressed from time to time. Asher is qualified for what he is trying to achieve under Kahn's guidance. He can be pleased with the way he functions. In this phase of his life there is little cause for the depressed response, if any.

The absence of his parents in Europe permits his being diverted from the family conflicts during the last years of training with Kahn, but it also prevents his having to face the conflict with his father on a deeper level. Thus, the completion of his personal liberation from the taboos of his childhood is delayed until the crisis in Paris (see Chapter 1) when he paints his two "Brooklyn Crucifixions," and also his liberation from Kahn's rigid rules of the artist's ethics (see A. Freud 1958:264). In addition to the conscious insights he reaches at that point, the urge to portray his mother as crucified suggests an unconscious image of her as tending to sacrifice herself. Such a tendency on her part would actually free Asher from some of the guilt suggested by his appearance at the foot of the crucifix. This is a grasp of family dynamics that he could not have achieved, at least not without therapy.

In keeping with the modesty of the family he describes, and probably with his own values, Potok is very discreet about Asher's sexual development during puberty and adolescence. We are made to sense, more than to see, that at thirteen Asher responds to the presence of a live, beautiful girl's naked body with an excitement and feelings appropriate to a boy of his background at his age. While his parents are very modest and discreet, Asher obviously is aware from early childhood on of a tender intimacy between them. As a young adult, after the exhibition of his two crucifixions, Asher indicates discreetly that he has met his future wife. She is a Jewish girl in the Hasidic congregation his father has organized in Paris. When he is about to leave Brooklyn after the exhibition of his two crucifixions, his father, despite his hurt feelings, tells him that he is aware of this association and that, as in-laws, the girl's family are highly acceptable to Asher's parents.

This does not mean to say that after having painted his crucifixions Asher Lev will be free from episodes of depression. Both the search for development as an artist and the clash of his orientation as an artist with his attachment and loyalties to his background will, time and again, provide the perplexities that cause the depressed response. It only means that despite his childhood depression the strengthening aspects of his background and his adolescent development provide him with the ability to resolve depressions productively.

Chapter thirteen

Family influences on development

In general, the organism attempts to reduce stress and associated anxiety both in optimal learning and in its defensive activities. But optimal learning and defensive activities are, in a sense, at the opposite ends of a spectrum. In the former, the input of new information tends to be maximal; in the latter, it tends to be minimal.

Peterfreund (1971:208)

Basic trust in the personal and the physical world that surrounds him is the air that the child must breathe if he is to have roots for his own sense of identity and for the related sense of his place in the world.

Lynd (1958:45)

Social participation from birth

As I proposed in Chapter 11, we appear from early infancy equipped to respond with depressed reactions to the persistent failure of a significant effort that is expected to yield, and earlier may have yielded, success. This was apparent in Spitz's description (1946) of anaclytically depressed babies and in other case descriptions, where invariably the effort that had failed was one of trying to elicit a familiar satisfying response from an attachment figure. It was evident that the social function of this affective behavior is served from the beginning: normally, the infant's depressed response alerts adult attention and care.

When we examine how early experiences in our family and society enhance or stultify our development toward coping with causes and process of being depressed, the following questions arise. First, what type of innate disposition will help a child develop the personality that makes productive work of depression possible, and what will hinder such development? Second, what is the role of the family in this development? Third, is the capacity for productive work of depression in the well-functioning adult a universal phenomenon or does it develop mainly in societies where cultural patterns and social organization require it? Fourth, what type of socio-cultural setting will protect against frequent cause for depression, against avoidance of depression, or inability to cope productively with being depressed; what will instead promote unfavorable developments? In this chapter the first two questions will concern us, while the other two are left for Chapter 14.

We know a great deal by now about experiences likely to be favorable or unfavorable to a child's successful adaptation to the requirements of our society, but we have very limited knowledge about the individual genetic or constitutional disposition that as infants and young children we bring to the interaction with others. Nor do we know how innate responsiveness to the functions and appearance of our own body, or differences in tactile, olfactory, visual, and auditory perceptiveness affect our development. But we cannot escape the impression that children are different from birth, that some may by native temperament be more alert, more responsive and enterprising, more resilient or sturdy than others; that some children are more sensitive – for better and for worse – than others, more imaginative; and that not only extent but also characteristics of intelligence and imagination vary (compare Gazzaniga, 1985). Children appear to play a significant part from birth in how they respond to, and how they are affected by, their experiences. For instance, although we cannot prove it, we cannot help wondering whether Margaret's response (Chapter 8) to her family could have been less difficult to remedy than Olga's (Chapter 9) to hers because of differences not only in their families' behavior and situation, but also in some of their own native dispositions. We cannot tell. In any case, their parents, their siblings, and other social surroundings played a decisive role in how they developed.

When I use the term "family," I mean the unit of people who live together and by whom the infant is taken care of. Most often this is the biological family, or at least a person or family unit with whom the baby is living for some length of time. And within this group, there is in our society usually one person who has the major responsibility for the day-by-day care of the baby, particularly for attention to the baby's need for stimulation, protection against overstimulation, and responsiveness in general; in other words, the person who does the mothering. In our society, this need not be but usually is a woman, most often the biological mother. In contexts where I refer to the person serving this function, I may use the terms "mother," "mother-figure," "parent," "significant other," "attachment figure," or "caregiver," interchangeably. For a baby who lives in an institution rather than in a family, the caregiver deserving the description of significant other or attachment figure may well be the nurse to whom the baby has become most attached.

An important factor in the infant's and, later, the maturing child's development is the match between the child's and the mother figure's interactional responses. The quality of this match – and soon also the match with the other parent – profoundly affects the child's earliest and continuing experience in the family, and determines the vicissitudes of its capacity freely to experience and express feelings, and freely to observe, explore, and draw conclusions; in other words, the child's capacity to learn without excessive anxiety or other handicaps. But how does an infant subjectively experience this interaction during the earliest months of life? To this we do not have certain and uncontroversial answers, although the extensive research into infant behavior that in recent years has been conducted and variously interpreted has led to new, challenging hypotheses. As a child grows older, it becomes easier for us to observe and understand the effects on subjective experience of his or her interaction with significant others. But by then we already see that he or she may be more or less vulnerable to potentially detrimental responses from parent figures or older siblings. How and when did this happen if it happened after birth? How does learning normally develop and how is the infant equipped for learning? What can have gone wrong with the development of this equipment? What is the infant's and what is the family's part in the successes and failures of their interaction? Our answers to such questions are of necessity hypothetical, but we must keep trying for more and more plausible hypotheses. Most of what I can offer on the basis of my own professional experience remains description of family interaction as reconstructed in the therapy of adults. But, as Stern (1985) points out, reconstruction is influenced by the theoretical expectations of the therapist. Therefore, it gives the reader a better perspective of my point of view, if I briefly comment on the position of three authors whose approach to the issues of development and learning I find particularly useful: Bowlby (1969,1988), Peterfreund (1971, 1978), and Stern (1985). They are psychoanalysts and apply the clinical concepts of psychoanalysis but differ from its prevalent metapsychology and conceptualization of infancy.[1] Partly their assertions follow similar lines; partly they complement one another.

Aspects of learning

Bowlby

Bowlby and his followers in developmental research emphasize the role played in the infant's and young child's development by his or her experiences with the attachment figure's responses in their social interaction. As Bowlby states (1988:4), the

> pattern of attachment consistent with healthy development is that of
> secure attachment in which the individuals are confident that their parent
> (or parent figure) will be available, responsive, and helpful should they
> encounter adverse or frightening situations. With this assurance, they
> feel bold in their explorations of the world and also competent in dealing
> with it.

This pattern is promoted by sensitive parents who are readily available and lovingly responsive to the child's signals.

A second pattern is that of anxious resistant attachment in which the individual is uncertain whether his or her parents will be available or responsive or helpful when called upon. Because of this uncertainty the child is always prone to separation anxiety, tends to be clinging, and is anxious about exploring the world. This pattern is promoted by a parent being available and helpful on some occasions but not on others, by separations, and, later, especially by threats of abandonment used as a means of control.

Where parents or their substitutes are constantly rebuffing the child's approach for comfort and protection, a third pattern develops, "that of anxious avoidant attachment in which individuals have no confidence that when they seek care they will be responded to helpfully but, on the contrary, expect to be rebuffed." This pattern "leads to a variety of personality disorders. . ."

In my clinical experience the third pattern, exemplified by Olga (Chapter 9) and to a milder extent by Margaret (Chapter 8), is particularly frequent in very persistent depression-proneness, but even the second pattern is an impediment in the work of depression.

Bowlby points out (1988:4) that "the pattern of attachment between child and mother, once established, tends to persist." He finds it usually established by the age of twelve months. The establishment of these patterns is, of course, a form of learning.

Peterfreund

Like Bowlby (1969: Part I), Peterfreund conceptualizes (1971:187) the human organism "in terms of hierarchically arranged, feedback-regulated, information processing control systems." He views "subjective psychological experiences, the phenomena of greatest interest to psychoanalysis, . . . as phenomena which correspond to vast and intricate programs of information processing." He demonstrates "that we can profitably approach the problem of learning by studying the changes in these control systems over time as they respond to the input of new information from various sources." These can be external and internal sources. The necessity for and process of learning is described in six steps:

1. *In the existing control systems, biological variables operate at normal or average values and within normal range. . . . 2. There is a new stimulus, a new source of information. . . . 3. A stress pattern results. . . . 4. A sorting, selecting, scanning, trial-and-error process takes place. . . .* 5. *'Natural' selection occurs.* A new program of information processing is found that restores the biological variables to their normal average operating values. . . . Stress is reduced. 6. *The new optimum program of information processing is firmly established via reinforcement and*

reprogramming at all hierarchical levels. . . . [1971:190] The essential point is this: In order to reduce stress, in order to attain the ultimate goal of homeostasis and survival, or any subsidiary goal, the organism must activate the appropriate adapted organismic program – the product of past learning and of phylogenetically evolved programming. But if the appropriate program is not present, the organism must proceed to learn; it must reprogram itself to reduce stress.

(1971:188–9)

If we compare these features of Peterfreund's concept of learning with my concept of the work of depression, it is apparent that the latter is learning under the *specific* stress of initially uncomprehended frustration of a significant, deeply personal effort.

Stern

Stern organizes (1985) his hypotheses about the infant's subjective experience of social interaction around the emergence of a sense of self, or rather of several senses of self which most often "reside out of awareness, like breathing," but "can be brought to and held in consciousness" (1985:5–6). On the basis of extensive literature on infant research as well as findings of his own research group, he suggests convincingly that at birth the infant is equipped with complex perceptive and integrative faculties which develop and proliferate rapidly. Some of these faculties differ from adult perceptive capacities but are highly effective in view of the immaturity of other parts of the organism. His discussion gives a central place to the "senses of self" that emerge in the pre-verbal infant and are "essential to daily social interactions" and "if severely impaired would disrupt normal social functioning." By "sense" Stern means "simple (non-self-reflexive) awareness"; by "self" he means "an invariant pattern of awarenesses that arise only on the occasion of the infant's actions or mental processes" (1985:7). Such senses include the "sense of agency": the infant does not mistake his or her action and initiative for someone else's; "the sense of physical cohesion"; "the sense of continuity"; "the sense of affectivity. . .", "the sense of a subjective self that can achieve intersubjectivity with another. . .; the sense of creating organization. . . the sense of transmitting meaning. . . . In short, the senses of the self make up the foundation for the subjective experience of social development, normal and abnormal (1985:7–8).

For our understanding of the functioning and failures of getting depressed, Stern complements Peterfreund's concept of learning most importantly by his emphasis: on the social responses we demonstrate from birth; on the development from the first few months of life of a sense of self and other; on the many components in the gradually evolving subjective experience of the self (at a later stage usually referred to as our "identity"); on the need for attuned responses from our attachment figures to our subjective experience of the moment; on the need for and joy in sharing subjective experience with our attachment figure(s), a need that during the first year of life becomes increasingly dominant. It seems to me, that while stress due to unfamiliar or otherwise anxiety-provoking stimuli motivates learning, the joy of sharing the subjective experience of successful effort and activity promotes the practicing that is a necessary component of effective learning.

Within the first three months two features of the infant's responsive equipment have, according to Stern (1985), become significant for its capacity to integrate external stimuli to an ever-increasing grasp of self and other, and of the material environment. He refers to one of these features as "amodal perception," and to the other as "vitality affects." Amodal perception involves the capacity to utilize perceptions of an object in one mode – say, touch – to form an expectation or recognition of the same object as it would be perceived in another mode – say, sight. For instance, blindfolded three-week-olds were given pacifiers to suck on, that had some nubs protruding from the nipples. When an infant was familiar with this pacifier, the blindfold was removed and the pacifier placed side by side with one that had a smooth, spherical nipple. After a quick visual comparison, infants looked more at the nipple they had just sucked. This remarkable capacity to grasp more comprehensive information about an object than the single sense yielded through which it actually had been experienced, holds for other combinations of perception as well (Stern 1985:47ff.).

At the same time, babies are emotionally very sensitive to changes and intensity of motion, rhythm, sound, light, and size. These emotional experiences, the vitality affects, as distinct from discrete categories of affect like joy, anger, and grief, are together with the amodal perceptions very significant in the communication between a baby and another. They constitute the preverbal – and later nonverbal – means for understanding and sharing that Stern (1985) calls "attunement." The latter is the channel for the sense of sharing that has developed in the baby within a few months. For instance, if a baby enjoys banging an object on the floor faster and faster, the mother does not need to do the same to convey that she is with it: she can instead accompany the baby's banging with words or sounds that become louder and louder as the baby bangs faster and faster, or follow the same rhythm. If she does this spontaneously, out of a mood that corresponds to the baby's experience, the baby's joy and interest will continue. If she fails or ceases to respond, or changes the rhythm and mood of her response, the baby's animation and interest in the activity may soon collapse. In this way, the parent's attunement, a communication that transcends the modes of our senses and dispenses with verbal thought, affects the extent of a baby's learning.

Infant research has also shown (Stern 1985:50) that three-week-old infants "would imitate an adult model in sticking out their tongues and opening their mouths." This has been observed repeatedly, and Stern makes the inference that there is an innate correspondence between what infants see and what they do. This appears to show how basic a component of our learning it is to use others as models. Our chances, then, to develop flexible patterns of learning, and consequently flexible patterns of coping with our getting depressed, depend to a high degree both on how significant members of our family respond to us from our birth into our adulthood, and on what kind of models their total behavior provides for us.

Helpful responses and useful models

How, specifically, can our family help us develop the patterns of response that protect us against depression-proneness and are conducive to a productive outcome when we do get depressed: self-confidence and trust in the reliability of others; reliance on the validity of our own emotions and thoughts as meaningful; the capacity to express them effectively; reasonably realistic expectations and aspirations; hope that effort will lead to rewarding results; some tolerance for frustration, emotional pain, and perplexity; curiosity and initiative; and a capacity to process information without excessive guilt, shame, anger, or anxiety, and without severe inhibitions? Such development is a long, complex process of integrating experience with maturation that we cannot pretend to understand fully; and if we did, it could not be described in detail here. But some features appear to be part of a reasonable hypothesis.

The helpful patterns of response I enumerated develop most readily if our birth, our sex, our looks, our endowment are welcome in our family, and if our parents have from their own family and cultural setting learned effective ways to make a child feel welcome. The patterns helpful to our coping with getting depressed develop most readily if we are allowed from infancy to exercise our abilities and talents as they mature; if the people most dear to us enjoy and respect us as we are; if our spontaneous explorations and curiosity meet with encouragement without undue interference, pushing, or overprotection; if our wish to share is accepted with pleasure when we initiate the sharing, and we also have the opportunity to enjoy sharing initiated by another; if we can discover that making mistakes is natural and can often be corrected, but that mistakes do not always have to be corrected; if we can discover that there is more than one way to be worthwhile and lovable, that different people are worthwhile and lovable for different reasons and if we have a chance to learn that while our emotions and thoughts are spontaneous events that cannot really be controlled and must be respected for what they are, action does not have to follow the impulses our emotions and thoughts may stimulate, but can and at times must be inhibited: that is, if our bad moods or excessive exuberance are understood and respected as such by others, while inappropriate action is consistently restrained in ways appropriate to our age and maturity.

The development of helpful patterns of response is also furthered if from early on we see those around us enjoy and respect not only babies but also themselves and each other; if they are self-confident and reasonably trusting, can enjoy what they are doing, can afford making mistakes and admit them, or get angry with one another without excessive guilt, shame, or anxiety; if they can afford to cry and be depressed, when there is cause, and eventually emerge from grief and depression with refreshed vitality; if they can be straightforward in speaking about any subject that needs to be talked about; if they are consistent in their attitudes and actions and live as they preach; in other words, if they can serve as models for the patterns of response that would help us escape depression-proneness and cope with the work of mourning and the work of depression.

But when can parents and other members of a family be expected to approximate such optimal conditions for a child's development? Good intentions are not enough. Many prerequisites for optimal or good enough conditions are a matter of good luck. Parents whose developmental needs during their formative years were understood and provided for are likely to understand and provide better than less privileged parents for the needs of their children, at least if these children are neither too different in temperament from themselves, nor too different from a loved and admired spouse or loved and admired relatives. If the difference in temperament between a child and one parent causes difficulties – and such difficulties can be particularly pronounced if another child in the family is a far better match for this parent – perhaps this can be compensated for if the other parent or a grandparent can compensate by well-attuned sharing with, and understanding of, this child, and as a model. In Fanny's case, the father could apparently compensate, but died too soon. Even an older sibling, as originally in Margaret's case, can to some extent compensate for or complement parental behavior, both as partners to attuned sharing and as models.

Other matters of luck are the social circumstances of the family at the time a child is born and grows up. Good relations within the extended family and between the generations are helpful; so is luck in finding the right partner in parenthood at the right time of one's life so that during the children's formative years marital strife and separation can be avoided; so is occupational success and economic security; so are good friends and a secure position in the community; so are good health in one's own and the extended family; and perhaps most of all, it is helpful if all children in the family are born without physical and mental abnormality, and if no child dies during the formative years of another child.

Favorable circumstances of this kind enable parents to enjoy their children and devote themselves to their needs. The richer and more satisfactory their daily life, the better it is for their child. At the same time, our development is not only a result of how we are treated as children and how we see members of our family treat one another. It is also influenced by the stimulation that the interests and activities of family members provide for us, and by the contacts with the community to which the social relations of our family introduce us. Here again, favorable experience and traditions taken over from earlier generations count. It is fortunate if interests and activities favored in a family match a child's talents and physical equipment, and the inclinations this endowment eventually promotes.

Inhibiting discouraging responses

In Chapter 9 I mentioned that I find people who suffer from frequent or extended periods of mild or severe depression to be burdened by psychological handicaps such as cognitive bias, which produces (among other difficulties) a distorted image of self and others, as well as unrealistic aspirations and expectations; inhibitions and repressions, particularly of emotional and sexual responses, but very frequently also of thinking, at least about certain subjects or in certain situations; a variety of pathogenic defenses; and excessive anxiety, guilt, shame, or anger. We saw that the combination and character of these handicaps varies from person to person. Although connections between the handicaps of certain patients and their life histories were suggested in earlier chapters, it is useful to look further at such developments.

Loss of attunement

As Spitz's studies documented (1945,1946), infants who from the first months of life are severely deprived of emotional response do not develop depression but often become severely retarded in their development or may even die. Neglect and mistreatment may lead to other severe disorders. On the other hand, people who can function passably or even exceptionally well in many respects, but are prone to become and stay depressed, have usually received a good deal of attention in infancy and later. But they have learned to function well only in those areas where functioning assured them of attention and acceptance by their attachment figures and to neglect and deny those of their inclinations or talents that would have aroused ridicule, contempt, rivalry, rejection, and, most of all, the threat of desertion, at times threat of desertion by suicide.

The emphasis on loss in the literature on depression is not surprising, inasmuch as depression-prone persons invariably have had experiences of happy interaction and sharing, but then lost this opportunity, which they may be slow to recognize or admit to themselves. There are parents who thoroughly enjoy interacting with, handling, and giving care to a preverbal baby, so that their infants thrive. But the same parent may be unable to relate adequately to a toddler, older child, or adult who can assert his or her objections or demands by verbal protest, verbal demands, aggressive action, or by walking away.

The loss for a child of the early experience of sharing and attunement with a surviving mother figure can also be due to other causes. There are adults who are capable of coping well with the needs of one child even after infancy, but not with those of more than one. There are adults who would attend well to the needs of their child or children, if their life circumstances were favorable rather than trying. There are mothers whose circumstances allow them to attend fully to their infant only for a limited period and who then have to return to work without being able to arrange for adequate substitute mothering for their baby. Some mothers have the capacity to make up by the quality of their interaction with their child for the loss in quantity, but other mothers lack this ability. Quite often the break for the child in fully satisfactory interaction with mother comes with the advent of the next child born or adopted into the family, but this need not be so. In fact, this early, lasting loss of more satisfactory interaction can, and often does, happen to only children as well. It need not come as early as during the second year of life, but can happen at any period of growing up.

From early infancy onward, loss of satisfying aspects of the interaction with significant others provokes efforts to recapture what now is missing, as we saw in the babies Spitz describes (1946). As a rule, a baby or a child beyond infancy is neither able to recover this type of loss nor to understand what caused it. This frustrated effort provokes a depressed response which cannot become productive. Soon the response is likely to be repressed, but it remains a hidden reservoir of being depressed that can become activated again when new cause for getting depressed arises. Then it reinforces the effect of the new cause.

Manipulation of development

Actual loss of former satisfactions in interaction is only one of the many experiences in the family that can prepare the ground for depression-proneness. Pressure can be brought to bear on a child from earliest infancy not to develop according to his or her innate temperament and, instead, develop a false self (Winnicott 1960), a personality that fits the parent's expectations or needs. A mother, for example, who part of the time is well attuned to her baby's activities but selectively withholds attunement either to slow down, or to intensify, the baby's spontaneous affect can powerfully enforce the beginning of a false self. She need not be aware of her doing this, or why, but an infant learns quickly to behave in ways to earn the pleasure of sharing, at the price of losing its genuine spontaneity or of acquiring a chronic and anxious exaggeration of effort and affect.[2] But while depression-proneness tends to have some of its most tenacious roots in experiences of the first year of life, this need not be the case; the damage to learning and the distortions of expectations can originate later.

As Stern demonstrates (1985), infants can experience their senses of self spontaneously during the preverbal period of their life, provided that misattuned or lacking adult responses do not confuse them. As speech develops, however, children are entirely dependent on adults and older children in learning to name their feelings and thereby bring them correctly into awareness, or alternatively in learning to distort or ignore them. This is where culture begins to wield its power, either mitigated, exaggerated, or distorted by the family. What is noticed or ignored in the family or community, what is talked about or forever nameless, what is welcome or shunned in the family or community now becomes a crucial influence in a child's chances to enjoy and develop its gender identity and other innate tendencies and talents, or to feel crippled or bad because of them. For example, many little boys nowadays are permitted to touch, parade, and name their sexual organs in the home. But as a rule, the little girl's sexual organs continue not to be given their right name; they are mislabeled or treated with silence, and as nothing to be proud off (Lerner 1977; Matthis 1981). The little girl's experience that interesting and stimulating parts of her body are to be ignored does not only cause shame and sexual inhibition, but it prevents happy gender identity and inhibits curiosity, thus interfering with healthy learning patterns. It creates causes for conflict, anxiety, depressed reactions, and interferes with productive work of depression.

Use of the child for parental relief or satisfaction

After the change to verbal development, the child becomes vulnerable to many family patterns that interfere with healthy learning and information processing: to the expectations, needs, fantasies, feelings, relationships, and actions of significant others, to their patterns of defense, their suspicions, fears, ambitions, rivalries, hate, contempt, isolation, or despair. Much of this can be found in case histories of the literature on depression.

As A. Miller (1980) emphasizes, parents who have early been deprived of acceptance and attunement tend to seek reassurance and relief by putting their children into the position of acting as a parent toward their parent or into the role of mother's helper. These demands are particularly hard to resist for a child who seeks to recover the lost bliss of maternal care during infancy, now demonstrated by mother's attention to a baby.

In a family with three children born in close succession, the mother, with heavy responsibilities in her husband's business, enjoyed playing with and feeding babies in arms, but after the first year rapidly turned over the care of each child to others and soon to the oldest child, Petra, whose brothers were two and four years younger than she. The mother, who worked hard and effectively in her husband's business, continued to enjoy the preparation of meals and nursing her children when they were sick. Long before Petra was able to understand what was expected of her, she was held responsible and reprimanded whenever her brothers hurt themselves or caused damage while Petra was with them or nearby. Apparently, the mother used her not only for practical purposes but relieved her own feelings of guilt by accusing little Petra of irresponsibility. Petra's eagerness to recover her mother's affectionate attention created a serious disturbance in her capacity to interpret perceptions accurately and draw realistic conclusions.

As an adult, Petra would accept work assignments without ever exploring whether the assignment could be reasonably expected to succeed or was suitable for her qualifications, let alone to her liking. If she failed in the assignment, she became very upset, only to take similar chances soon again. Despite good intelligence, she neither thought of or knew how to inform herself about what the assignment entailed, or how to inquire whether it really was in keeping with her duties under her work contract. Even if she had recognized that an assignment was unsuitable, she would have been unable to take up with a superior what was appropriate to expect of her. Other than at school, where she did well under the guidance of a sympathetic teacher, Petra had not had the experience as a child and adolescent of getting adequate explanations of what she was to do – for example, control her brothers – and why. That something had been expected of her, she recognized only when she was reprimanded, but she still did not grasp just what she should have done.

As a child, because she did not get answers to her questions, she had soon stopped asking them. Like all children who have lost a treasured closeness to their attachment figure, Petra took for granted that something was basically wrong only with her, particularly since her father favored the older boy. In order to avoid answers that she expected would hurt, she refrained from asking questions. She repressed her curiosity about what made other people tick. Thus, she could not learn from bad experience.

Petra's parents were capable and performed well in their work, but they felt insecure in personal relationships and in the community. They were depression-prone. Much of the time they sulked silently when displeased. They did not talk about their feelings and had no proper words for them even when this could have explained matters and facilitated reconciliation. Their feelings could only explode now and then in an angry argument which was suspended immediately if an outsider approached. Appearances had to be perfect, also the behavior of the children in the presence of outsiders to the family. Thus, Petra's inability to protect herself against unreasonable demands was not only a consequence of her own experience at the hands of her parents, but from the example they set she had also learned to behave like them in many ways.

Triangles

In recent decades, family therapists have contributed essential insights into the role of family dynamics and family history in human behavior. The role of a pathological system called "perverse triangle" (Haley 1967) is particularly significant: at least one member of the triangle belongs to a different generation, and a coalition is formed between two members of different generations against the third: a child and a parent form a coalition against the other parent; a parent and a child against another child; a parent-in-law and one spouse against the other; a grandparent and a child against a parent; the coalition is demanded of the weaker partner by the stronger one, but its existence is consistently denied, which creates a "double bind." Haley and his colleagues have studied the role of such triangles in the origin of schizophrenia. I find pathological triangles across the generations also prominent in the families of depressed patients. But in these families the existence of a coalition is not denied forcefully enough – if at all – to create a double bind. Rather, there is undisguised hostility, silent or vociferous, used as a justification of the coalition across generation lines. The excuse is the need to get or give protection.

"The pattern undoubtedly is passed down over many generations. However, the pattern must also be continually reinforced if it is to continue. At a minimum, two people each of a different generation must co-operate to perpetuate it" (Haley 1967:23). At the same time, I find that the roots of parental feelings and behavior that foster development of depression-proneness in a child need not only be due to a parent's exposure to disturbed patterns in his or her family of origin. In addition, the parent's personality development may have been affected by traumatic experiences suffered at the hands of the community or caused by other uncontrollable misfortunes, such as racial persecution. The behavior of grandparents can likewise be traced to difficult experiences within and without their family.

Damage to the parent's development

In the context of this chapter and this book, it is impossible to discuss or exemplify the countless variations of family interaction that can cause a child to develop those personality handicaps that disturb learning in general and the work of depression in particular. But it is important to take up some of the early hardships we can find, or at least hypothesize as having occurred, in the lives of the parents of depressed persons I have described.

We know nothing about the history of Olga's father, but late in her analysis Olga revealed significant data about her mother's history which Bloch (1978) shares with us. Olga's mother was the oldest of five children and fifteen years older than the youngest in the family. Her parents were very poor. They were Jewish. Only the boys were given a chance to go to school. Olga's mother had to renounce her desire for an education and had to go to work very early. Because her mother was ill, she also had to take care of her siblings until her marriage. They later treated her like a mother, with the same awe and distance shown by Olga and her siblings. Olga's mother recalled with bitterness that at the age of five she was made to give the only piece of food in the house to her youngest sister, a baby. She was still five when she dropped this baby, who died soon thereafter of the head injury the fall had caused. The neighbors accused the five-year-old of having murdered her baby sister. It is unlikely that under these circumstances that she got much warmth and appreciation from her own mother, particularly after the death of the baby. Olga's mother was "dominated by boundless feelings of guilt." Although her "acceptance of a role that amounted to virtual slavery may have been dictated by necessity, it may also have been an attempt at expiation that prevailed throughout her life" (1978:166). She became a chronically and severely depressed recluse, and it is no wonder that she transferred her resentment and jealousy of her siblings to her own children, particularly to Olga who, during the first years of her life, received her father's attention.

She may even have envied Olga who was five when a baby brother died of meningitis, rather than due to Olga's behavior. One wonders what some of her mother's attitude had to do with the intensity of Olga's conviction that she had caused her brother's death.

We know much less of the actual dynamics in Fanny's family. As already mentioned, her mother was a full orphan at the age of fifteen. She later moved with her older brother to a distant part of her country where she met her husband. This made her vulnerable to her early widowhood and poorly equipped to help Fanny cope with the loss of her father.

About Fanny's paternal grandparents I only know that she knew and loved her grandmother, who doted on her son and lived into her nineties. As was the custom in the circles of her parents, Fanny had a nursemaid who later was a servant in the house of friends of the family. In middle age this woman was emotionally quite disturbed although able to work. When her employer died, she was about sixty and took her life by hanging. Fanny was not attached to her.

In Margaret's and Norman's cases, we know nothing about the background of their parents. But the pattern of Margaret's parents as well as Norman's mother, which was tacitly to prohibit disquieting information that could cause guilt or painful identification with a son or daughter, suggests damaging early experience.

In Petra's case, finally, the background of both parents involved early losses by death and migration, physical and emotional deprivation, sibling rivalry, and early heavy responsibility for younger siblings.

Conclusion

In the light of the complex unfavorable influences to which a child's development can be exposed from infancy on, it is not surprising that overt or hidden fear of rejection and disregard by the therapist causes many severely depression-prone patients to remain silent for a long time about their lonely early suffering within their family. In fact, distrust of the therapist, often denied or unconscious, may for a long time be the only clue available to the therapist of an early disturbance in the parent–child relationship. Only after prolonged, intensive therapy may the most significant recollections of this early drama begin to reach the patient's awareness and enter the therapeutic dialogue. Whatever the individual combination of detrimental influences may have been, as a rule they have caused the patient from childhood on to feel a great burden to their parent figures, responsible for the latters' and their own misery, and obligated to justify their existence by satisfying the needs of others, rather than their own. They have not learned to recognize their own needs, let alone assert them. Why they tend to seek out equally damaging relationships later on will be discussed in Chapter 16. In other than successful long-term therapy, these patients succeed in disavowing and disguising this experience and tend to give an idealized picture of their childhood, as Olga insisted on doing (Chapter 8) in describing her mother.

Chapter fourteen

Socio-cultural influences on development

True identity ... depends on the support which the young individual
receives from the collective sense of identity characterizing the social
groups significant to him: his class, his nation, his culture.

Erikson (1964:93)

Illness, both mental and physical – although based on universal
psychobiological factors – is in its expression culturally patterned. One
becomes "sick" or "crazy" in a well-defined, culturally delimited way.

Fox (1975:180)

The work of depression affected by culture

Now we turn to how culture, subculture, and society at large can protect against
or foster depression-proneness and symptoms of avoided depression. Since the
term "culture" is used and defined in many different ways, I must state how I
use it. When I speak of "society," I emphasize the legal, administrative,
economic, and other formal organization of a community or nation. When I
speak of "culture", I have those features in mind that, affecting our cognitive
and emotional responses, underlie all formal organization: I mean, social,
religious, academic, and occupational traditions, beliefs, values, and mores
which guide the members of a society in their expectations, decisions, and
spontaneous actions. The powers that influence them may be exerted as a result
of cultural traditions more than as a result of formal organization and law.

A good deal of research on the incidence and symptomatology of syndromes
of depression in different cultures all over the world has been undertaken in
recent decades. Singer (1975) reviews this literature, and concludes that many
studies suffer from methodological shortcomings and are still inconclusive in
their findings. At any rate, depression in the context of culture has been studied
only as a mental disorder, not as an adaptive process. Consequently, the
developmental implications of cultural climate that interest us here still appear

to be virgin soil. The points I shall make can only be hypothetical. Without pretending to have scientific documentation for my own impressions and without attempting a comprehensive analysis, I shall present some of my impressions of the role that cultural influences on family relations and social experiences outside the family play in personality development affecting processes of depression. These impressions rest largely on informal, personal, and professional observations, but they have also been influenced by my acquaintance with the writings of American and English sociologists and anthropologists.[1]

In earlier chapters we found that, as a rule, successful work of depression requires benign external circumstances while a person is depressed (Chapters 4 and 12) – particularly understanding of and supportive responses to the depressed person by significant others. We also found that it requires a fairly flexible and secure personality on the part of the depressed person, which is usually the result of benign circumstances during the formative years. Yet, however favorable our native disposition and endowment and however well-intentioned our parents, as children we do not have a chance to develop freely in ways that are oriented to favoring our major talents and tastes or to protecting our greatest weakness. All of us are limited by what our society expects and permits according to its cultural values and traditions, the resulting laws and methods of enforcing them. Although each culture and subculture allows for variations of behavior, some definite limits are nonetheless imposed and some definite demands made on everybody. Other limits and demands may vary greatly according to the person's age, sex, occupation, or social rank. To fit into these limits, the native characteristics of one child may need much more restraint or support than those of another child. For adaptation to the requirements of our society without too much violence being done to our individual potential, we are as children totally dependent on sensitive adult guidance. We learn the cultural do's and don't's first from our interaction with family, family substitutes or delegates, and relatives; later also from interaction with peers, neighbors, teachers, and clergy. We absorb them through religious rites, myths, and other traditions. In our culture we also learn some of the values and mores from literature, from film and television, and later from interaction with employers and coworkers. But why do some children succeed in assimilating and integrating these many clues of what is appropriate and inappropriate behavior; why can they confidently relate to others and accept their role in society without crippling effects, while other children fail in this development? Are only the generations of families responsible for what happens to children?

An examination of the role played by society and its mediators in fostering or hindering this adaptation suggests answers to these questions. The effectiveness or ineffectiveness of the family in bringing up its young appears strongly affected by the security of its role and status in society, while the stability of society rests on the contribution of its citizens. We know today that children thrive when demands on their learning are in keeping with their level of maturation; when adults inside and outside the family respond to them with sensitive appreciation to each child's innate traits, with comprehensible communication, with consistent expectations, restrictions, and rewards; when the attitudes and actions of significant adults toward one another, toward the child, and toward themselves serve as reliable and reasonably fair models for what is expected of the child. We know that in a child's immediate social environment contradictions and inconsistency of adult behavior, including their feelings, cause insecurity, confusion, and anxiety in the child and can lead to emotional and cognitive pathology; that modes of communication not only in the family but also in the schools are of vital importance. But as clinicians treating depressed patients we are often less alert to the favorable effect of wider social support and the detrimental effect of ignorance, injustice, inconsistency, or contradiction in our patient's socio-cultural setting. Before examining these, I shall take up another question.

Recovery from depression in an American Indian setting

So far, I have spoken of productive work of depression as if this were a universal prerequisite for adequate adult functioning. Actually, while essential for adult coping with the demands of an individualistic culture in a process of rapid change like ours, I doubt that this capacity needs to, or even can, develop to the same extent in every society. The following example from a culture that is not individualistic and has been resistant to change may put this issue into perspective.

Fox reports (1975:189) the effective cure of a woman's severe depression of many years' duration by ritual adoption into an additional clan of her Pueblo Indian tribe in Cochiti, New Mexico. As in the case of depressed infants and young children reported in Chapter 11, the social function of her depression sufficed – although with great delay – to ensure complete recovery, apparently without personal adaptation on her part. I shall describe the nature of this cure only briefly, referring the interested reader to the author's text for further explanation of the intricacies of intermarriage and clan relations in the village of Cochiti (1975:180ff.).

Fox describes the social patterns and organization of the Cochiti Indians as he found them in the 1950s. On the surface, the Catholic religion brought to them by the Spanish American conquest had been adopted, in some instances even the Protestant religion of the North American white conquerors. The Cochiti were enthusiastic baseball players and television watchers, and yet, important aspects of their Indian culture were still remarkably intact. Their original Pueblo Indian beliefs and rituals pertaining to physical and mental illness or disorder were unchanged by these foreign influences, and their social organization remained matrilineal (see Fox 1967 and Benedict 1934). In this instance matrilineal descent meant that not only the clan to which one belonged, but also one's ownership of housing or the right to live in a given house owned by someone else was passed down from mother to first-born daughter. Family units living together were primarily composed of grandmothers and their sisters, their daughters, and sons, and the daughters' children. Husbands were attached to the household in a more casual, not necessarily permanent way. Mothers and daughters were very closely attached to each other throughout life, with the daughter dependent on her mother's guidance and support particularly during trying life situations, such as childbirth. Maternal aunts, however, and other female members of the mother's clan might substitute as mothers, if necessary.

Men were responsible for religious and medicine ritual. In Benedict's description (1934) it appears that this responsibility was absorbing most of a man's time and energies; and that the observance of ritual and traditions attracted far more public and private attention of men, women, and children alike, than aspects of private life. According to Benedict this culture rejects individualistic tendencies of any kind. Fox stresses that there was a deep-seated belief in witchcraft as the cause of all physical and mental disorders that came on suddenly. This caused general apprehensions of being the victim of witchcraft, or having inadvertently become a witch, or being accused of witchcraft. There were two male medicine societies in the tribe responsible for different aspects of curing people from the effects of witchcraft. Disturbances that came on gradually, or, like the case of depression described by Fox could be understood as due to social causes, were dealt with by the ritual of adoption into one or two clans in addition to the person's native clan, thus providing the claim to further protective relationships.

Not knowing names typical for Cochiti women, I shall refer to this woman as Sally. Fox met her in 1958, seven years after her cure, and was able to collect more detail about her background and life experience than about other women he met who had been cured of symptoms of depression by similar methods. Sally was the older of her parents' two children. Her early life was thought to have been secure and happy: her mother was energetic and beautiful, her father was an important ceremonial official. Sally's intelligence was below normal but she was a serious and conscientious child. Under the guidance of her mother, she early took care of her boisterous sister, three years her junior. She was, at the most, twelve years old, when her mother died after an illness during which Sally nursed her, possibly with resentment of the burden. After her mother's death, until her father's remarriage which did not improve matters for her, she also was responsible for the household.

Sally remained inconsolable about her loss. Her first symptom was insomnia; she wandered about the house at night, complaining. During the day she was tired and inactive. Later she began to put on her best clothes and jewelry in the morning, and to sit on the stairs combing her hair, crying and talking to herself. She had stomach pains, moaned, and kept vomiting all over the house. She talked almost exclusively about not having a home. (Due to a number of circumstances, Sally was not living in a house owned by her grandmother or inherited from the grandmother by her mother and then by Sally.) Prone to many anxieties since her mother's death, she began to fear that after her father's and her stepmother's death she and her sister would become homeless. There was no evidence to support this fear, but the lack of title to her housing apparently symbolized the general insecurity caused by the loss of her mother's active support.

Sally and her sister were not attractive and remained unmarried. But at the age of twenty-four, Sally bore an illegitimate son. A first childbirth without her mother would normally be frightening to any Cochiti woman. Sally was assisted by her mother's cousin's and her paternal uncle's daughters. Shortly after the delivery, Sally's father began to go seriously blind, which made him helpless. At this point, Sally became so disturbed that she was taken to a hospital run by Indian medicine men. When she was discharged she was unimproved. Her infant son had to be nursed by a maternal relative. Then Sally's relatives decided to take positive action.

The first step took apparently a good deal of negotiation in keeping with the implications of lineage and clan ownership. Matrilinear title to her housing was to be secured for Sally. But when this was finally arranged, it did not suffice to cure Sally entirely. A "clan cure" by adoption was necessary, meaning that she would become a member of an additional clan, or of two, without losing her primary membership in her mother's clan. Finally, a couple were found who were willing to bear the expense of the ritual and the responsibility for a new daughter. Through an elaborate ritual involving many gifts to her, Sally acquired a new mother and the right to call mother even all new female relatives. This put an end to all of Sally's symptoms. Seven years later, despite her stepmother's death and her father's approaching death, she had had no recurrence of organic symptoms and was functioning normally. "Before the cure, she was 'wasted away to nothing' and 'pretty near dead sometimes' "(Fox 1973:196).

The birth of her sister may have been difficult for Sally. Later, her mother's attention and approval had to be earned at the price of taking care of a demanding child only three years her junior. I gather that in her cultural climate, which aspired to harmony and an evenness of emotions, this difficulty could not be expressed by a child. In addition to these frustrations, bearing the burden of nursing her dying mother, and then for a while taking over her mother's role in the household, must have been much more than Sally was equipped to manage. We do not know her interpretation of that situation. She may have felt that her mother's death cheated her out of hard-earned rewards for her efforts. One has to bear in mind that according to the Pueblo Indian traditions that Benedict and Fox describe, Sally was after her mother's death indeed living in a socially and emotionally underprivileged situation: no grandmother, no aunt, in fact no older woman of her own clan, to live with in the same household. Sally's symptoms disappeared without relapse when she had received title to the house in which her mother had grown up and when she received a mother substitute who of her own free will had chosen her as a daughter and welcomed her with lavish gifts. That the new mother and clan were not shared by her sister may also have been significant. This seems to support the impression that Sally had felt deeply rejected and cheated of her rights by her mother's death and its consequences. The social functions of fathers in this society are not likely to include any psychological attention to a young girl in mourning. Also, her father was early affected by his going blind. Sally was helplessly frustrated and realistically unable to improve her situation by personal initiative of her own, as this would have been socially unacceptable. Thus, her remaining depressed and disturbed until this mobilized the proper persons to take initiative in such circumstances was probably the only way open to Sally toward having her needs eventually met.

The work of depression, if leading to improved self-understanding and self-expression, to more independent thinking, new planning, and personal initiative, can be effective by these means only in an environment where such behavior is expected and rewarded, while the society in which Sally lived responded to and rewarded only dependence on and compliance with group caretaking and group decision making. Yet, one wonders why in Sally's case it took twenty years before her disturbance mobilized group action on her behalf. Was this a weakness in her family, or could it be that some weakening of traditional group cohesion by the impact of the North American culture surrounding the Cochiti community can account for the delay? Or was it entirely due to the fact that to the Cochiti observance of traditional ritual was far more interesting than details of private life (Benedict 1934)?

Whether in such a culture effective work of depression is possible that produces results less conscious than in our culture but nonetheless adaptive is hard to tell. Even so, such questions are worth raising. The answers could throw light on how, in view of a depressed person's cultural environment, we should expect that person to develop in order to overcome depression more successfully. Under what conditions is our customary approach to therapy appropriate, and when does it add insult to injury?

The influence of socio-cultural features on development

Our individual view of what is expected of us in our culture and society, what will be rewarded, what will give us security, a measure of power and freedom, and a satisfactory role in our community, is evidently decisive in the aspirations we develop. But if we are to reach our goals they have to be reasonably realistic. Inconsistencies and contradictions in our expectations have an important part in determining when and why frustration of our aspirations will cause us to get depressed. Our individual views can be personal or subcultural distortions of broader cultural patterns, but to some extent they are invariably rooted in the realities of our society: its power structure, its economic structure, its technical development, its ethical values, its religious beliefs, its consistency or inconsistency, its fairness or injustice, the opportunities it offers some of its members but denies others, and so forth.

If we are to become capable of productive work of depression, the characteristics I have repeatedly emphasized should be promoted by the cultural attitudes and social structure prevalent in our community: self-respect, confidence in our ability to conduct our lives as we see fit, and trust in the validity of our feelings; hope that effort will lead to rewarding results; selective trust in the reliability of others; realistic expectations and aspirations. To what extent does our society meet these needs?

Despite variations according to nation, religion, class, and subculture, most children in the Central European, Scandinavian, and Anglo-Saxon countries I am familiar with, are today brought up in nuclear families from which they are expected to become relatively independent as young adults. They are expected to become self-supporting through work outside the family – with some exceptions if they grow up on a farm or in a family business. Ideally, they are expected to acquire some occupational skills, but here the realities of class differences are far more decisive than the common view of reality will have it. To an increasing degree they are expected to make their own choices of friends, hobbies, of sexual partners, of having children and with whom, of political and religious affiliation. Increasingly, children are even expected as early as in secondary education to choose their elective courses at school. How society equips children to meet these demands varies greatly from child to child.

I shall sketch some of the influences of social support and of social discrimination on personality development that I consider relevant to productive and unproductive depression. By emphasizing the damaging effects on children of discrimination I do not mean to suggest that discrimination and exploitation of weaker groups is more characteristic of western societies than of others. Social organization necessarily involves distribution of power. It involves some protection of weaker groups but also their control and often their exploitation – groups such as children, young men, women, the aged, and certain minorities. Excessive discrimination and control may be the harder to avoid, the larger the population and the more heterogeneous a society has become, so that innate controls on aggression which function in small, homogeneous groups no longer operate successfully. We see this illustrated by the long-distance, mass destruction characteristic of modern warfare. All I want to show is how, in our particular mass society and culture, its contradictions and injustices affect the development in the young of a capacity to cope with massive frustrations beyond their control and comprehension.

Social privilege

Many children in our society are brought up by parents who are secure in their social role, in their economic situation, in their personal relations, in their marriage; parents who enjoy status in their subcultural group and immediate community; they are parents who are flexible enough to take some of our cultural prejudices with a grain of salt; parents who experience this particular child's temperament and endowment as congenial; parents who do not compete with their children and who enjoy them. When these children enter schools where they are taught the country's social and political ideals of democracy, liberty, equality, justice, brotherhood, generosity, fairness, independence, self-reliance, and creativity, they find these values natural and reassuring, because they are in keeping with the atmosphere in which they have spent the first, most formative years of their life.

Unless these children run up against an emotionally disturbed teacher or a rigid, punitive school system, they will easily adapt to the tasks and rules they are expected to meet. They will enjoy the stimulation and challenge of schoolwork. They will be liked by their teachers and accepted by their peers. Their trust of others and their self-confidence, developed within their family, will be strengthened by their school experience. Later, they are likely to meet success in higher education and in the occupational and other activities of their choice. If such children run up against an unfavorable classroom or school climate, they often feel free to describe this to their parents, who will try to support the child against school authorities, and if possible see to it that the child is transferred, in order to minimize damage.

For such children, the general expectation they meet that they will perform adequately with increasing independence is an implicit confirmation that they have the capacity for success and independence. It is an incentive to develop their potential, to learn enabling skills. They develop all the qualities necessary for flexible information processing and for productive work of depression, should cause for getting depressed arise. They can afford to be fair to their peers, with all the rewards this earns them.

Unfortunately, such a combination of secure social position and secure family relations is not the rule. These children represent a privileged minority as members of a social elite in their nation, community, or subcultural group. They do not necessarily come from an economic or power elite, but from creative, successful groups in various walks of life.

Social discrimination

The majority of children, however, are exposed to less favorable circumstances. Some of them may come from a more or less underprivileged national, racial, religious, or political minority. They have early been exposed to parental frustration, anxiety, shame, anger, or poverty due to discrimination, without comprehending the causes for their parents' tension and discontent. They may, in addition, have been exposed to parental anxieties and helplessness, particularly if their parents are first-generation poor immigrants or members of a chronically underprivileged minority. These children may have met discrimination themselves and have been bullied by peers as early as in nursery school, or when playing out of doors, for looking different and using a different language. When they enter school, the social ideals taught there are not borne out by their own personal or group experience and therefore fail to make sense.

On the basis of their own experience the parents of these children may not believe that these ideals and values will be applied to their own and their children's needs. Or else they may expect their children to have better chances than is warranted. In either case, these children soon become torn between their parents' and their teachers' convictions. Often they are less appreciated by teachers and peers than the secure children. They do not get the same help at home with homework as privileged children do, nor the same rewards; they get less stimulation, less companionship in academic efforts, often not even a quiet place to read their lessons or write. Despite effort and talent, their parents may have had no opportunity to acquire academic training or learn an occupational skill, or even if they had, they will not get employment as easily, if at all, as the privileged members of society. If, nonetheless, family relations are harmonious, this may counteract some of the damaging effects of social discrimination. But often parents and grandparents are emotionally scarred by their experiences of social injustice and violence. Erikson's case Sam (1950) or the character of Asher's father, Aryeh, in Potok's novel *My Name Is Asher Lev* (1972) illustrate this. Some of the parents' frustration, shame, and confusion will affect their behavior toward their young.

Yet, cause for depression and the inability to cope with it is not due to economic deprivation in itself, but to the inability to grasp the cause for one's hopelessness or helplessness, the inability to discuss it and express feelings about it and the negative self-image developed under such circumstances. In the public schools of San Francisco suburbs, for example, there are many students of Mexican extraction. Their grandparents and parents have been unable to find employment in California and have been on relief all their lives. At the same time, television feeds these youngsters the sight of unattainable and incredible luxury. For children in such a situation the suggestion that they could perform as well and become as independent as their privileged peers, if only they tried hard enough, is far enough from the realities of their life to be thoroughly confusing. It leads to their drawing the mistaken and damaging conclusion that somehow they must be worthless, dumb, and bad. This arouses shame, hopelessness, and protest. In self-defense, they may become obstinate and defiant, or else apathetic. A vicious circle is set up, in which the negative expectations of the child and of adults who make unreasonable demands on him or her reinforce each other.

I have sketched two extremes. Most children will fall somewhere between these extremes. For some of those who become depression-prone, social injustice will be the major cause for their developing depression-proneness or the symptoms of avoided depression; for others, personality disturbances in their family despite a situation of social privilege may be the dominant cause for their depression-proneness or symptoms of avoiding depression.

Disadvantages attached to gender and sexual role

So far, I have not mentioned the types of injustice or discrimination that are based on a person's sex. Again, this is not in keeping with the ideals our children are taught to adopt and take as realities. In recent decades the discrimination against women has received increasing attention, although its existence is not yet part of general consciousness. The personality development of girls in our society is in many ways affected by culturally determined general attitudes and beliefs that make them vulnerable to feeling incomprehensibly inadequate – and consequently depression-prone. These attitudes and their effects have been examined by a growing number of authors, both feminists and others. I mention only a few, all of them psychoanalysts: Bernay and Cantor (1986), Blum (1977), Chasseguet-Smirgel *et al.* (1970), Chodorow (1968), Galenson and Roiphe (1977), Lerner (1977), J. B. Miller (1973,1976).

I find Chodorow's work particularly relevant to an understanding of the cultural influences that promote cause for, and inability to cope with, getting depressed. She examines the effect of the self-perpetuating division of labor between the sexes on the development of gender identity[2] in modern western societies. As women are unconsciously induced to retain almost exclusive charge of mothering while men are diverted from home life and parenting into public life, this arrangement serves to maintain the current economic and political organization of our society.[3] Chodorow emphasizes that, despite important contributions, anthropological and sociological research and discussion are limited by their dominant focus on features of intentional behavior accessible to the acting person's awareness. Freud and ego-psychologists, on the other hand, though studying and discussing unconscious processes, do so with a theory based too exclusively on physiological components of behavior at the expense of attention to innate social tendencies of mankind. Chodorow's psychoanalytic views favor object-relations theories (Guntrip 1961; Balint 1965,1968). Her thorough study and conclusions support more informal impressions of my own, that pre-date my acquaintance with her writing.

Chodorow emphasizes that the early development in a girl of her gender identity is unconsciously directed by the fact that her first significant experience of relatedness to another person is attached to a person who responds to this baby as someone "like me," while the baby herself slowly discovers that this adult is "like me." In contrast, the boy is responded to by the mothering person – biological mother or other woman – as "different from me" and gradually he

191

discovers that she is different from him. Chodorow discusses the many profound consequences that these largely unconscious comparisons have on the personality development of either sex. This cannot be pursued here. In the frame of this chapter I can only sketch some advantages and some disadvantages for men and women of this division of sexual labor and gender identity.

The advantages for men are strongly emphasized by feminists: that men have more freedom and initiative in sexual activity and gratification; that on the average they have more opportunities than women to develop their intellectual, technical, artistic, and athletic talents; that they have more opportunities in political and economic pursuits than women of the same class; that the experience and expression of anger, disapproved of in women, is permitted in men; that violence toward women and children tends to be ignored or minimized by predominantly male police, courts, and juries. To the extent that these advantages strengthen a man's self-respect and self-reliance, this will give him some protection against frequent cause for getting depressed. In an educated man, intellectual flexibility may also – though it need not – contribute to his solving an inner deadlock.

The disadvantage in this state of affairs, the enormous price that our men pay for these privileges, is rarely observed, let alone emphasized, by men or women, nor by Chodorow either. Only the disabling effect on men of the taboo on their showing fear, grief, or depressed reactions is increasingly recognized, at least by Swedish feminists. Here I shall take up two other areas.

Despite rapid change in this respect, a man is still widely expected to succeed in providing the entire or major economic support of a family, although in Northern Europe this is far less so than in Central Europe and in the Anglo-Saxon world. Steady employment, success in business or farming, academic accomplishments, and other careers are the values by which he is made to measure his personal worth. The damaging effect of this emphasis is borne out in Sweden by the frequent depression – if not psychosomatic illness or premature death – of men in the lower and lower middle classes who are approaching automatic retirement from work at the age of sixty-five. Their children no longer need them, the companionship with coworkers is lost, they feel alone and worthless in a meaningless existence (compare Hazelton 1984:140, for the similarity with men in the USA). Unemployment hits their self-respect even harder, even if their wife can support the family.[4] In the USA this is illustrated by the fate of Vietnam War veterans who have difficulties in meeting the standards set for male occupational success. For many men a good marriage relationship is deeply significant and reassuring, but for many others, I have found, the capacity to attract desirable women and maintain a lasting relationship with such a woman is only part of cause for real pride, but secondary to the pride in occupational success. Moreover, in many segments of western culture the deep sense of support stemming from lasting friendships develop only within the same sex, if at all. Contact with members of the same sex diminishes when employment ceases. The sum total of these features makes a man dependent for his self-confidence on matters beyond his control: access to education during childhood and adolescence; supportive, powerful contacts to push him ahead in his career as a young adult (in the USA, for instance, access to the right fraternity when young); market fluctuations; technological and political changes; the incidence of war; the national, religious, racial, and economic background he was born into. But the extent of this dependence on accident beyond our control for success and happiness is vigorously denied, particularly in Protestant countries. This often causes people to experience their inability to realize their aspirations as a personal failure and as proof of their worthlessness. Although these are problems for adult men, their existence is early obvious to and affects the young and promotes a sense of hopelessness and meaninglessness in many sons, and uneasiness in daughters.

Wanting to succeed despite the hazards of uncontrollable circumstances may suddenly cause helpless confusion and resentment, which would normally elicit the depressed response. But in most segments of our culture, a man feeling and behaving depressed is rejected as weak, unmanly, or sick. This is documented by the studies undertaken by Broverman et al. (1970), and by Hammen and Peters (1977,1978). Thus, many men resort to the avoidance of depressed feelings by overwork, other overactivity, or the use of drugs or liquor; or else they develop a psychosomatic illness. But beginning with the heartbreak when not accepted into the football or baseball team, boys are kept in line by their unawareness of the trap that is created for them by the discrepancy between the ideals of manliness and their realistic chances.

Likewise, large-scale modern warfare is not generally seen as a consequence of our western ideals of success in competition that, with the good graces and cheers of many women, trap our men. Although it goes counter to the values of all religions adhered to in our society, men are expected to do military service regardless of their convictions and judgments. They must learn and if necessary proceed to kill innocents by cruel, often long-distance means and to risk exposure to the same treatment. It is their sex, not their suitability or willingness, that requires this of them unless, again, they belong to an elite and can stay out of the holocaust by planning and conducting war, war industry, government, and the like. The younger and the more underprivileged, the more likely a man is to be placed in the midst of dangerous activity. True, men are genetically and historically those who protect the tribe, fight an attacker, and one another. Even primates discriminate against their young males, pushing them into dangerous edges of the band's territory, but those who survive at least get a chance eventually. And what has the original fighting to insure survival of a small, intimate tribe to do with modern warfare? If they were not conditioned for it from infancy by men and women alike, how genuinely would young men want to engage in warfare where their personal prowess is almost entirely irrelevant to their survival?

Little boys are trained to hit back at other boys rather than be submissive "cry-babies." But if a five-year-old boy hits back at a sturdy little girl who took his toy, a kindergarten teacher – at least in the USA – may say reproachfully, "one doesn't hit girls" (who at that age are often taller and stronger than boys). And many adults do not accept but frown at the valid and necessary communication in a boy's – or girl's – frustrated anger at a parent. Until adults accept this anger, boys will learn either to become self-destructive (compare Solnit 1966), or to displace it onto weaker peers, and later onto women, children, minorities, society at large, or foreign nations.

Women, although they are also inclined to fight one another and actively encourage male battle against men, are spared active participation in the atrocities of war, although they suffer some of them passively.[5] But passive exposure causes neither the conflicts of engaging actively in warfare that goes counter to the morals one was taught, nor the torture of lasting guilt. No wonder that many men resent women for escaping this and that they take revenge in more than one way.

Finally, the consequences of gender identity and the division of labor between the sexes in our society deprive many men of the capacity for emotional intimacy that many women develop out of their early intimacy and identification with the women who adequately mothered them (provided that this was the case). Many women accuse men of being emotionally unresponsive, as if this were their fault. Yet those men who have had the good fortune as little boys to be allowed to develop their innate potential for the supposedly feminine trait of good mothering, bring up sons who can share the mothering task with their wives and still function well in their occupations. Most men, however, are today deprived of the deep satisfaction that accompanies the arduous labor of mothering.

The advantages to women of the structure of our society I see as the following: exemption from military service; greater closeness to their children, often until the end of their lives; greater closeness to members of their own sex; and greater freedom to experience feelings, other than anger, and to express them. This means that when they have cause for grief or for being depressed, they can normally confide and thereby get help in coping, more so than in our society is typical for men.

The price for these advantages is high and gives much cause for getting depressed. But the discrimination and exploitation of women, particularly but not exclusively women belonging to discriminated groups, is far too complex an issue to discuss here in any detail. With regard to employment opportunities, education, freedom of expression, and power, we can look at women as one of the various social minorities I have referred to. In these respects the situation of women has improved greatly in recent decades. In the formal sense of legal rights, they have in some countries become the equals of men, but in terms of more hidden cultural attitudes they are still exposed to countless frustrations in the application of their legal rights to employment, education, organizational work (for instance, union representation), political representation, and leadership in general. All this restricts a woman in developing and enjoying her intellectual, artistic, and technical endowment. Often she does not grasp that this is so and that it causes her frustration. She becomes depressed. There is, for example, the frustration when she reaches out for goals that are on the surface open to her, but subtly and at times incomprehensibly frustrated, while the reality of these conditions is denied by those responsible for them. Furthermore, a girl's attitude toward herself is not only affected by the attitudes of the men around her, but even more so by the attitudes of women who have made the standard image of woman's role and limited endowment their own.

In many regions of Switzerland, for example, women voted in the 1970s against the introduction of suffrage for women. Or, when I lived in the USA from 1940 to 1963, a middle-class woman there had cause to feel adequate, successful, valuable, and normal mainly if she was pretty, had attracted a capable man to marry her, if she made him happy and helped him be successful; and if she had healthy, happy, successful children with leadership qualities. This ideal was strongly upheld not only by teachers and clergy, but by social workers and psychiatrists, ready to equate unhappiness with personal failure. With such ideals – more or less prevalent also in other western countries – a woman is as dependent as a man on factors beyond her control. Only in her case, the dependence on the uncontrollable is most crucial with regard to her intimate life: she is dependent on the accident of good looks; on meeting a suitable partner at the right time in her and in his life and development; on the man's continuing capacity and motivation for economic and occupational success and for maintaining their relationship; on the multiple factors beyond his control that affect his achieving success; on the health and native endowment of her children and the many factors beyond her own good will that influence their development for better and for worse. When her husband is transferred or wants to move to another town or country, she is expected to move along and not react with grief and loneliness to the loss of her social network and to becoming an outsider in a foreign environment. This way of life gives many women frequent cause for becoming depressed. Their depression in turn affects their children – boys in one way, girls in another. It disturbs the children in the development of a secure and contented identity and does not fit into the ideals they are taught to expect of life.

It must be repeated again that I consider injustice, discrimination, material deprivation, and painful disappointments as such not as causes for depression and depression-proneness. What causes depression is the discrepancy between what children – and adults – have learned to believe and expect, and the reality they meet. This discrepancy, when uncomprehended, causes chronic lack of self-esteem, or the loss of self-esteem that since Bibring (1953) has been associated with severe depressions. Men and women can bear a remarkable amount of misfortune and grief, as long as they need not see them as result and proof of their own inferiority.

I do not pretend to know the answers to the unrealistic and discriminatory treatment of men and women in our society. Men and women are different, although we still know far too little about what is truly genetic difference and what is culturally determined. Quite aside from the differentiation of functions in procreation, men are physically, and perhaps cognitively and emotionally, better endowed for certain activities, while women are for others. Provided men and women get a chance to develop and apply their innate potentials, differentiation of their roles in society on a broad scale appears inescapable and necessary. I only want to point out that many features of the current differentiation of roles and distribution of labor between the sexes appear to have outlived their greatest social usefulness.[6] For many men and women this creates unrealistic expectations of themselves, of their mates, and their children, which lead to disappointments, conflicts, bewilderment, and in the end give cause for the depressed response or the symptoms of avoided depression. Then their own cultural attitudes and those of others interfere with their capacity to discover why they are depressed (or have to drink) and what they can do about it.[7]

Further features

In closing, it should be mentioned, without entering into any description, that there are further features in our society that cause problems of adaptation. For example, the rapid changes in sexual behavior; the alienation between the generations that has come in the wake of these and other rapid changes; the negative attitudes toward depression and deep mourning; the moral code for behavior toward parents and authority, if exaggerated; and the demands for regular, punctual, continuous availability for work, if exaggerated. But what I have described in some detail should, I hope, alert the reader to the complexities in judging a person's depression and in trying to help.

Part III

Aid to the work of depression

Chapter fifteen

Self-help and informal first aid

For truly creative thought, the influx of new information must be allowed, and randomization must be permitted. From this a high degree of biological ordering can be achieved.

Peterfreund (1971:197)

Prerequisites for a remedial process

In the preceding parts of this book I have proposed and illustrated that getting depressed is a normal and potentially adaptive response to a very specific though largely unconscious perception: we sense that some expected and intended process within ourselves is not proceeding as it should or not yielding the expected results; but we do not comprehend this state of affairs. I have proposed that our basic depressed response to this perception creates, by its various reactions, a frame of mind and a physical state promoting the work of depression. Under favorable circumstances, this internal labor can facilitate our discovering what is amiss and why, so that we come to cope with the breakdown more effectively.

If we accept these premises, how does this affect our attitude toward either being depressed ourselves, or seeing others being depressed, and how does it affect our efforts to help ourselves or help others to emerge from an episode of depression "stronger, wiser, and more stable" than we were when we went into it (Winnicott 1964:126)?

First of all, we might compare our response to the unconscious frustration of an emotional and cognitive effort with our response to the disturbance of a physiological process. When our digestive system cannot properly take care of some food intake, our organism reacts in several way: it tries to eliminate the content of stomach or bowels, or both, as quickly and thoroughly as possible. This process may cause not only vomiting and diarrhea, but also stomach pains, nausea, dizziness, weakness, headache, and fever. Instinct or experience may cause us to respond to these symptoms by refraining from eating or by drastically restricting our diet to foods and beverages that are easy to digest and soothing to stomach and bowels. We may also rest, keep warm, and avoid exertion. Such symptoms appear both when we have eaten harmful food and when our capacity to digest healthy food is disturbed by some other irritation of the digestive organs, such as laceration, infection, or inflammation of the digestive organs, or by a disorder of other organs.

When we look at the concept of productive and unproductive depression, there are remarkable parallels with the responses of digestive failure. It is not the vomiting, diarrhea, or fever that are an illness in themselves. On the contrary, if we were unable to vomit, get diarrhea, or a fever, we might die of some of the poisons or infections. These unpleasant reactions tell us that our body is making an effort to remedy a disturbance and that this effort requires our consideration. Likewise, if we were not equipped to withdraw into ourselves, lie awake, or dream restlessly, and generally slow down until the cognitive and emotional problem is solved, the continuation of our psychic functioning would be in serious danger whenever part of our information processing – our psychic digestion – temporarily comes to a dead end. This is why depressed reactions require consideration as much as do symptoms of physiological dysfunction. The remedial effort they announce should be given a chance by a restriction or change of our activities.

This is, however, not as easy as it may sound. In Chapter 1 I used Potok's description (1972) of his character, Asher Lev, as a young adult in a crisis, to illustrate these points: Asher was able to cope with a recurring and intermittently disabling depression due to complex loyalties and other conflicts. He withdrew from most social contacts. He took long walks on the streets of Paris. He remained stretched out inactively on his bed for hours at a time until, with the help of several bursts of pictorial expression of his thoughts and feelings, a liberating understanding of his family history and a resolution of his conflicts emerged. Far away from the needs and demands of his parents and from intrusion by other members of his religious sect in Brooklyn, he was free to withdraw from all disturbing influences. Also, he was economically secure and did not, like most others, need to go to work to make a living. Few people are in a position to shield the remedial work of their depression so completely against interfering diversions.

In Chapter 3 we saw how psychotherapist Bertha coped with an acute, though mild depressed response. She was not in a position to withdraw as much as Asher was, but there was no need to do so either. The problem she needed to recognize and solve was minimal compared to Asher's. Her professional experience helped her to respect her need to pay attention to herself when depressed, but had she been working in a clinic, rather than in private practice, she would not have been able to cut out as many activities as she did. Aside from therapy sessions there would have been conferences and other obligations that could not readily be postponed. In the same way as earlier her preparations for the meeting with her thesis supervisor, clinic demands might have diverted

Bertha's thoughts from introspection and interfered with necessary withdrawal and inactivity. Consequently, it might have taken her much longer to realize what the problem was that required appropriate action. Had there, in addition, been children or a distressed adult in her household who needed her attention after working hours, this might have delayed her insight even further. Or else, the accumulation of insomnia that might have been necessary for the work of depression to proceed despite family demands might have become a hazard to her health.

In Part I, I have pointed out that every affect has a personal and a social function. I have stated repeatedly that getting depressed has the dual personal function of alerting us to an inner problem and at the same time conditioning us – if all goes well – to respond in ways conducive to solving the problem. In addition, getting depressed has the social function of alerting others to our having a problem and to our not being on top of the task of solving it. The work of depression which normally leads to a solution may be aided by the personal or the social function of the affect: by our own response to our difficulty or by the response of others to our struggling with this difficulty; or by both. The first I shall refer to as *self-help*. The second I shall call *informal first aid* when it is given by people who are not entering a professional contract with the depressed person. When there is a contract between the depressed person and the helper, designating the former as patient and the latter as therapist, I shall refer to the procedures aiming at giving aid as *therapy*.

Self-help

How can we help ourselves when we get depressed? It is first of all important to bear in mind that, as shown in Part II, being depressed is not the same as worrying, grieving, or being unhappy, although remaining depressed for a long time may make us unhappy as well, or cause us to worry. When we are unhappy and grieve we usually know what we are missing, what is hurting us, which of our wishes are being frustrated. Then our task is to find out what we can do about it, or how we can get used to the situation, if nothing can be done about it. We may be too numb and aching to do something immediately, but the task remains nonetheless that we mobilize ourselves into appropriate activity. When we get depressed, we do not know what the inner deadlock that perplexes us is all about, why we are slowed down and have other depressed reactions. Before we can try to do anything helpful, we obviously need to know first *what* requires our attention. How do we find out? And how can we possibly be expected to help any process in ourselves that is unconscious?

We do not know what is going on in our stomach when it gets upset. Yet, if we don't react in an optimal way instinctively, we can still learn from experience or from others what to do and what to avoid so that our digestion may get the best chance to mend. The same is true for being depressed. Some people react instinctively in ways that give an intensified information processing of the unconscious issues of disturbance an optimal chance. They tend to withdraw without much ado from demanding current activities that would normally absorb them. For a while they engage in quite different activities that for them are just right to relax them and to allow their mind to work unconsciously on their hidden unsolved puzzle. They may suddenly decide to chop wood or clean the house, to go skiing or for a long walk, knit a sweater, fix the roof; they may plunge into baking a large supply of cookies, play the piano, or perhaps develop some films. They are silently doing things that engage surface skills and routine without more than physical effort. Or they allow themselves to rest, to stare at the ceiling or through the window, or listen with reduced attention to the radio. They need not know at all that by this moratorium on their usual involvements they are protecting an internal process of psychic digestion and reorganization. They simply do not feel fit or in the mood to do anything else and do not feel called to force the impossible. They dare to follow their inclination, and it works for them. Things fall into place and the puzzle gets solved, they do not know how. Often they emerge from the inner crisis with a solution without anyone else having recognized that their need for submersion into solitary activity, and their absentmindedness or preoccupation could deserve the name of being depressed. The matter-of-factness with which they switch tempo and focus for a while commands respect and conveys the message that they should be left alone. Or else they feel free to talk to a trusted, good listener about their bewilderment until this helps them to reach insight into what the unknown but absorbing problem is.

In many ways the work of depression is a creative process: it involves our abandoning preconceived positions, reorganizing memories and fresh perceptions, and finding a new synthesis that makes sense under changed circumstances.[1] Thus, it has a great deal in common with what we are used to calling creative work – for instance, writing a book. In the latter case we know a good deal about what we want to accomplish, but there is a lot of uncertainty about how it should be done. We may start out with definite ideas of how the book should be organized and what it should contain, but in the end something quite different may have emerged from a steady inner process that rarely reached awareness. If we are inexperienced in writing a book, we may get quite anxious at first when we seem to lose the thread and seem to have come to a dead end in our writing. Only gradually we learn to relax and to trust, that if we are patient something fresh will emerge in due time. As we stop straining, things begin to flow more evenly. In the same way patience and relaxation may result in depressed reactions and feelings having a productive outcome.

That for many people things do not work themselves out spontaneously and that they do not readily learn from experience or from others to rely on a hidden process to take care of itself like an upset stomach is not surprising. As mentioned earlier, our society impresses on us from early on that we should always be active, alert, interested, punctual, reliable, effective, and sociable. We should not feel sorry for ourselves, or indulge ourselves, or be lazy, or poke around listlessly. We should always know what we want to do, and do it. If we get depressed these demands with which we have become identified can make it very difficult for us to pay serious attention to the occurrence, let alone give in to the withdrawal and slowdown it calls for.

When we have a fever, it is quite likely that we have been taught to leave our usual tasks alone and to take care of our body, because the fever signalizes that some bodily operation is out of gear and wants to mend. But if our depressed reactions signalize that either a cognitive or an emotional operation is out of gear, most of us are expected to ignore the message until a physical or mental breakdown is the consequence of this lack of attention to the inner crisis. Only then is it acceptable to collapse. This is why we may be unable to give the work of depression a chance at an early stage, unless understanding support from others helps us to accept our being depressed and to listen to its message without waiting for a collapse.

Therefore it is important, when we notice that a spell of depression does not resolve itself after a while, that we find a good listener whom we can use as a sounding board. For some people writing a diary or letters, praying, or meditating may serve a similar purpose effectively, but others do need a live listener and one who may participate with some helpful questions or advice. Such advice need not necessarily be followed, to make it useful. If we find the advice to be wrong, the effort to understand why it is wrong can redirect our thinking in a useful way.

Talking to another person can be particularly helpful because, when we believe that we know why we are depressed, we actually only know why we are unhappy, worried, or afraid. It is disquieting that until the work of depression has reached a productive outcome we can neither tell whether a depressed episode of ours is going to be productive or not, nor what caused it. Another person's patient and confident listening can be reassuring in this discomfort.

Our episodes of being depressed, whether they become productive or not, tend to register in one way or another with many of the people with whom we interact while we are depressed. Their recognition of our being depressed is not necessarily conscious, and even if they consciously perceive that we are not in a comfortable frame of mind, they may not use the term "depression" for their perception. Some of them are very helpful to us, others are not. The latter may be afraid – without awareness of that fear – that contact with our depressed feelings might stimulate the emergence of their own hidden causes for getting depressed. They try to avoid becoming aware of their perception that we are acutely disquieted by a sense of internal failure. They react to our depressed reactions exactly as they often do in response to our hidden or overt grief when we are mourning: they avoid us outright, or else they become cheerful and talkative, trying to divert us from what we are brooding over. They may be unable to observe us quietly, to ask us about ourselves, to listen to us. They hope that what they refuse to notice will disappear.

Being treated in this way adds to our strain when we are depressed. It makes us feel lonely, undesirable, and inadequate. It may increase our sense that something is wrong with us, and adds anxiety or guilt to our depressed response. This makes it difficult to concentrate, consciously and unconsciously, on what it is that does not function as it should. It diverts our attention from the original cause of the depressed response. Now we must struggle with the problem of being unable to communicate with and get support from those who turn away or try to interfere with our depressed behavior. Unless we are confident that this is due to the limitations of those who do not understand, rather than our own, this will create a new, separate cause for getting depressed.

Under such circumstances the best self-help may be that we talk to a person who, due to his or her professional training and experience, can be expected to be a good and sensitive listener. Such a person may be equipped to serve as a sounding board, to understand, give support or advice, or be able to judge whether other professional help is called for. People one might turn to first are social workers, counselors, ministers, psychiatric nurses, psychologists, or physicians. When we confide in a friend or a professional helper, one of the most significant contributions we may receive is actually this: interested, understanding listening and an occasional pertinent question can mobilize us to explore our ideas, feelings, memories, hopes, and apprehensions more fully than we do without such an echo. But again, some members of each of these professions will give a far more sensitive response than others. After all, they also are influenced by the attitudes toward being depressed that are prevalent in our society, or they may have their own anxieties about getting depressed themselves. They may think that we are exaggerating, or that we are pampering ourselves. Or they may, particularly if they are nurses or physicians, have been trained to believe that our difficulty is not an emotional and cognitive problem but a purely physiological one. After a short interview they may send us home with some medication.

Should we come to the conclusion that it is necessary or desirable that we enter therapy, it is sound self-help not to expect that therapists can actually solve our hidden problem for us. They can only serve as more or less adequate instruments for us to use in our search for better self-understanding. And if the contact with a professional person does not prove helpful or at least promising, it is further sound self-help not to conclude that the fault is ours alone, but to try again, with someone else. Even if part of the failure of our work with a given professional were to be our own, another professional helper might be a better match for us. On the other hand, it is unwise to quit a therapy without open explanation and discussion. Many a therapist who fails to be helpful can become helpful, when given the help of the patient's honest criticism. Breaking our contract with a therapist instead of resolving it in mutual agreement means often that we are throwing away a great deal of the time and effort both have invested. Breaking the contract with the therapist without first making the effort of reaching a mutual understanding will not improve our capacity to recognize why we get depressed and to cope better with depressed episodes. But having made the effort can be a step in this direction even if the therapist should not understand and accept our decision.

Giving informal first aid

As we have seen, the largely unconscious and uncomprehended deadlock in functioning that causes a person to become depressed requires for its solution an intense concentration of his or her unconscious mental activity. It requires avoidance of other strain, avoidance of diversion, and it needs rest, and patience. As observers of this struggle we give the best support to the efforts of a depressed person when we are patient, too. Exactly as with a person in deep mourning who is grieving, and who may be but need not be depressed at the same time, we should be available for talk and exploration, without on our part insisting on such talk. Often a mourner needs to be left alone, and so does a depressed person.

In our society, more often than not, depressed people feel inadequate because they have been taught that it is a weakness to be depressed. Often they feel more or less ashamed, perhaps even guilty about it. Therefore, it can give them well-needed support if, instead of pressing them to solve matters by talking about them, we encourage them to take their mood seriously and to cut out unnecessary activities and commitments. They often need our permission to take good care of themselves, to remain silent, perhaps to stay at home from work, perhaps even in bed, so that they may get the peace and quiet needed for their inner search.

In view of our customs and values, this is by no means easy for us to do for another person. We are inclined to think that if we encourage such "self-indulgence" and withdrawal, the other may never get out of bed again; that we will become responsible for having driven a "sick" person deeper into sickness. Of course, if our depressed friend or relative actually stays in bed or away from work indefinitely, we are entitled to draw the conclusion that this is not a depression doing its work productively, but that here being depressed may remain unproductive and therapy become advisable. It is human not to want to wait too long for such a discovery. On the other hand, if we do not tolerate, and at times encourage, a limited period of a depressed person's staying at home and perhaps being prostrate part of the time, we never get the chance to discover whether our depressed friend has the capacity to emerge from this depression in due time with a happy smile, a good deal of new energy, a new plan, and new understanding. Suddenly it all may fall into place and the puzzle be solved.

But what should be done if a person's depression goes beyond a low mood, a certain amount of withdrawal, exhaustion, sleeplessness, poor appetite, and lack of interest; if, due to added anxiety, guilt, or despair, this condition becomes increasingly disabling over an extended period of time without any apparent growth in insight and understanding?

The suffering caused by being depressed unproductively can vary from occasional nagging discomfort to constant despair and apathy, from mild physical symptoms to progressive psychosomatic illness. At the present time, in our society, we meet not only productive, but also unproductive, and avoided depression all around us. Psychiatrists, psychologists, and social workers are not alone in being called upon to help depressed youngsters and adults, and to help those who damage themselves by their methods of avoiding depression. Usually, friends, spouses, parents, teachers, nurses, physicians, ministers, employers, or fellow employees are the ones who must give emotional and practical first aid before it can be determined whether psychotherapy is necessary, available, and acceptable to the depressed person or the avoider.

When we feel justified in assuming that in a given instance the work of depression will not succeed without expert assistance, we should make every effort to motivate our depressed friend to seek professional help, or if our depressed friend has a spontaneous wish to do so, give every support to this. Also, once psychotherapy is instituted, it is important not to disturb that new relationship by curiosity and interference. Again, this is easier said than done: even psychotherapists who would not welcome interference in their work with patients can at times find it difficult to resist the temptation to be inquisitive or show criticism of a colleague if their own child, spouse, or friend is that colleague's patient.

Exactly as for the depressed person, the problem for the observer is that productive and unproductive depression are not distinct and mutually exclusive as a pear and a plum. They are the extremes of a continuous range, and a given person's depression could at a given time lie anywhere within this range. Thus, when someone close to us is not his usual self but is showing depressed reactions, we are not faced with a simple, clear-cut choice between having to leave him or her alone and having to find a suitable therapist or hospital. Quite the contrary; another person's depression can be very perplexing. The bewilderment of the depressed person feels contagious. This is trying, and as observers we may find the problem alien because we do not bear the potential solution of the puzzle within ourselves, as the depressed person does. This frustration makes us impatient with someone else's depression. We find it hard to see a constructive meaning in it and tend simply to wish it away. If we are living with the depressed person or are otherwise very close to him or her, this may be so distressing that it may be advisable, and even to the depressed person's advantage, that we seek professional guidance in this situation for ourselves. At least it may be helpful, in this dilemma, to know what Winnicott (1964) has said: "one can help a depressed person by adopting the principle of tolerating the depression until it spontaneously lifts, and by paying tribute to the fact that it is only the spontaneous recovery that feels truly satisfactory to the individual" (p. 125). And to the statement I have quoted earlier, that "a person may come out of a depression stronger, wiser and more stable than he went into it," he added, "A great deal depends, however, on the freedom of the depression from what might be called 'impurities'" (p. 126). By "impurities" Winnicott meant essentially what in Chapter 9 I have described as handicaps in information processing.

Some guidelines for informal first aid

When we try to respond to the needs of an acutely or chronically depressed person, it is important that we accept our ignorance of what makes him or her depressed. The person in question became depressed when some intended, significant behavior for uncomprehended reasons failed to materialize or when it proved ineffective. The intention and its significance result from this person's deepest but by no means fully conscious values and strivings. The depressed response is caused by the unconscious meaning that the frustration of the intention has for him or her. While the depressed person remains depressed, these matters have not reached awareness. Thus, it is rarely fruitful that we try to press our depressed friend to give us an account of what is wrong. In a close and trusting relationship, we might make a correct guess of what the depression is all about, but at best this is a guess we should not be too sure of. Also, there is always the risk that the very relationship in which we are with the partner might be causing not only the significant striving, but also its frustration. In that case there are probably some blind spots in our efforts to understand.

In the difficult decision whether we dare be patient and let things ride until they work themselves out spontaneously, we may ask ourselves the following questions:

1 Is our depressed friend having to deal with difficult circumstances, such as marital or family discord; major loss through death or separation; stress at work, economic difficulties, or poor health?
2 Does our friend, in addition to some of the depressed reactions described in Chapter 3, also demonstrate anxiety, grief, guilty feelings and self-accusations, shame or anger that is hard to comprehend?
3 Has our friend earlier had periods of depression that lasted for some time without resolving themselves in a way that in retrospect made them understandable for both that person and for others? Were any of these periods disabling?
4 Does it seem difficult for our friend to develop and keep friendship or love relationships; to have satisfactory sex relations; to show a normal range of feelings from joy and affection to those of anger, grief, and hatred; to be discriminating in whom to trust or distrust; to succeed at and relish work and keep a job? In other words, is he or she even without depression not functioning comfortably but has handicaps of the kind described in Chapter 9?

If the answer to most of these questions is no, then the depression of our friend should be left to his or her own devices. Then we need only try to follow the signals we receive about how and when we might be available to our friend, and when to keep out of the way. If this proves difficult for us, we might do well to get involved in some absorbing, satisfying activities in order to feel better ourselves and thereby protect our friend's work of depression from the burden of guilt about our dismay.

If the answer is yes to question 1 but no to questions 2 to 4, our friend might cope better if help were made available to diminish the environmental or health problems. In the case of discord in the family, for example, family therapy, marital counseling, or group therapy for couples might be helpful. The stresses of mourning after loss or separation could he diminished by alerting a close friend or relative, or perhaps a trusted minister to serve as a listener. A social worker could prove very helpful both when mourning, employment, or economic difficulties seem to impede successful work of depression. Finally, in the case of a health problem, improved medical services might be very effective in speeding the work of depression, provided this does not lead to excessive medication against the symptoms of depression. Unless they are disabling, depressed reactions should remain available as signals to everyone involved.

If the answer is yes to several of the items in questions 2 to 4, then getting and staying depressed is not the basic problem, but is a consequence of other personality problems. In that case our friend would be well advised to enter individual psychotherapy with a psychoanalytically trained therapist who is interested and skilled in treating depression-prone people.

Finally, a word of caution: even by a personal friend or acquaintance who is a psychiatrist or other mental health professional worker, a person's desperate, angry grieving due to a disappointment or loss is easily mistaken for depression, if that friend does not listen very carefully. Moreover, a griever may admit defeat or loss more readily when in the role of patient and to a stranger who is a professional. The following is an illustration reported by Lamers (1982:107ff.).

Example of a frequent error

A woman in her seventies whom I shall call Tessa was referred to Lamers by a friend of hers, a psychiatrist who saw her as seriously depressed and probably in need of antidepressant medication. At the time of their first interview, Lamers noticed Tessa's recurrent tears and shifting moods. He suggested that she might be grieving rather than depressed. Indeed, she was grieving the loss of a recently acquired boyfriend to a girlfriend of hers who "stole him away" at the time Tessa was introducing him to a small circle of her friends. Now she missed her boyfriend and was angry with her girlfriend. Then, in tears, Tessa reported that her loved dalmatian dog had also died in recent weeks. "I'll never have another," she sobbed, "I'm getting too old to train another puppy." When Lamers commented on the loss of companionship, Tessa began to talk about the myriad changes in her life during the decade since the death of her husband. Once again, she felt truly alone.

During the second visit Tessa reviewed the many losses suffered decades earlier as she left her homeland without her family, only to learn by and by of their deaths in concentration camps. Lamers goes on to say that she

"felt as alone now as she had on leaving her native country and as empty as she felt on learning of the death of one family member after another. I could not help but feel compassion for her and began to hope that the strength that had once enabled her to survive multiple losses might again be available to her. For, now she saw little reason to go on and began to talk of the time when she, too, would die.

She did not come alone to the third session, but carried in her arms a small dalmatian puppy. We talked of her decision to live. And she told me that she did not want to live alone. She was not interested in merely 'surviving' until death came for her. Nor could she ever cover over the grief of former losses. But she still wanted to get out for walks and missed the companionship of her dog. She was willing to try again with the full realization that she would always be vulnerable to loss."

This shows how a careful differentiation of affects can facilitate the therapist's understanding and promote the patient's self-awareness and capacity to communicate effectively.

The symptoms of grief and of the depressed response overlap in the disturbances of sleep, appetite, or breathing, and in the irritability and sense of helplessness each can cause. But for the observer who takes some time to ask questions and listen, and who has a clear concept of the difference in cause and function of the affects, the differentiation is no problem. Unfortunately, due to their basic training and to the habits of thought created by excessive work-loads, many psychiatrists and psychologists tend to jump to the conclusion of "clinical depression" whenever a person appears in despair and, for reasons the observer does not understand, demonstrates a longing not to have to go on living. Mourning a great loss or repeated losses, most people have moments when they wish life did not have to go on. They rarely talk about this, because they sense that few people would want to hear it. Thus, when this normal and passing phase of mourning becomes apparent, it tends to be taken for a sign of sickness by those who have not experienced it; if noticed, "depression" as a syndrome is diagnosed. The agony of total reorientation to living is taken for suicidal risk, while in other people genuine risk of suicide is often ignored.

The effective service of a few sensitive interviews that Lamers provided for Tessa is not always made available to mourners. All this basically strong woman needed under trying circumstances was the opportunity to compare her current situation with her earlier losses and to recognize that the repetition explained her overwhelming feelings when late in life she once more lost much of what recently had given her stimulation, comfort, and strength: a new affectionate relationship with a man, her trust in a woman friend, and the companionship of her dog. I have seen a couple one generation younger than Tessa deeply mourn a dog although they had a good relationship with each other, steady employment, children, and grandchildren. Like her, however, they were immigrants and had suffered dramatic losses during a war.

The only aid to her mourning work Tessa required for her to become able to rally her strength was the opportunity to sort out her feelings by expressing them to a sensitive listener and to review for him and for herself how her many losses had forced her repeatedly to start her life afresh. But in a situation as trying as hers, it is quite possible that had she not so soon after her most recent losses met Lamers, a specialist on processes of mourning, she might have become depressed for some time.

The loss that brought Tessa to Lamers was not a major loss of the kind that in the course of mourning brings about a phase of personality disintegration (Bowlby 1961,1980) which elicits the depressed response. When Tessa found a therapist who by his perceptive listening and pertinent questions helped her express her painful emotions, she quickly related them herself to her earlier life experience and, once she had understood that the new losses had revived pain belonging with severe earlier losses, she recovered some zest for living. But had she only met people who considered her behavior exaggerated or sick, Tessa might have become confused by the discrepancy between their attitude and her own sense of reality. Her anxiety about a lonely future might have become more intense.

Lamers, however, correctly understood Tessa's condition as one of mourning, rather than one of depression. By the less experienced observer they are not easily distinguished because the behavioral symptoms of grief and depression can overlap. The griever may appear restless, unhappy, and self-centered owing to preoccupation with memories, pining, and the search for new directions. The depressed may appear restless, unhappy, and self-centered because of preoccupation with some disturbing sense of dysfunction within and the effort to find explanations. The picture can be complicated in either case by signs of anxiety. Only attentive interaction with this person – friend, client, or patient – enables us to find out whether we are dealing with the depressed response, with grief, or with both.

Chapter sixteen

Professional aid to the depressed

The semantics of psychoanalysis and psychotherapy commit us to the view that the client is a "patient" and the expert helping him, a "therapist." However, the opposite idea, that the client in search of this sort of help is *not* sick and that his helper is *not* a medical therapist, is nearly as old as psychoanalysis. Freud never tired of resisting efforts to assimilate psychoanalysis to a medical psychiatry.

Szasz (1965:46)

Making a patient into a passive receiver of analytic "wisdom" tends to duplicate what many parents unfortunately do: take over a child's right to discover, learn on his own, make his own errors, and recognize his own uniqueness.

Peterfreund (1983:170)

Types of professional help

With the reservation that I agree with Szasz's comment quoted above, I follow the traditional semantics of using the terms "patient" and "therapist," although, as I will try to show in the remaining chapters, aid to learning that can free a person from depression-proneness requires a mutual process of learning between two, or more, people who increasingly become attuned to each other in significant understanding. Successful psychotherapy that helps a person outgrow depression-proneness is exploration and growth shared by therapist and patient.

Unavoidably, issues will be raised in these chapters that apply to psychotherapy in general, not only to work with acutely depressed or depression-prone patients. But the reader needs to bear in mind that the focus of this book is nonetheless on the vicissitudes of the basic depressed response rather than on psychotherapy or other therapy *per se*. Consequently, this and the following chapters will selectively emphasize those aspects of the interaction between therapist and patient that enhance learning, effective communication, increasing self-reliance, and the capacity to utilize available and appropriate human assistance. If this is successful, causes for getting depressed will become much less frequent and the work of depression more productive. The process of change by such learning in intensive psychotherapy will be the major focus, but other approaches to freeing people from acute depression will be taken up briefly.

Dealing with environmental factors promoting the depressed response

In a given instance of inability to cope productively with being depressed it may be that no more than lack of necessary information requires correction. In other cases it may be the depressed person's state of health, or social and economic conditions that need to be remedied. It may be the interpersonal relations within the family or work team. In such instances, what the patient looks for and the consulted professional worker is likely to offer, subsequent to an exploration of the patient's circumstances and limitations in coping on his or her own, are means to remove or reduce the circumstances that provoke the ineffective efforts to cope and, thereby, cause the current state of being depressed. One may administer or provide referral to health services; refer to or render social services to improve occupational, housing, or economic difficulties; provide marital counseling or family therapy. Such types of aid are particularly necessary when the depressed person appears neither able to cope on his or her own, nor able or motivated to learn to do so. Perhaps, as is often done in social work, the case worker will, while practical services are provided, at the same time teach the depressed client a better use of his or her own resources, should similar circumstances recur. If environmental circumstances are not too unfavorable, such assistance suffices to resolve depression in many instances where it has been acute and recurring.

Orientation 1 of intensive therapy: removing acute depression

On the other hand, with or without current severe environmental problems, there may be a disturbance or arrested development of personality, so that some environmental difficulties are automatically provoked from within and then responded to with inappropriate coping efforts enhancing frequent, often severe depression. The opportunity to learn from the physician, social worker, minister, or from other counselors, better ways of using one's own resources cannot be utilized. Learning and insight are blocked by the emotional and cognitive handicaps discussed in Chapter 9. Unless one resorts exclusively to medical therapy with various drugs or ECT, which may remove depressed reactions without recognition and modification of handicapping emotional and cognitive patterns, or unless the entire family is willing to participate in family therapy, individual psychotherapy of some kind may be chosen as the optimal remedy. Depending on the theoretical orientation of the therapist, even intensive individual therapy may have as its primary goal the removal of a single acute depression, or of recurring depressions when they occur, and therefore deal with cognitive and emotional handicaps and their history only to the extent that this is necessary to free the patient from acute depression or its too frequent recurrence.

Orientation 2: overcoming depression-proneness

In contrast, acute and recurrent depression may be seen by the therapist only as a symptom of basic disturbances in cognitive and emotional functioning. Even when the patient is not depressed, this may deprive him or her of optimal learning, effective communication with self and others, pleasurable self-reliance, and secure, stable personal relationships. These basic problems in functioning will then be the primary focus of therapeutic attention, provided that an evaluation of diagnostic, social, and other factors have made insight-oriented, intensive, and psychodynamic psychotherapy the treatment of choice for a given depressed or depression-prone person.

Perhaps "aid to inner reorganization" or "redevelopment" would be a better term for this than the customary term "treatment," if we mean by this the carefully protected provision of opportunities for spontaneous development of a person's highly individual cognitive and emotional potential, and if we mean by "treatment" something one person does or applies to another (compare Szasz 1965). Psychoanalysis and psychoanalytic psychotherapy of Freudian and other schools belong here, provided that their application has not become what Peterfreund calls (1983:2) "stereotyped" – in the sense of invariably trying to fit the patient's responses into pre-existing theoretical expectations – but rather are "heuristic in the sense of serving to discover or learn." In therapy, the latter approach aims "to initiate and foster a process whereby patient and therapist work together to learn, discover, and understand as much as possible about the individual patient" (Peterfreund 1983:2).

The concepts of orientations 1 and 2 are theoretical abstractions. Actual therapies are not necessarily clear-cut examples of either approach. Nonetheless, the two abstractions are helpful because of some significant differences despite the many features they share. Aspects of orientations 1 and 2 of intensive psychotherapy will be illustrated in the next chapter.

Basic aspects of psychotherapy

The patient's transference, repetitions, unconscious hope

Before comparing orientations 1 and 2 further, some aspects of the interaction between therapist and patient need to be discussed. The patient's responses to the therapist reflect, of course, basic features of human response; to parental and other authority figures one is dependent on; to those we trust, love, distrust, or hate; to strangers and anything unknown. For instance, all of us may interpret and experience interaction with significant persons in our current life in terms of past experience with significant others, and fail to take into account the differences between a past and a current partner. The meaning we have long ago attached to the feelings or actions of the former we now attach to the feelings or actions of the latter. In psychoanalytic terminology, this is referred to as "transference" (Freud 1912).[1]

Inadvertently, transference of feelings and inferences helps us in our unconscious wish and hope to repair injury and disappointments we have suffered in the past. In transference, the repetition of interpersonal constellations allows us the conscious or unconscious belief or illusion that a given new relationship duplicates an old one in some significant sense. We respond as if by attaining in the context of the new relationship a better outcome than the original relationship has had, this will put straight what went wrong in the past. In successful therapy, this is actually the case to some extent. But it is not only there that we seek such solutions, but in many unsuitable arrangements. Perhaps we get married to a person who not only has some of the favorable traits of one or both of our parents, but also the most negative ones. Daughters of alcoholics who saw their mothers beaten and exploited often marry alcoholic men. People who in attachment theory are called "anxiously attached," tend to attach themselves as adults to people who are as unreliable, though lovingly available at times, as their parents were. The unconscious hope behind inadvertently seeking out partners in such a repetitive manner – for instance, in marriage, sex, work – is that this time the old drama is to have a happy ending. Unfortunately, it usually doesn't, so that preconceived distorted views of self and others are once more reinforced by disappointment. Often, if a referral does not preclude it, a therapist is chosen by the patient on the basis of a transference established before or at the first contact. This is important for the therapist to bear in mind, or the therapy may go on indefinitely though remaining unproductive, be broken off prematurely, or end with a pseudo-cure.

Both transference and the other patterns I have sketched here are aspects of what Freud has frequently referred to (for instance, 1922,1932) as "repetition-compulsion." Transference is exemplified in Chapter 8 by the way in which Margaret, to begin with, experienced and responded to Dr G.'s behavior, and in Chapter 9 by Olga carrying on her angry battle with her analyst, as if she were faced with her mother. Bowlby (1988) and Stern (1985) describe, each in his way, how the tendency for transference and repetition acquires significant features of its individual adult character in the early experience within the family. Bowlby might say that, due to the attitudes and behavior of their parents, Margaret's and Olga's attachments had become anxiously avoidant, so that they were afraid of closeness to and distrustful of attachment figures. Stern might say that their disturbance stemmed from lack of attunement or from misattunement in the parenting they received. According to Sandler (1976:44–5) the patient has

> unconscious images or fantasies, in which both self and object in interaction have come to be represented in particular roles. In a sense the patient, in the transference, attempts to *actualize these in a disguised way* within the framework and limits of the analytic situation.

Dependence and helplessness in the role of patient

Although it operates to some extent in all of us, the tendency for transference and repetition compulsion is more pronounced in personalities with a distorted view of self and others. It becomes particularly virulent in the interaction with a therapist. As patients, we are vitally dependent on our therapist's adequacy to the therapeutic task for the improvement of our capacity to attain a better life. Yet, we are not really in a position to judge how competent our therapist is to help us with our specific difficulties, however well reputed he or she might be. Usually, when we enter therapy, we are so distressed that we do not even inquire systematically into the issue of the therapist's competence. Even if we wanted to explore the issue, as patients most of us lack the knowledge about psychotherapy that would enable us to reach a valid conclusion, even if we tried. In other words, the patient's situation is truly reminiscent of the child's situation: as children, we cannot choose our parents nor judge whether they are competent as parents. Since we are totally dependent on them for our survival, development, and well-being, all we can do is hope, and when they don't respond to our protest, try to ignore their failure to be helpful. Of course, as patients we can give notice and leave a therapist, whereas a child cannot change parents, but by the time we give up hope for our therapy, we may have invested a great deal of effort, time, and money; become attached, though deeply disappointed; and fearful of repeating a poor choice with another therapist. Therefore, we may hang on to an unsatisfactory therapy, just as we remained attached to unsatisfactory parents, wavering between hopeful, trusting love and contemptuous, mistrusting hate for the therapist.

Thus, one of the many features of the relationship with their parents that depression-prone people repeat in the interaction with their therapists is their getting caught in a conflict between, on the one hand, wanting to judge the therapist objectively and, on the other, wanting to leave well enough alone, idealize the therapist, and take the entire blame for anything that doesn't feel right in the therapy. The repetition of ambivalence and the inner conflicts it creates is soon in full swing and becomes permanent if the therapist does not watch out. In individual therapy, the patient has no opportunity to observe the therapist in interaction with other people and other situations. This increases the difficulty for the patient to reach a valid evaluation of the therapist's personality, which further enhances the virulence of transference responses in therapy. That the therapist rarely, if ever, sees the patient in interaction with others creates a similar hazard for the therapist's judgment, whether a certain behavior observed in the patient is typical of all of the patient's relationships, or mainly provoked by the therapist. Awareness of these hazards and processes, however, can give the therapist the perspective necessary for reconstructing, despite the patient's repressions and fear to remember, what experiences the patient may have been exposed to as a child.

Where fuller insight and modification of personality is the aim, it is important for the therapist to be aware, and help the patient become aware, of the presence of ever-shifting transference. For a while the therapist may be experienced as being just like the good or the bad mother one has had or believed one had; then all of a sudden, the therapist is cast in the role of one's past or present father, of one's grandmother, one's little or big sister or brother, or that wonderful or devilish teacher one had for an unforgettable year.

But it is equally important for the therapist to watch for, recognize, and if advisable admit to the patient, that by no means all significant and insignificant impressions the patient gets of the therapist are aspects of transference. For one thing, our patients are very alert in their conscious and unconscious observations of our behavior – our motives, our emotions, our tastes, our ambitions, and our blind spots. For another, their transference reactions rarely become virulent without having been touched off by some actual behavior or characteristic of ours that – often in an insignificant, but at times in a very significant way – is reminiscent of past formative experience. Searles is particularly astute (1975) in observing such phenomena (compare also Little 1951:38).

The therapist's transference and countertransference

For a long time in the history of psychodynamic therapy, the therapist was expected to be the cool, composed, objective, mirror-like observer whose work was not to be disturbed by emotional involvement of any kind. If he or she experienced in or after a session with a patient intense feelings such as anxiety, anger, fear, affectionate identification, sexual arousal, a sense of helplessness, depression, or confusion, this could only be a neurotic dysfunction on the part of the therapist calling for therapy. In many quarters this attitude still prevails. But the behavior, the needs, the history of our patients do arouse strong feelings, at times because we do not understand them, at other times exactly because we do, albeit unconsciously or preconsciously. Freud was aware of this and used (1912:99) the term "countertransference." For a long time, this term was mainly used when the therapist reacted as if the patient were a replica of a person in the therapist's past; in other words, with actual transference feelings independent of the patient's behavior and the interaction between the two. This is, of course, detrimental to the therapy, if it is not recognized and overcome soon.

Increasingly, however, the term "countertransference" has become reserved for an important feature in the process of therapy: that the patient's experience and behavior, and particularly its unconscious intentions, have an emotional impact on, and a significance for, the therapist. At first, however, this is not comprehended or does not even reach the therapist's awareness. Perhaps, the emotion that has been aroused is sufficiently disquieting to be at first defended against, although the defense can be overcome either through some self-analysis or supervisory consultation. Then this effect of unconscious messages from the patient and their meaning for the therapist can be understood, and enhances the therapist's understanding of the patient's life history, the patient's current needs and experience, the therapist's mistakes as observed by the patient, or other facets of the interaction between the partners in the therapy.[2] The therapist's experience of strong emotion aroused by the patient has become accepted by many as a natural part of the process of intensive psychotherapy. What is now expected of the therapist in this context is that he or she tolerates these feelings without losing composure or attentiveness in the patient's presence, and takes time to explore and analyze them without acting on them blindly. This tolerance by the therapist of own feelings and thoughts, as well as the patient's feelings and thoughts, has been called by Winnicott (1965:ch. 3; 1971:chs 6 and 9) "holding."

Bion's term "container and contained" (1970:72ff.) refers to very complex processes that, if I understand him correctly, differ somewhat from, although they overlap with, Winnicott's "holding." The term "containing," when applied to the analyst's function, is now used by many authors – for instance, by Casement (1985) – as very similar to "holding."

Very helpful contributions on the subject of countertransference have, among others, been published by Heimann (1950), Little (1951), Money-Kyrle (1956), and Sandler (1976). It is included in their discussions of therapy by Langs (1978), Basch (1980), and Casement (1985).[3] In the following chapter, Peterfreund's case illustrating one aspect of orientation 2 includes the utilization of countertransference.

Modes of communication

I have repeatedly mentioned that great discrepancy between aspirations and inappropriate efforts to realize them is a significant factor in giving frequent cause for the depressed response and in this way makes a person depression-prone. Another contributing factor of great importance is a disturbed system of communication with self and others. One source of difficulties is the use of language and verbal thought. Words are on the whole rather limited in expressing our perceptive and affective experience accurately enough for another person to understand us with empathy. Words are colored by subjective meaning. If we expect that anyone should be able to understand quickly and accurately the emotional implications of what we have said, and if we assume that lack of understanding invariably implies that the other person is indifferent, looks down on us, dislikes us, or is stupid, we are in trouble. If we take for granted that we, on our part, have immediately understood correctly what was meant by what we heard another person say, we are in trouble. If we believe we can correctly interpret the thoughts and feelings that cause another person's posture, motions, facial expressions, tone of voice, or silence; or that anyone who cares must readily understand our body language; we are in trouble. Such beliefs isolate us: they are doomed to frequent frustration and make us very lonely.

From the moment of their first contact patient and therapist are engaged in a complex pattern of verbal and non-verbal communication. In the process of their initial interviews and arriving at a contract how to proceed, patient and therapist are exposed to a great number of further impressions of each other created both intentionally and unintentionally. From this initial set of beliefs, expectations, hopes, aims, cautions, and apprehensions their interaction unfolds.

When trying to help a patient discover his or her blind spots in the understanding of the hazards as well as the potentials of communicating, we must as therapist be alert to the many problems and pitfalls of communication between partners in therapy; alert, for instance, to the fact that not only our conscious but even our unconscious attitudes communicate themselves and influence our patients. In the work with depressed or depression-prone patients, for instance, one set of attitudes is of particular significance: our attitude towards being depressed. If the therapist – perhaps because of unresolved personal problems with getting depressed – consciously or unconsciously looks upon being depressed as something weak, sick, and unnecessary, that should be overcome as quickly as possible, then the patient, longing to be liked and approved of by the therapist, will try to be a good patient and may seem to be improving rather quickly. He or she may become more active – often too active – and more cheerful, less depressed, or not depressed at all, and feel rewarded by the therapist's satisfaction. This so-called transference cure (accepting the role of the good little boy or girl who is no trouble) may eventually collapse and depression return. The chance is lost of engaging in the slow, laborious, painful, but more truly remedial process of discovering how people really communicate, both on and under the surface. Even if depression does not return because new defenses against the experience have developed, such relief from depression leaves the patient barred from the opportunity of learning to relate to self and others in a new, free, and more independent way; and developing greater creativity, flexibility, and joy in living.

Modes of learning

Learning is, of course, intimately intertwined with communication, but there are features that are independent of communication with others – for instance, our practicing a skill on our own. Learning is important in the context of overcoming depression-proneness, because the latter is enhanced by inhibitions of learning. As indicated earlier, all successful therapy is a process of cognitive and emotional unlearning and new learning. In general, some of our learning occurs in response to our own observations and experiments, other learning results from our receiving spoken or written directions, or adopting another person's behavior as a model. Still other learning is dependent on specific experiences in the dynamic interaction with another person.

Effective communication is vital in most forms of learning. For the therapist it is important to appreciate what forms of communication can help a given patient to feel understood; and to appreciate when a patient becomes ready to receive and integrate new forms of communication.

For a child, learning involves trying and mastering new knowledge, new skills, and new socially acceptable attitudes, and often involves the giving up of earlier beliefs, behavior, and expectations. Like the adult, the child learns partly from his or her own observations and explorations, from imitation, identification with, and submission to others. As we saw in Chapter 13, much of the child's learning is dependent on the child's significant relationships. Optimally, the child's learning progresses at specific, genetically programmed developmental stages from more limited and immature functioning and understanding to increasingly complex and mature patterns, although from time to time reemergence of earlier levels of development are normal. Behavior belonging to earlier stages of development is not totally abandoned, but can surface again under periods of physical or emotional stress.

The new learning of a patient in successful therapy resembles our learning during childhood and adolescence in many ways, but lacks the assistance of developmental phases adapted to specific learning needs. In contrast to the child's situation, the first stages of trying out formerly inhibited behavior may be quite unsuitable for an adult patient to apply outside the therapy relationship. The patient's learning often moves backward insofar as it may begin with modifications of relatively recently acquired understanding and behavior patterns. Patterns that developed under the impact of very early experience are modified only very slowly and painfully. They have been the backbone – for better and for worse – of our way of being and part of whatever security and stability we have in functioning. To let go of them is frightening. For this to take much time is not a matter of choice on the part of the therapist or the patient, but necessitated by the way our organism functions. Only when the patient has acquired a new understanding of earlier experiences can he or she move forward to new learning.

Obviously, if a person's long-established, complex cognitive and emotional patterns are to be modified by means of the personal interaction of two people, this is an adventure that involves how *each* participant learns and communicates. Sooner or later both partners must dare be as honest as possible in looking at themselves and at each other, as genuine as possible in dealing with each other, and as curious as possible about what is happening between them and what it

219

means. Changes in the therapist as a result of new learning, although often the conscious and/or unconscious aim of the patient, are not the primary goal of the therapy, but as a rule, they are necessary for, and dynamically significant in, the success of the therapy. Aside from winning trust, the capacity of the therapist to learn and to change serves as an important model for the patient. The patient's hidden hope and need to experience in the therapy what would have been vital to receive as an infant or child, can be met only if despite the patient's covert or overt distrust and fear of closeness, despite habitual misinterpretation of human behavior, despite mistaken expectations and conclusions, gradually the therapist's effort to understand facilitates new trust, new insights, new self-respect, new expectations, and new patterns of communication. In this complex task it is important for the therapist to remember to what extent our encouraging the patient to talk about a problem (as we saw in Lamers's case in Chapter 15), our readiness to listen, and an occasional pertinent question can mobilize in the patient the capacity to explore his or her responses and find suitable solutions.

In summary: if and to the extent that therapy improves a patient's capacity to learn and communicate, this will not only improve his or her ability to establish, maintain, and trust personal relationships, but also develop the patient's capacity for self-analysis, which is a model for, if not identical with, the work of depression. All these changes reduce the frequency of cause for getting depressed.

My suggestion as to what, as a therapist, one should try to do and avoid is an ideal set of standards that no therapist can expect to meet at all times. We make mistakes all the time. We have to live with them and try to make them productive. As Winnicott proposes (1965:258): "In the end the patient uses the analyst's failures, often quite small ones, perhaps manoeuvred by the patient. ... So in the end we succeed by failing – failing the patient's way." With perfect parents and perfect therapists one would remain hopelessly inferior and unable to become independent.

Further comparison of work with orientations 1 and 2

Now we return to the differences between the alternative orientations in therapy. I said that with orientation 1 one tries to work toward an improvement that frees the patient from excessive depression under given circumstances and, perhaps, enables him or her to modify these circumstances, so that a more satisfactory, more creative daily life becomes possible. This can often be accomplished without therapist and patient fully understanding the deeper causes for the depression-proneness.

Management and utilization of transference

A short-term therapy does not allow for emphasis on the full expression in the therapeutic relationship of these deeper causes and on working them through in that context. In fact, it cannot permit strong ambivalent transference ties to develop. These cannot be severed without harm to the patient before the conflicts causing the ambivalence are understood and resolved. Thus, orientation 1 focuses on the patient's behavior in his life outside the consultation room and on teaching the patient new modes of understanding and handling these situations. In as much as hidden patterns of early origin are not touched and resolved, a relapse is likely to occur, when an unusual cause for the depressed response arises, one that was not dealt with during the therapy. Being dependent on what the therapist has specifically taught the patient, the latter may in unforeseen circumstances be left without guidance in trying to cope. Under benign circumstances, and if additional professional intervention has modified the environment, this need not happen, or it may not happen until several years later, as exemplified by Arieti's case Doris, described in the next chapter. Therapies using this approach with severely disturbed patients took Arieti between eighteen months and three years to complete (1978).

With orientation 1, then, the therapist actively helps the patient maintain a trusting attitude, which may be realistic or an idealizing transference, or both. The development and expression of exaggerated doubt, distrust, resentment, and disappointment is avoided. The latter reactions are called "negative" transference in professional terminology, although their appearance during therapy according to orientation 2 is just as essential for effective therapeutic work as the presence of positive feelings, transferred or realistic.

With orientation 2, illustrated by the cases of Margaret and Olga in Part I, and of George and Mrs D. in Chapter 17, behavior outside the therapy relationship is also carefully examined, but these impressions are utilized to throw light on the meaning of the patient's behavior toward the therapist. From the resulting understanding of this behavior, many of the patient's emotional and cognitive handicaps are then traced to their earliest beginnings. To the extent that the early traumata are emotionally reexperienced in the relationship with the therapist, they can become understood and can gradually cease to become activated in current relationships. This frees the patient for new learning, for greater creativity, independence, and competence in coping with unexpected crises and the depressed reactions they may provoke. But at first and for a long time, giving the transference full range usually creates intense, ambivalent feelings toward the therapist, so that the contact cannot, without doing damage, be terminated as early as in orientation 1. Reaching the treatment goal of security and greater independence may require intensive therapy of several years, at times up to ten years, or even more. It further requires that the therapist, perhaps through a personal therapy where trying transference reactions were experienced, tolerated, and understood, has overcome early handicaps in his or her own personality development. Otherwise, because of defenses against experiences similar to the patient's, deep empathy with what the patient goes through during therapy is rare. Even in orientation 2 – that is in character analysis – some of the patient's vulnerabilities are likely to persist to some degree, but it is none the less unlikely that during a later depressed episode, when the patient is on his or her own, he or she reverts to most of the earlier emotional and cognitive handicaps without understanding any of their causes, as will be seen in Arieti's case, Doris. But except in research and training institutions, a therapist in an organizational structure has rarely the choice to apply orientation 2.

Utilization of learning modes

Another differentiation between the alternative approaches to therapy can be made along the lines of learning and teaching. With orientation 1 the therapist is throughout the therapeutic contact essentially conceived of by both therapist and patient as the person who knows what the patient must learn and do to have a better life. The therapist assumes the responsibility of demonstrating how this should be accomplished. Among the several modes of human learning, mainly the mode of the learner trusting and following the guidance and example of benign and/or powerful authority tends to be utilized. The self-reliance, conviction, and determination of the therapist can be experienced as a vital support by patients for whom this is the most suitable approach. It is my impression that Beck's technique (1967) primarily uses this approach, while Arieti (Arieti and Bemporad 1978) combines elements of both orientations.

In work with orientation 2, learning from direction is least important. It is vitally important, on the other hand, for the therapist to recognize that the patient will often use the therapist as a good or bad model; and to recognize the patient's capacity to learn on his own. As emphasized by Basch, Casement, Langs, and others, this independent learning should proceed with minimal interference from the therapist's activity. The permission to try out by oneself becomes a model for what one allows oneself. The emphasis is, within the safe frame of the therapeutic contract and environment, on the mode of increasingly providing learners with the necessary emotional space (see Casement 1985) and opportunity to explore, try out, and experiment in their own rhythm and time; to waver in following and opposing, accepting and rejecting the therapist as an aide and model; to discover through the experience of the interaction with the therapist many components of their own personality and life experience; until they emerge with increasing self-assurance and independence, with new meaning in life, with new goals, less conflict, and less confusion.[4] In the course of this process the therapist participates originally also as a benign authority, but gradually the two become partners in interaction of equal importance though with different responsibilities; partners in a shared adventure of search and discovery. Toward the end of a successful therapy, the patient clearly has the lead.

In our society depression-proneness and acute depressions are common, but the number of therapists who have received a training adequate to the task of thorough character analysis is limited and the cost of such treatment very high. Therefore, the great value to the patient, to the patient's environment, and to society as a whole of the usually shorter psychotherapy according to orientation 1 should not be demeaned by therapists who are inclined to choose alternative 2 for patients who can utilize it and have the economic means it requires. In the closing chapter I will return to the subject of alternative methods of treatment, but before doing so, some further case examples may help to clarify some of the issues raised in this chapter.

Chapter seventeen

Case examples

In brief, we are never truly "neutral" observers and interpreters. In every word and comment we implicitly convey something of our life experience, our standards and beliefs, something of what we feel about the patient as a human being. How could it be otherwise?

Peterfreund (1983:108)

The analyst is certainly able to do a great deal, but he cannot determine beforehand exactly what results he will effect. He sets in motion a process, that of the resolving of existing repression. He can supervise this process, further it, remove obstacles in its way, and he can undoubtedly vitiate much of it. But on the whole, once begun, it goes its own way and does not allow either the direction it takes or the order in which it picks up its points to be prescribed for it.

Freud (1913:130)

Aid to a severely depressed woman in late middle age

The therapists of Margaret (Chapter 8) and Olga (Chapter 9) worked with orientation 2. Arieti's case, Doris (Arieti and Bemporad 1980:230ff.), is an example of a successful therapy conducted predominantly according to orientation 1.

For his most extensive description of his treatment of severely depressed patients, Arieti chose the case of a woman who was in her late fifties at the time of referral by her husband. She was far more disabled than either Margaret or Olga when they entered therapy. Arieti tells us that "although described in detail, the case of Doris Fullman is not examined in all its possible aspects. Some inferences have been omitted because they are relatively easy to make. . . ." (1980:230). As the interested reader can read Arieti's full description in the original, the following is condensed.

Initial phase of therapy

Doris was a housewife, married for over thirty years and mother of three adult children, a son and twin daughters. She was referred by her husband. At that time she had been continuously hospitalized for almost three years and was currently kept in a unit of patients constantly watched for the possibility of suicide. The current episode of Doris's severe and unproductive depression had started soon after the death of her dominating mother. There had been repeated episodes of depression in Doris's life, the first severe one at the time of the birth of her first child, the son, now twenty-six. She had been in treatment with a psychotherapist for fourteen years without finding it helpful. During her current hospitalization every type of available therapy had been tried unsuccessfully.

After Dr A. had conferred with hospital staff, arrangements were made for Doris to be accompanied from the hospital to his office for weekly interviews. He proposed to her that this should continue until the time when she could return home. Then she would be expected to come at least three times a week. This optimistic outlook was a surprise to Doris but no doubt reassuring. Despite her doubts about such a possibility, she agreed. Dr A. met Doris in a warm, unhesitating, and accepting manner. He made no demands other than that she try to report her thoughts and did not insist on pursuing subjects she did not appear ready to delve into. She knew Dr A. by reputation and had come with positive expectations. She gave pertinent information although with effort; but some significant data emerged only gradually.

At the beginning of therapy, conducted face to face, Doris showed no interest in leaving the hospital. She felt no desire to return to her husband and children and no desire to go on living. She was not angry at her husband, she said, for going on a cruise without her on a boat she loved, only angry at herself for being sick. But she was angry at her mother whom she had never been able to please although she had tried very hard to do so. To be approved by mother was "absolutely essential." Doris felt very guilty after her mother's death for having put her in a home for the aged. She was plagued by intense feelings of guilt and inferiority in many contexts. She felt inferior to her husband because he was a successful businessman while she was inadequate in every way. She felt inadequate as a mother. When her son was born she was too depressed to love him as she should. When her daughters were born, she took better care of them, not out of love, but only to atone for her neglect of her son. She felt unattractive as a sexual partner because ever since her marriage her husband never took the initiative for sex relations, although he would perform if she made overtures. She felt socially inferior because she came from a lower class than her husband. Her mother had always criticized her and told her what to do even when she was over fifty. She had tried to comply for fear of her mother's rejection.

In the second session, speaking of her mother's constant disapproval of her, Doris remembered that when she was five a boy had lifted her skirt and kissed her knee. When she told her mother about this the latter said with contempt that she knew what kind of woman Doris would grow up to be. Doris contended that at the time this meant nothing to her; that she did not feel guilty about this episode until she was eight. At that age she had thrown a pen at her brother. The pen hit him in the eye and he lost it. She was neither reproached nor punished by her parents. (This is the only time when by implication the father is mentioned in Dr A.'s report.) The incident was never mentioned. Thus, Doris was left to her terrifying conviction, which she confessed to Arieti in the fourth session, that she had hit her brother's eye intentionally: in response to his tormenting her she had first threatened to throw her pen into his eye if he did not stop, and then thrown it. Since then she felt guilty, guilty, guilty about everything. She had no love for anyone. She had never accepted her husband and children, and they never accepted her.

Dr A. had recognized that Doris's way of life had always been to submit to the needs and demands of others; first to those of her mother, later primarily to what she saw as the needs of her husband and children. She seemed to feel that she had to care for others to atone for her existence. Now, Dr A. responded in an accepting, reassuring way without demanding further discussion of the incident with the brother just then. He told her that she never followed her own wishes and, in fact, she did not let herself know what she wanted. She wanted only what others wanted. This would have to change and he would help her.

The next time Doris reported with a smile that for the first time she was feeling better. In the fifth session Doris disclosed that she had become pregnant for the first time at the age of thirty-two, five years after her marriage, not out of a desire to have children but in order to console her husband who was depressed about the death of his brother who had started their business and was the senior partner. She also reported that when she married her husband she was not sure that she loved him, but she wanted to cheer him up when he was in despair after his fiancée, with whom he was very much in love, had broken their engagement.

In the sixth session she reported the overwhelming insight that she could not have hit her brother's eye if she had wanted to, that it was an accident. Dr A. told her this was a major breakthrough and that she would be able to go home within six weeks, a plan which was carried out.

Continued therapy

"In the following months there was a gradual but steady improvement, and a quick readjustment to life" (p.236). Dr A. learned that Doris was the child of poor Russian immigrants who had left their country when Doris was eleven. "She still remembered an uncle who remained in Russia; he loved her very much and did not make demands on her like her mother. The memory of this uncle had remained with her as something to revere" (p.237).

After her return home, Doris reported much more about her marriage and her sexual frustration. "Since her childhood, her mother had been able to convince her that she was much too interested in sex and that sex was dirty" (p. 236). Gradually, she became able to express complaints about her husband rather than blaming herself for the unsatisfactory situation. For a transitory period she became too self-assertive and easily angered, but apparently these reactions did not appear in relation to Dr A. She would express strong opinions in ways that offended others. She became excessively suspicious and jealous when a woman tried to call her husband whom she had met during the cruise. Doris had to review her attitude toward her marriage. Dr A. told her she could both improve her marriage and become less dependent on her husband, relying more on her inner resources. She succeeded in this and various other areas. Thus, she gave up smoking entirely although she had been a chain smoker at the hospital. She taught Andrew, her husband, some romantic habits and learned to accept taking the initiative sexually. Dr A. had helped her see that Andrew was not as domineering as she assumed, but that she herself had put him in the dominant position to replace her mother.

Doris's treatment continued for some time "mostly for the purpose of preventing her from slipping back into a mood of depression when small disappointments occurred." Doris "became capable to distinguish disappointments from sadness and depression." In view of her age and her long history of depression Dr A. had expected that in some areas only "satisfactory compromises" would be reached. "Nevertheless the treatment seemed to exceed expectations " (p. 241). She became proud of having been the mother of her successful children. She became self-assertive, she showed brilliancy of intellect and a practical knowledge of many subjects. She became a successful bridge player and was active in many ways.

Having been completely free from depression for nine years after termination of treatment, Doris suffered a relapse of severe depression. "All her complexes and cognitive constructs," which Arieti "had hoped had been weakened to the point of not disturbing her again, came back. We had to reexamine again her whole past, the relation with the mother, the burden of guilt originating with the accident of the brother, her marriage, the difficulties she still had in believing her husband cared for her, and so on" (p.242). At first, Doris's disappointment in Arieti whose judgment she had trusted made the work more difficult than before. Dr A. told Doris that he "should have been more cautious and prepared her for the possibility of a recurrence" (p.243).

What brought on this relapse was a severe case of herpes zoster (shingles), causing excruciating pain and bleeding during defecation. Cancer was suspected. When after numerous examinations this rare but benign condition was diagnosed, Doris did not believe it. She thought her life had come to an end and that she had not fully lived. A year earlier she had had a few minutes of depression when she went on a cruise with her husband on a ship that was not as beautiful as the *Aurora*.

Treatment had to be more intensive than the first time. Tape recordings of the sessions were used for Doris to listen to again later during the same day. She decided to let her husband listen to them, too, with favorable effect on his understanding of her and of himself. Arieti does not tell us how long this second phase of the treatment took, but one gets the impression it was only a matter of months. The sessions not only concentrated on "reexamination of the past from different points of view, but also on a detailed reconstruction of her present life" (p.243). As a result, Doris's relations with her husband became much more satisfactory, with great improvement of their ability to communicate. When treatment ceased, she was sixty-nine and about to go on a cruise around the world with Andrew.

What modes of learning and what aspects of transference were utilized in Dr A.'s treatment of his patient Doris which effectively relieved her of constant severe depression? He helped her leave the hospital after eleven or twelve weekly sessions. Within less than two years of frequent sessions he restored her to a life she probably enjoyed more than the entire fifty years since the incident with the brother's eye. How was this possible?

Modes of learning

Arieti (1980) asserts that in cases of severe depression it is of crucial importance that the therapist establish an immediate and intense rapport with the patient.[1] He should assume "an active role from the beginning," be firm, make "clear and sure statements." When a good rapport is established, the therapist must "aim at a quick discovery and understanding of the patient's basic drama" (p.216). This process of discovery has many aspects in common with the process according to orientation 2, except that, as described in this case, it is more focused on conscious or preconscious behavior and on the history the patient brings up spontaneously, rather than utilizing and interpreting repetition in the transference of earlier experiences.

Arieti's description of Doris's therapy demonstrates that he was remarkably qualified to implement his principles. First of all, one gains the impression of an unusually warm, secure, sensitive, and flexible therapist who was explicit and firm in his communications. He was eager to understand his patient, ready to admit a mistake. He was at ease in his technique of taking the lead and offering the patient a very pertinent reeducation in her behavior. He was quick to grasp the nonverbal communication inherent in Doris's behavior and to adapt his own behavior to it. He worked very effectively with the verbal communication Doris presented spontaneously. He was not only very sensitive to Doris's anxieties but also quick to recognize many important dynamic features. While he sought sufficient background information to grasp the central patterns of her behavior, his explanations and counsel concentrated on aspects of her life that either were, or could readily become, conscious. Whenever he deemed Doris ready to work with them he shared his impressions frankly with her. His confidence must have been contagious.

Arieti educated Doris partly by direct instructions, but also by letting her experiment with these instructions in her own way without causing her to feel like a failure – for instance, when her new self-assertiveness became exaggerated. But her experimentation did not become independent. In all likelihood he remained the model for her decisions.

Management of transference reactions

Doris's intelligence does not suffice to explain why the firmness of Dr A.'s guidance enabled her to be so successful in following his lead. As an additional explanation, it seems probable that, consciously or unconsciously, Doris experienced Dr A. as a reincarnation of the lost uncle in Russia who loved her very much without making demands. By being a good patient rather than acting like the naughty child she thought she was after having hurt her brother, she may have wanted to keep this new uncle favorably inclined. It is also possible that Doris believed that Dr A. was so kind and encouraging because she was indeed a good patient, but that he would turn his back on her like mother if she did not succeed in following his lead. That her father, except for his existence being implicit in one reference to "parents," was never mentioned suggests that he may have been a weak man, no protection against mother, or was otherwise disappointing. Dr A. may have represented a wished for good new father and good new mother all at once. These may be some of the inferences Arieti omits (1980:230) from his case description because they are easy to make; or perhaps he meant that Doris could not tolerate or benefit from reexperiencing in the transference painful tensions in an early significant relationship.

Be this as it may, Doris was fifty-eight years old when treatment began. She did not come on her own, but was referred by her husband and assisted in coming by hospital personnel. She did not come with the expectation that Dr A. would help her develop more effective behavior patterns but in the hope that he would relieve her from suffering. She was a housewife with an unsatisfactory but stable marriage. Her children were grown. She did not aspire to a different occupation. There was every reason to help her adapt to this life in a better way, but no reason to work toward the more basic changes that might have been appropriate – and perhaps necessary – had the patient been a much younger woman who, despite a similar family of origin and individual history, and despite some similar behavior patterns, had come with different goals for her therapy; perhaps a single woman who wanted to attract a suitable man with whom to form a family; a woman with a broken marriage and young children who wanted to become a better mother and have better relationships with men; one who wanted to become able to establish different relationships in general and become more effective in her occupation; or the like.

In Doris Fullman's case, it was probably wise to concentrate on helping her look in a different way at some aspects of her current circumstances and to discover better methods of dealing with them. It seems that there was good reason for Arieti to discontinue each of the two phases of Doris's therapy without any attempt to make her independent of him as a benign and guiding parental figure. Despite its omissions, her version of her history is suggestive of unconscious anxieties, anger, conflicts, and misconceptions, having their origin mostly in early childhood. An effort to let them surface by being less active and benign as a therapist, so that old patterns of behavior might become more fully understood in their cause and purpose, and eventually replaced by more effective responses, would in all likelihood have caused her periods of intense negative feelings in the transference, and anxiety. In her life circumstances, the consequent suffering might have been out of proportion to the potential gain. Most of all, there is no evidence that it would have been in keeping with her own goals. Although Doris was able to change her social behavior and expectations, there is no evidence in the report of an improving capacity to establish new links between past and present perceptions or between her own responses and those of others; and thereby for better work of depression, should she have significant cause to get depressed. To these questions I shall briefly return further on.

Aid to a mildly depressed college drop-out

The next case is an illustration of orientation 2, although the patient's youth and developmental history required a management of his transference that differs from what we followed in the case of Margaret (Chapter 8).

Basch describes (1980) two years of therapy in face-to-face interviews with a young man, George, who sought therapy at age eighteen. Except during the final months, when frequency tapered off to twice, then once a week, they met three times a week. Basch gives a record of essential portions of their dialogue in many of their sessions. He lets us follow how his decisions to proceed – what to ask, what to assert in words, and what to convey nonverbally through his behavior – grew out of his impressions of George's strengths and difficulties, as well as of George's life circumstances and history.

Initial phase of therapy

George was sent to Dr B. by his family physician. He had asked for a psychiatric referral without mentioning his reasons for the request. To Dr B. he readily explained that he was afraid he was going crazy because of his symptoms: sleeping difficulties, withdrawal from activities and interests, and a sense of unreality and meaninglessness.[2] He thought this was what he had read on schizophrenia during a college course. Dr B. did not immediately reassure George about his not being schizophrenic, but waited to do so until the end of the session, a delay George was able to tolerate. He was co-operative in the interview, could develop a topic spontaneously, and showed a capacity to relate to authority in a trusting way, so that Dr B. considered him able to benefit from intensive therapy. Dr B. found it important not to let George get caught in an emphasis on his symptoms of depression, although, in a suitable context, he ascertained that George was not suicidal. He supported George in talking about his life situation and how it had developed, rather than about symptoms. At the end of the session, George was told that he was neither crazy nor schizophrenic, but that he had been wise to seek help in as much as he did have problems.

When George returned for the next session, he was disappointed and annoyed, because the relief about not going crazy had not freed him from his symptoms. This was used to explain more about what therapy entailed and how they would proceed, which George accepted. He asked what was wrong with him and was told it was a depression. To his questions about antidepressants, Dr B. said he thought the depression had causes that could be dealt with psychologically.

As the relationship developed, Dr B. noticed that the symptoms of depression subsided gradually without George discussing them any further. There was a great deal George was more eager to discuss. As a rule spontaneously, but at times subtly elicited or clarified by Dr B., the following picture emerged. George was an only child, because his mother had to have a total hysterectomy due to complications at his birth. His parents had met when his father was an office boy in the maternal grandfather's law firm, where Mother was a legal secretary. A plan that Father would become a lawyer and enter his father-in-law's firm may have been a major factor in her choosing him for a husband. The young couple lived with her parents while Father attended college, but soon the war broke out and Father was sent to the European war theater. When he returned from service, George was three years old and resented Father's presence intensely. To him, his grandfather, who his mother idolized, remained the father figure. Grandfather was a distant and immaculate person who did not like small children and avoided touching or being touched by them, giving as a reason that his clothes might get dirty. As the therapeutic dialogue gradually uncovered, three-year-old George, used to having his mother entirely to himself, rejected his returned father not in an oedipal sense, but as a child resents the intrusion of a new, big brother. He would scream and squirm violently if Father tried to hold him on his knees or embrace him. He insisted that Father wave goodnight to him from a distance, like Grandfather. As a result, his father, an emotionally shy man, and George never became physically close. At the same time, George felt that Grandfather never approved of him because he could not behave like a grown-up. He was eight when Grandfather died, and he had never felt close to him.

Mother could never reconcile herself to her husband's decision, after his discharge from the army, not to return to college or become a lawyer. He wanted to develop a business of his own, which he did successfully. He was very active in his manufacturing company. His wife did not hide her contempt if he returned home with machine oil on his clothes. When George was a schoolboy, it was bewildering for him to find that neighbors, friends, and peers appreciated and admired his father who was very helpful in practical and mechanical matters, but then at home to see his mother's chilly contempt of Father's activities. This chilly atmosphere drove him away from home to group activities with other children, but Mother reproached him for any time spent other than studying and reading, although his marks were good without much effort. Yet, he remained "a loner" at school. He was so afraid of rejection that he could not take the first step to associate with someone he found attractive; he was dependent on someone else taking the first step. But when he was fourteen a pretty, fifteen-year-old girl, Nancy, took the first step toward making friends when they met in the school library. She had similar problems, and they were soon inseparable friends, and remained so until graduation three years later. They could confide everything to each other. Due to George's restraint, there was only some kissing and hugging, but no more sexual contact between them.

Pressured by his mother, whose approval he could not win by any other method, George became very interested in reading and debating, and finally thought he wanted to enter a pre-law course in college and then study law. Mother expected that he would some day enter the law firm her father had built up. After graduation, in order not to be separated from Nancy, he wanted to go to the state college she was to attend. But when he received a scholarship from an outstanding college in the East and a letter that he was welcome there, his mother succeeded in convincing him that for his future career it was very important to accept this offer. He and Nancy agreed not to feel tied to each other, but date others as well. Nevertheless, when he felt very lonely and estranged at college, Nancy's letters became all he was living for. For the first time ever, he could not concentrate on his studies and did not hand in his assignments. As her letters became increasingly infrequent, he came closer and closer to failing. Then, when she broke off by letter, he collapsed emotionally. Weekly interviews with a psychiatrist and antidepressants did not help. College authorities suggested that he take a leave and return when he felt all right again. Without packing a single suitcase, he got on a plane and returned home, very much to the dismay of his mother. After staying inactively at home for three months, he applied to Dr B., backed by his father's willingness to pay for the therapy as long as

George thought it was meaningful. Only Mother disapproved, as if George could pull himself out of the dumps as soon as he decided to do so.

Continued therapy

Once George's depression subsided he demonstrated – comparable to Margaret's development (Chapter 8) after the most frightening phase of her therapy – a remarkable capacity for introspection and for using Dr B.'s questions and clarifications to establish historical and causal links in the recollection and understanding of his experiences. He was curious. He was courageous and honest in revealing apprehensions, aspirations, feelings of inferiority, and fantasies, including sexual ones. Consequently, his development in therapy was rapid. He soon decided not to return to college for the time being, as he did not want to become a lawyer and did not know what else to study. Then he realized that before committing himself to legal training he had for two years thoroughly enjoyed working at his father's plant after school hours and during school holidays. At that time he had actually been very favorably impressed by his father's personality and his competence in business. But under the pressure of his mother's dissatisfaction he had spent the summer preceding graduation from high school as office boy in the legal firm, without enjoying it.

Then George decided not to stay at home all day during his therapy, but for the time being to work full time in his father's business where he was given increasing responsibilities in various departments. At the same time George worked with Dr B. on his difficulties in social contacts with peers and in dating. Dr B. helped him recognize that in both areas he reacted emotionally as the three-year-old who yearned to receive from an attachment figure exclusive attention and admiration; but if he was not perfect and competent in every way he expected to be rejected and ridiculed. Supported by Dr B.'s full attention and responsiveness in these discussions, he experimented with new modes of reacting in peer groups and with his new girlfriend. While Dr B. was on holiday, he decided to try intercourse with his girlfriend and then was greatly relieved, when he reported the adventure in the eighty-fifth session, to discover that Dr B. approved of his having decided to take this momentous step on his own independent responsibility. Finally, sessions were reduced in frequency on George's own initiative. Not long thereafter, he left town, and therapy, to study business administration with the goal of eventually becoming a partner in his father's company.

Management of transference reactions

Dr B. saw George's difficulties as largely due to a developmental arrest brought about by the lack of opportunity in his childhood to identify with an admired male attachment figure. Therefore, he found it important not to encourage an ambivalent transference in George by silence and anonymity, but rather by his own behavior to facilitate George's idealizing identification (compare Kohut 1971,1977) with an "understanding, helpful and admired mentor that adolescents need and that he had not previously found" (1980:144). George had not had the opportunity at the proper age for an idealizing identification with a male figure. Although George had admired his father as a schoolboy, his mother's contempt for the father's activities had soon alienated George from his father again.

As George related with increasing trust to Dr B., he reported a "bad dream" about a woman who kissed him but then turned into a man with Dr B.'s voice. He was helped to express his anxiety that becoming dependent on and attached to Dr B. must mean that he had homosexual leanings. Dr B. made clear that the trusting and helpful nature of their relationship reawakened the very natural yearning for physical tenderness from his father that he had suppressed in his childhood. It had nothing to do with adult sexuality.

When George later expressed fears of failure and ridicule if he were to try intercourse with his new girlfriend Betty, Dr B. explained the influence of his mother's and grandfather's attitudes and perfectionism on his view of self and others. When George countered that his father had been easygoing and helpful as a teacher, Dr B. told him that the foundation for the difficulties George had in experiencing himself as a worthwhile and lovable person who could be taken seriously, were laid before the age of three, when his father had returned from the army; Dr B. added that he was puzzled by the trust and confidence with which George had nonetheless been able from the beginning to cooperate with him. At this, George recalled his grandmother about whom he had not thought for many years.

She was an unassuming woman who was frequently bullied and humiliated by her husband. Then she would retire to doing housework in some other room. When still living in his grandparents' house, little George would seek her company on such occasions. Alone with him, Grandmother was a different woman: cheerful, talkative, singing or reading stories to him, playing games with him at which she would invariably find ways to let him win. To her, even when no longer living in the same house, George would come with his sorrows and triumphs, to her he showed his early scholastic achievements with pride. By her he always felt loved, and understood as the boy he was, without having to meet demands. Then, when he was nine, she suddenly had a stroke. Overnight she became senile and incompetent. When he visited her at the nursing home, she did not recognize him. He never asked to see her again. At her funeral four years later he felt nothing, and he never thought of her again.

After the significance of this relationship and its loss was discussed in this session, George did some mourning. A week later, he was told that a month hence Dr B. would take two weeks of vacation. Although always prompt, he arrived ten minutes late for the next session, in an angry mood, complaining about events at work. When Dr B. related the anger to his impending vacation, George asked "what vacation?," having forgotten this information. He saw no reason to be angry at Dr B. whose vacation was well deserved. He had forgotten all about it. But he had also forgotten to bring the check with Dr B.'s fee for the month. To the next session he arrived in a fury at Dr B. He insisted that Dr B. stopping his car next to George's car at a red light, had ignored George's friendly waving and stared right through him. When George finally accepted that this was an error, because Dr B. did not drive a blue Buick, he still felt angry. Dr B. explained that children experience a loved adult's illness and disappearance as rejection. Now he was belatedly experiencing this anger at his grandmother's not recognizing him. Then George mourned not only the lost relationship with her, but the injury to his development that it had caused.

Modes of learning

When George was puzzled by any of the experiences and problems he brought up spontaneously, Dr B. used them to explain, depending on what fitted the context, how children generally interpret and are influenced in their development by such experiences, or how adults function. Dr B. did not give George any instructions on what he should do, other than encouraging him to share his thoughts whenever he felt ready to do so. Instead, Dr B. demonstrated – somewhat reminiscent of Father's demonstrating a way of life as scout leader or head of a company – how things can be looked at, examined, communicated, and understood. Both in the choice of topics during sessions and in the activities of his life outside of therapy, George was given the freedom of independent choice and responsibility. Within the frame of the professional setting, Dr B.'s attitude toward George repeated not only the positive features of his father's responses, but also those of his grandmother.

Thus, George's emotional and cognitive development was able to pick up where his mother's attitudes and values and his grandmother's stroke had interrupted it. He outgrew the handicaps that had prompted his getting depressed at college: the inability to recognize that alienation from his father had led to inadequate educational planning; the inability to establish age-adequate relationships with peers of both sexes.

Comparison with Doris

Looking briefly at Doris, compared to George, we can see that in Basch's terms also Doris suffered from a developmental arrest. She had to grow up without a woman she could idealize and identify with. In her case, even the early security experienced by George with his grandmother appears to have been lacking. Her contact with her uncle is unlikely to have been as intimate from earliest infancy. Then her negative view of herself had been constantly reinforced over more than fifty years. So it is not surprising that one could not help her in the way possible with George. Although they are applying different theoretical concepts to their work, it seems to me that Arieti's and Basch's perceptions of their patients follow similar lines.

A successful reconstruction

My last case is chosen from Peterfreund (1983). It illustrates how the correct reconstruction of traumatic conditions in early infancy, among other functions, serves the purpose of "corrective emotional experience" (p.108; see also Basch 1980:82). The following is a condensation of a significant psychoanalytic episode Peterfreund reports.

Mrs D. was a "gifted expressive young woman with unusual access to her inner life" (p.104). She came into analysis shortly after her marriage because she felt confused, uncertain, excessively tense, and hyperemotional. She was the older of two daughters of divorced parents who occasionally joined in meeting their daughters as a family. On these occasions both parents enacted a pretence of gay, friendly togetherness. The father was an extremely narcissistic, hypomanic, impulsive, and infantile person, who could not relate genuinely to anyone, but a brilliant businessman. Before Mrs D. married her husband he appeared to be open, friendly, concerned and involved with people, but soon after the marriage he withdrew from her, unrelated, hostile, and depressed. She was slow in recognizing that he was a disturbed man resembling her father. They were divorced during the analysis.

Until some time during the seventh and within the last year of her analysis a constellation of distressing feelings had repeatedly come up but had eluded genuine understanding. Then one day, Mrs D. came in to report enthusiastically that her mother was getting remarried on Christmas. The mood in which she talked about this did not fit what Dr P. would have expected in view of how he had come to see her and her family. When he confronted her with the seeming inappropriateness of her response, the following became clear. She had not been told the news directly by her mother, but learned accidentally from her sister not only about the marriage plans, but also that their mother was selling the family home without having consulted her daughters. Mrs D. did not like the man in question. She was very upset about this when she called her friends to tell them. But before coming for her session with Dr P., she had called her mother and talked to her as the good, pleased, dutiful daughter. The mother had told her she would be married at Christmas and Mrs D. had told her that this was a fine time to get married, although actually, it was the only time of the year when the daughters together could meet both parents as a family. During the session, Mrs D. spoke to Dr P. as if it were necessary to continue acting like the dutiful, sweet daughter even with him.

Some months prior to this session Mrs D. had been unexpectedly and inexplicably deserted by a man she expected to marry. She had been extremely upset and since then felt that she was living only to come to her analytic sessions. In recent sessions she had been speaking about her mother who was tense, anxious, and impatient, and could explode and fall apart if Mrs D. tried to express different moods and feelings or complained in any way. Mrs D. had during these sessions been very displeased with Dr P.'s interpretations, which she felt were bad; the words he used had no meaning for her. Now again, Dr P. was trying to bring to her attention that she was "guarded" in her relationship to him, as if she were afraid that he might become irritated and explode the way her mother did. Then "with great turmoil and anguish, she spelled out the constellation of experiences she had been attempting to delineate for many months" (1983:112).

She said that a great part of her didn't feel his presence, wasn't aware of his existence. Nor did she know who she was, where she was, or where he was located in space. She had no inner sense of him, no sense of contact and warmth between them. It wasn't that she was guarding herself from anything; she couldn't find Dr P.; didn't know how to make contact with him; felt helplessly blind, and wondered whether there was a time in her life when she had been blind with no one aware of it. If he used the word "guarded," it became something she must reach, she must work all by herself to get to it, in a frantic life-and-death feeling; she must be able to do it, must, must, must. The word "guarded" is an outside view of her, not her inner experience, and when Dr P. uses it he shows no awareness of what is going on inside of her. It pushes her into an abyss, an endless abyss. She didn't know how long she could keep going.

Dr P. was struck by this despair and at a loss how to understand and reach her, at the same time feeling that if he did not understand her feelings of this hour, he might never understand her. In his mind he tried to match the feelings she had expressed with such intensity with all the traumatic situations of her childhood he knew of, a tonsillectomy; a celiac syndrome followed by many enemas; an accident when she fainted; and a serious strabism, on which much analytic work had already been done. But none of this quite matched the current response. Where had not knowing where one was and this desperate groping its origin? Dr P. knew that the mother had been unable to touch and fondle this daughter, an unwanted baby, but that was not enough to explain these feelings that seemed to stem from a very early period in life.

Dr P.'s sense of anxious urgency on this occasion and his intense feeling of relief when he found the answer to the puzzle has the quality of countertransference that was used constructively.

As Mrs D. walked out of the office, this chain of Dr P.'s associations turned to thoughts of how she had been fed early in her life. Suddenly he saw, that if she had been fed by a propped-up bottle, the experiences she reported might have their origin in the bottle's falling and being unavailable. The idea came to him "as a deep, insightful experience, a coalescing with conviction, and a sense of relief..." (1983:114), it fitted the psychology of the mother. The next day, when hearing this hypothesis, Mrs D. confirmed it completely. She had been raised on a rigid schedule. Neither parent came to comfort her when she cried desperately at night.[3] That she was fed by a bottle propped up near her face was a well-known family story. She recalled that when her sister was fed the same way, she would secretly slip her hands into the crib "to help her get the bottle back when it fell." Her mother, having propped up the sister's bottle, often went to vacuum the house, proud of her efficiency, though unable to hear the baby if she cried.

Thus, when Dr P. spoke of Mrs D.'s being guarded, he was not reaching the depth of her experience and was experienced by her as the unrelated mother, and his words as if they were the bottle that eluded her. His accurate reconstruction, on the other hand, evoked a deep sense of warmth in her, as if he were reaching out and attempting to make contact. He presents this vignette as an illustration of how "every piece of good analytic work may implicitly and automatically carry with it a corrective emotional experience – new experiences, new information that makes updating of working models possible." He presents it also as an illustration of how the constant correction of errors allows the process to move on. The patient would not have worked so hard to make herself understood, if she had not felt that somewhere he "truly wanted to help and understand her" (p.116).

Peterfreund gives us a detailed description of his own experience of working with this perplexing incident. The reader who wants further evidence of the therapist's responses and coping, when in their interaction the patient reexperiences an early trauma, will find a detailed description of an equally dramatic incident in Casement's report (1985:123ff.) of his work with Mrs B.

Dr P. contacted Mrs D. (1983:236) fourteen years after termination of the analysis with a follow-up inquiry. She was married, had two children and was doing well professionally. Although she also conveyed disappointment in two aspects of her analysis, she saw as the greatest among many gains from the analysis the stabilizing and integrating experience of their joint explorations. It had taught her to relate to others in ways that made for shared growth and discovery.

Comment on case examples

With these and earlier case examples (Chapters 8 and 9), I have tried to highlight several aspects of the therapeutic work with depression-prone persons. Particularly important in illustrating my hypothesis about function and failures of the depressed response are two points.

Margaret, Olga, George, and Mrs D. exemplify that people will outgrow their depression-proneness, if they are able and are given a chance to learn from the interaction with their therapist, how to observe self and others; how to establish – consciously or unconsciously – significant links between old and new information from within and from without; and how to become increasingly self-reliant in this type of information processing.

People, on the other hand, who do not have this capacity, inclination, or opportunity are likely to remain more or less depression-prone despite therapy, but they may be greatly helped – as were Norman and Doris – in overcoming an acute depression, when they have cause to trust the sincerity of a therapist who is convinced of the efficacy of his approach and treats them with warmth, concern, and respect.

Chapter eighteen

Concluding comments on professional aid

We serve the patient in various functions, as an authority and a substitute for his parents, as a teacher and educator; and we have done the best for him if, as analysts, we raise the mental process in his ego to a normal level, transform what had become unconscious and repressed into preconscious material and thus return it once more to the possession of his ego.

Freud (1937:181)

In Chapter 16 I gave an outline of features in individual psychotherapy that are most important for the patient's success when using professional aid to overcome his or her distress. In Chapter 17 I followed this up with case material from the professional literature to illuminate my points. Now, in closing, I want to comment on aspects that may influence the therapist's decisions when approached for help.

Alternative methods of therapy

Family therapy to modify interpersonal responses

Some reader and at times a patient might ask: why the laborious, time-consuming effort of intensive individual psychotherapy with depressed patients, when family therapy appears to help so many people more quickly to get along without depressions in their families and work relationships? Is this not preferable, particularly to orientation 2 of intensive, psychoanalytically oriented individual psychotherapy? I do not have the training and experience in family therapies to consider this question other than hypothetically. If the painful but heavily disguised unmet needs of long standing for empathic understanding and for affirmation of each family member's individuality are met in family therapy, if insight into and tolerance of individual development

240

as well as family fate across two or three generations is reached in that therapeutic process, then this is undoubtedly preferable to individual therapy. It can help more than one person directly and free a family's interaction from being pathogenic.[1] In individual psychotherapy, the patient designated as the disturbed one in his or her family may after discovering and modifying his or her own part in the pathogenic family process still be left with the task of establishing a *modus vivendi* with the pathogenic family, although the latter may improve due to the change in the patient. Yet, I cannot help assuming that success in the therapy with a given family requires as resourceful a designated patient and family, and as skillful a therapist as individual therapy with the goals of alternative 2. Otherwise, even seemingly successful family therapy might prove comparable to orientation 1, rather than 2 – that is: considerable improvement but risk of relapse; cessation of unproductive depression as long as improved circumstances prevail, but continuing depression-proneness. Of course, if the family is available and motivated for family therapy, this type of limited outcome may still be preferable to the limited outcome of alternative 1 of individual therapy.

But be this as it may, there are countless unattached adult people suffering from depression-proneness because of their cognitive and emotional patterns, who have neither their family of origin left or available for family therapy, nor a family of their own with whom to enter family therapy. Unless they are severely depressed, repeat suicidal attempts, or have manic episodes, depression-prone persons are often experts at keeping their family unconcerned about them, even if family members are residing nearby. Many of them do not, like anorectics or some schizophrenics, alarm and distress family in ways that would motivate the latter to participate in therapy. Consequently, the therapist in individual therapy who has the role of partner in the patient's reenactment of formative events in his or her life and uses the interaction as a social laboratory, may at the same time be the patient's only confidant and reliable human contact, which complicates matters.

If Margaret had not found her friends, Pat and Rita (Chapter 8), this would have been her situation, and therapy could not have progressed as fast as it did. Her parents would not have been motivated to enter family therapy and make productive use of it. Nor would Margaret have dared to ask them for it, before her therapy had helped her a good deal, at which point, since she was ready to start a life at a distance from them, there was no need to consider their participation in therapy. What helped Margaret was that Dr G., in a role resembling a parent's authority, executed that power and responsibility in a way that enabled her to understand herself and her past differently and adapt her current expectations and actions to this new view. Even in Norman's case (Chapter 8) it appears unlikely that family therapy including not only his wife but also his mother and sister could have been arranged.

Other methods of therapy

A comparison of orientations 1 and 2 with the methods and requirements in the treatment of the depression-prone patient, such as cognitive therapy, behavior therapy, bio-energetic therapy, the use of paradox, and other methods lies outside my competence. But I would like to quote the following authors:

Basch (1980:180):

Therapists with different orientation may be doing the same thing but calling it by different names. I hardly think, for example, that the experienced behaviorist overlooks the whole person any more than my colleagues and I do. We don't forget that the patient is, by the way he behaves, creating the world in which he lives, and I doubt very much that the behaviorist forgets that today's behavior has a past history. I think that the transference exists as much as a therapeutic tool in other forms of therapy as it does in dynamic psychotherapy. I believe that the successful therapist with a nonanalytic orientation probably uses transference in sophisticated fashion without daring to call it by name, similar to the reluctance of some psychoanalytically oriented colleagues to admit that they influence their patients through anything other than genetic interpretation.

Peterfreund (1983:60):

I suspect that adequate specification of the different types of processes now being practiced by Freudian analysts may reveal that, although important differences exist between so-called Freudian and non-Freudian therapies, there may well be important common denominators to all effective therapies regardless of the names under which they are subsumed.

Factors to be considered in the therapist's planning

Hazards in communication between therapist and patient

By direct and indirect verbal or nonverbal means, depending in their form on technique and personal style, the therapist conveys his or her interest in getting to know the patient, and also some conscious or unconscious limits of this receptivity. By direct or indirect verbal and nonverbal means the patient conveys his or her longing to be seen and understood by a person who can be trusted. At the same time – with or without awareness – the patient reveals the tendency to hide and disguise events, feelings, and thoughts in order to avoid expected disapproval, disbelief, rejection, contempt, or other injury. There are also hidden efforts to influence the therapist's response. Out of the unavoidable conflict between wanting to reveal and to conceal, but unaware of the process, the patient reenacts with the therapist the interpersonal dynamics – actual events and the patient's interpretation of events – that in early childhood, in later formative years, and to a lesser degree ever since, have fostered the development of troublesome emotional and cognitive patterns (compare Sandler 1976). Invariably, these patterns of response to experience have in childhood been the only methods available to the patient for adapting to his or her circumstances, and have served some of their purpose: they may have been what parents and siblings or other significant persons demanded or expected; they may have reduced anxiety and frightening feelings of protest; they may have facilitated submission to what this child could not escape; they may have helped the child to get some of its needs met and to control impulses that were unacceptable; they may have protected against punishment, ridicule, or humiliation; and, perhaps most of all, kept conscious and unconscious hopes for desired changes alive and, thereby, protected against emotional disintegration and collapse. Olga, for example, was helped by the distortions of her images of self and mother not to see her total isolation and loneliness within her family. Before the support of an analyst she slowly had learned to trust made it possible for her to bear the emerging hate and grief, she could not have borne this isolation without emotional collapse.

True, many important conscious and unconscious messages that go back and forth between two people are carried not by the apparent meaning of the sentences and exclamations exchanged, but rather between the lines, or by hint and innuendo, by disguised allusions of which the speaker is him- or herself unaware. Messages are conveyed by affect, timing, rhythm, speed, vocal volume, or intonation, or by silence. They are conveyed by actions: tenderness or violence of bodily contact; remembering or forgetting; doing things on time, too early, or too late; by being submissive or obstreperous; asking for necessary information or never asking; and so forth. One significant form of disguised or "coded" (Langs 1978) message from the patient to the therapist involves the patient's conscious or unconscious observations of therapeutically inappropriate behavior on the part of the therapist. Casement describes (1985) in this context the disguised expression in therapy of the patient's unconscious hope that the therapist will learn to do what is necessary for the patient to have his or her growth needs satisfied. Learning during therapy to be more conscious of these objectives and to express them more openly will lead to the patient's communicating more directly in other relationships as well.

For two people to be able to understand these messages easily, requires as a rule that several of the following features be present: that they know each other intimately over a long time; that they either share family and/or cultural experience, so that they use language, gestures, and manners in similar ways; or that they have at least a good many interests and tastes in common, if some of the other features are lacking; or that there are similarities in temperament. If we look at this impressive list of prerequisites that I have become aware of by living in four countries on two continents, and by my work as therapist, it is apparent that human communication is full of hazards. For a person who in his or her own family has not often had the experience of satisfactory, reliable communication that can later be used as a measure for successful as against unsuccessful communication, it is difficult to learn what or who is wrong, when communication misfires. It is helpful to be aware of these hazards when we make our service available to a given applicant.

The patient's complaints, motivation, and strengths

When depression-prone people seek or are referred for our professional help, they have or give very different reasons for needing help. They may be troubled by their loneliness, by disturbances in intimate or other relationships, by difficulties in applying themselves to important activities, including sexual life, by disturbing thoughts, by compulsions or psychotic symptoms, by anxiety, or by conversion symptoms or other bodily symptoms diagnosed as psychogenic by a physician they have consulted. Some of them take a chronic but perhaps mild state of being depressed so much for granted that it is not mentioned, or perhaps not even recognized as a problem. Others complain only about being anxious or depressed as requiring therapeutic intervention, while further symptoms of disturbance in their functioning are taken for granted. As applicants for therapy describe their difficulties, some of them believe that this state of mind is an illness, and that they will be cured as soon as they feel cheerful and active again. Nothing is further from their mind than the efforts of unlearning and relearning a way of life. Others, when suffering from such a state of mind, attribute their misery to unfavorable life circumstances alone, often to the behavior of their parents, spouses, employers, coworkers, or neighbors. They may attribute it to their poverty, or to their being socially isolated or discriminated against. They want help in changing their circumstances, not themselves. Helping them to realize their own contribution to these circumstances can take a long time. Others come to us because they suspect, or are convinced, that some of their difficult circumstances are of their own making; they want to understand how they mismanage their life and what to do about it; they want to find out whether their feelings are appropriate to their realistic situation. Perhaps they do not even recognize that their circumstances are unsatisfactory but insist that these are benign, while they nevertheless are incomprehensibly miserable. They want help in changing; their major focus is not on being depressed and on wanting to get rid of depression, but on learning to cope better with their relationships and work so that there will be less cause for getting and staying depressed. It may take a long time to help them see that some painful factors in their life cannot be eliminated by their changing. Olga's therapy (Chapter 9) illustrates this. Although they may unduly blame only themselves for their situation, it is this last type of patient who is best equipped to undergo major change of personality with the help of psychotherapy. They are prepared to struggle and discover.

In psychoanalytic terms: by different patients different symptoms are experienced as ego-alien or as ego-syntonic. Jacobson's patient, Mr V. (Chapter 4), for example, was concerned about the periods of depression that interfered with his creative projects, but saw nothing unusual in his work relationships, although the latter provided recurrent cause for getting depressed. Also Norman (Chapter 8) sought treatment to put an end to the symptoms disabling him in his professional work as well as interfering with his family life, but readily abandoned his original curiosity in the possibility that his prior functioning could have precipitated these symptoms. Margaret, on seeking therapy, was mainly concerned about her uncontrollable changes of mood, her nightmares, her inability to perform well on the job, and was secretly afraid of becoming schizophrenic. She became interested in her inability to mourn and the underlying causes in her family relations and personality only with Dr G.'s help. When seeking Bloch's help (Chapter 9), Olga was primarily alarmed by her relationship with a woman friend and by feeling depressed. She needed much therapeutic help before she began to recognize that her images of her mother and of herself were distortions that marred her life.

Reasonable choices for the type of therapy to be made in view of such differences are very helpfully discussed and illustrated (1980) by Basch. Unless the patient's current life circumstances are realistically perplexing, the symptom of recurring or persistent moods and reactions of depression will be viewed as an indication that misconceptions, discrepancies, and conflicts between aspirations and actual functioning, cognitive bias, as well as cognitive and emotional inhibitions, are easily activated. Yet, evidence of the patient's strength has to be weighed carefully against these weaknesses.

The patient's social circumstances and vulnerability

The patient's life circumstances also affect the chances for the success of therapy. What type of personal relationships, work opportunities, and economic security are available to the patient during periods of stress caused by the partly very unsettling process of therapy if long-term intensive therapy is chosen? In particular, does the patient have any stable and satisfactory family, friendship, or work relationships to lean on during stormy periods of the therapy? Or might the relationship with the therapist become and for a long time remain the most reliable and stable, if not the only significant, interaction available to the patient? Does the patient have satisfying work, interests, and hobbies that provide periods of diversion and comfort to make stressful periods of therapy more bearable? Can the patient's family be expected to support the therapy or to interfere? Can the patient from his or her own income pay a customary fee for extended therapy, and if not, can other suitable arrangements be made? If several of these questions have to be answered in the negative, is the therapist's personal life and health adequate to bear the strain that the patient's deprived situation creates during stormy phases of extended therapy, including open threat or hidden risk[2] of suicide? The therapist must consider whether alternative 2 of intensive psychotherapy can progress and suicidal risk be coped with under the existing circumstances. Finally, is there a known risk that the therapist may have to cut the therapy short in his or her own interest and thus repeat an earlier trauma of desertion? If so, how should this risk be dealt with?

These considerations do not only apply to the work with depression-prone patients. But because the latter often function well in many areas and on the surface can cover up their great vulnerability in various ways, their vulnerability to new losses and disappointments is easily overlooked. They have usually suffered damage from repeated losses of or disappointments in significant relationships during vulnerable phases of development. If premature loss of the therapist can possibly be avoided, the earlier damage should not be reinforced by such repetition, at least not without appropriate protective measures.

The therapist's competence and social circumstances

The inexperienced or insufficiently trained therapist is easily tempted by the patient's suffering as well as by the patient's apparent personal resources to expect much quicker, lasting results of their interaction than proves realistic. This expectation, conscious or unconscious, particularly if shared by the therapist's supervisor or consultant, creates or reinforces equally unrealistic hopes in the patient. When these hopes become disappointed, transference anger at the therapist will be increased by realistic disappointment.

Yet, one should not be too pessimistic, either. In many cases depression-proneness can be greatly reduced or even overcome, and at times much faster than expected, as, for instance, in Margaret's case (Chapter 8). In most instances, however, this will require much time and patience. One must carefully consider what one may be getting into. Is the patient motivated for the unavoidable turmoil? Are the patient's social circumstances likely to give some support under the impact of this turmoil? Are the therapist's competence or supervision, and his or her social circumstances, likely to hold up under the impact of crises within the therapeutic interaction?

With regard to the questions of the therapist's competence, orientation 2 is particularly indicated in the treatment of psychotherapists during their training, or if they seek re- analysis some years after completion of training. Applying this alternative can in some cases also be an invaluable work experience for therapists who wish to reach a fuller understanding of the developmental dynamics of depression- proneness. It enables them to become acquainted with the sensitivities of the depression-prone patient to the therapist's responses, and to learn to understand the specific difficulties in therapy arising from the therapist's own exposure to the depression-prone patient's conflicts and behavior. These insights can then be used constructively in the practice, teaching, and supervision of therapies with more limited goals. This is evident in Basch's diagnostic and therapeutic discussion (1980). Thus we owe a great debt of gratitude to our patients from the mental health professions who so frequently wish to continue with the treatment of their own cognitive and emotional handicaps, even after the agony of severe or frequent depression has greatly diminished.

In the long run, insight-oriented deep therapy provides the therapist with the satisfactions of challenge, constant stimulation, discovery, growth, and of becoming a participating witness to another person's discoveries and development. But this is earned at the price of recurrent perplexity and turmoil. Therefore, it is important that the therapist be qualified by his or her personality, training, and experience to cope with these demands; or that competent and congenial supervision be available.

Finally, the task will be immeasurably more difficult and the risk of having to tolerate failure will increase if the therapist's social life is not sufficiently rich and nurturing to hold the therapist up during periods of accumulating stress in therapeutic work. A period, for instance, of mourning a divorce or the loss by death of a mate or child is no time to take on new cases of potentially demanding therapy. Nor are the combined physiological, psychological, and social changes that overtake us with advancing old age. Nor can we foresee just how quickly they may suddenly progress. Poor health can at any age seriously reduce our attention, our judgment, and the capacity to hold or contain the impact of the patient's anxiety and analyze our own countertransference. For a short time our work with patients can, like other stimulating activity, be a stabilizing diversion from crisis in our personal life, but it must not be allowed to serve our own needs in this way for any length of time.

The resources in the community

Whether it is safe to take on the responsibility for a given patient's therapy is affected by the resources available in the community. Is there a hospital we can count on to have space available if a patient of ours needs a period of hospitalization; a hospital with understanding, well-trained ward personnel – a hospital, for instance, where a suicidal patient placed there during the therapist's vacation or illness will not, contrary to the original agreement between the three parties, be discharged before the therapist has returned? Is there a hospital available where competitive attitudes of personnel responsible for so-called environmental therapy will not jeopardize an individual therapy in progress?

Do we have access in our community to colleagues who are available to step in as "babysitters" for a patient in crisis during an unavoidable absence of ours; a colleague who will refrain from deciding without a careful discussion of the three parties involved that the patient will be better off continuing as his or her regular patient, thereby repeating for the patient the pathogenic triangle of rival parents whom the child can set up against each other? Or, if a patient requires chemotherapy during a period of crisis, is there a psychiatrist available who will not insist on continuing that regime longer than desirable from the point of view of psychotherapy?

By this I do not mean that if such professional resources are not available, we must never accept a patient for the intensive therapy we deem necessary. We should go ahead, if we believe that we will be able to cope, regardless. But we will have to be prepared for the risks this implies, and for meeting demands during crisis with whatever, possibly unconventional, measures this may call for. We must also be prepared for possible failure.

Comments on literature

Many of the aspects of psychodynamic, insight-oriented intensive therapy I have in mind are extensively discussed and exemplified by Basch (1980), Casement (1985), and Peterfreund (1983). As in other areas of human know-how, the skills and theory of psychotherapy develop from generation to generation as the contributions of creative therapists over the past century are integrated and further enriched by living therapists. Therefore, I am mainly referring to the work of living authors. Among them I have chosen those I have found most in keeping with my own experience,[3] and most helpful in my own work and thinking. I wish I could say more about challenging recent contributions – as, for instance, those by Kohut (1971,1977), Langs (1978), and Szasz (1965), and about earlier authors, particularly Freud and Winnicott, but this would take us too far afield from my emphasis on restoring the function of the depressed response.

Basch (1980), Casement (1985), and Peterfreund (1983) impress me as analysts who have therapeutic styles and theoretical orientations quite distinct from one another but share, none the less, the same attitudes toward the patient's "growth needs" (Casement 1985) and potential, as well as toward the function, personal experience, and human limitations of the therapist. They share a "heuristic" approach (Peterfreund 1983), and the strength and humility to disclose their mistakes where necessary for therapeutic or didactic purposes. They have the capacity to be forever learners and, despite the anguish this can cause at times, they securely carry at the same time the responsibility of being therapists and teachers. They give enlightening case examples. While having these characteristics in common, they address the subject of the psychotherapeutic process from different angles, and for different audiences. Consequently, they highlight different features of the process and, thus, complement one another. Taken together, these three books give to the prospective, the inexperienced, and the experienced therapist a vivid, challenging, and, to my mind, very useful and supportive view of when and how therapy works. Though clearly meant for an audience of experienced psychoanalysts, Peterfreund's book is none the less illuminating in its case discussions to therapists of limited experience or of other schools of thought.

None of these authors claims to have all the answers to the puzzles of psychotherapy, and each refrains from condemning every approach to therapy that diverges from his own.

Conclusion

Condensing the message of this book into a few lines, I want to repeat this: We have a precious genetic heritage in our tendency to take pause and, if necessary, withdraw when we are perplexed about our functioning. Although unintentional and often distressing, this tendency can help us become more observant of our perceptions, thoughts, feelings, and memories of the moment and integrate them in new ways to solve the puzzle, so that life can become more meaningful. Therefore, it is essential that we respect the development of this capacity in our children; that we help our partners and our patients to exercise it; and that we dare exercise it ourselves.

Notes

Introduction

1 Pathological conditions in which the basic depressed response fails to lead to an adaptive outcome are referred to by members of different professions with a variety of diagnostic terms, such as "dysthymia" and "major depression" in DSM-III; "severe depression" and "mild depression," for instance, Arieti and Bemporad 1978; "depressive illness," for instance, Bowlby 1961, "depressive disorder," "clinical depression," for instance by authors in Anthony and Benedek (eds.), 1975, simply "depression," for instance, Feighner *et al.* 1972, or Klerman *et al.* 1984; or "borderline case" vs. "caseness" of depression in the study by Brown and Harris 1978.

2 Coyne's experimental research gives support to the everyday observation that depressed behavior is usually met by members of the environment with "non-genuine support" (1976:187), followed by irritation and avoidance.

3 Potok's novel gives us an opportunity to identify with the severe depression of a young woman following bereavement and with her recovery; with her son's severe depression and recovery between the ages of six and fifteen, and the productive outcome of his milder depression in young adulthood. These aspects are discussed in my summaries, while his father's efforts to cope with his own depression-proneness are mainly indicated by implication. The novel illustrates features in family relations that may cause a depression and prevent it from having a productive outcome, and also features that tend to enhance the capacity to emerge from being depressed with a productive outcome. It also demonstrates the role of social and cultural influences in the origin of depression and in the course it may run. While documentation to support my theoretical position needs to come from real life, this novel can help the reader empathize with, rather than only intellectually grasp, the experiential aspects of the subject of my discussion: the cause and function of depression, its work and process, the development of its function during the formative years, and factors promoting either a productive or an unproductive outcome of a depression.

Chapter 1

1 Davis writes (1970:110):

Inflammation, for instance, has long been regarded as reflecting adaptive

250

processes, in this case in reaction to invasion by micro-organisms. To take another example – the cold, pale skin of the patient in "surgical shock," until a decade or two ago regarded as due to a failure in the peripheral circulation to be corrected by warming up the patient, is now seen as adaptive, blood being diverted from the periphery to serve the vital functions. No attempt is made to correct what is seen as an adaptive process.

Likewise, in dealing with symptoms of depression, we need to consider when they do or do not serve an adaptive function.

2 Sandler and Joffe (1965:92) used the terms "basic depressive reaction" and "depressive response" for "a state of helpless resignation in the face of pain, together with an inhibition both of drive discharge and ego functions." My use of a very similar term, however, conveys different implications.

3 I realize that in this I differ from Tomkins's and Izard's views and shall take this up in Chapter 5.

4 Klerman (1977: 50) states:

One principal source of confusion attending discussions of the affective states is semantic – the terms *anxiety* and *depression* denote multiple meanings. This unfortunate characteristic contributes to unnecessary ambiguity and conceptual confusion.

Both terms, anxiety and depression, refer to four levels of psychological phenomena: (1) anxiety and depression are normal emotional states; (2) as symptoms pathological anxiety and depression occur in a variety of clinical conditions, psychiatric and non-psychiatric; (3) there are a number of anxious and depressive *syndromes*, and (4) some specific diagnostic entities, i.e. *anxiety neuroses* and *neurotic depression*, have special psychopathological status.

5 I find it clearer to reserve the term "depressive" either for those of a person's behavior patterns, or for those factors in his or her situation that tend to exaggerate or prolong episodes of depression in that person quite apart from what precipitates each episode to begin with.

6 Hill states (1968:452):

A clear distinction must be made between circumstances in which depression has developed and circumstances in which, given understanding of the patient's situation, it might have been expected but has not occurred. In the latter circumstance we commonly observe those first line defensive neurotic postures, such as "acting-out," means of obtaining comfort or gratification by excessive eating, drinking, or sexual activity; various minor delinquencies and antisocial acts; hypochondriasis and hysterical or obsessional symptom formation. Some of these would appear to be age-specific, as the "acting-out" behavior of adolescents bears witness.

Chapter 2

1 On this point there still exists controversy, as illustrated in the field of cognitive psychology by the argument between Zajonc and Lazarus. While the former argues for the primacy of emotion (1984), which he deems independent of cognition, Lazarus (1984) replies that cognition of some kind is a prerequisite for any emotion to be aroused. Zajonc observes (117) that "Lazarus's definitions of

cognition and of cognitive appraisal also include forms of cognitive appraisal that cannot be observed, verified or documented." His criticism would also apply to my definition.

2 Relating the observation of infants to neurophysiological processes and development, Basch (1976) describes the baby's crying, smiling, gestures, and facial expressions as innate, universal "affective behavior patterns"; as "automatically generated signals" serving to mobilize the mother to attend to the baby's needs. It is "a system of communication antedating and independent of verbal language." Although the baby's behavior reminds us of our own states of emotion, as if the baby were angry, fearful, or happy, the baby's nervous system actually does not yet allow the baby to be aware of self and to experience feeling in the way an older child or adult does. But when conceptualization becomes possible as speech develops, after age two (769), "there is a beginning translation of various behavioral patterns into emotional experience." That is, in emotion we are aware of finding ourselves in a particular situation and of reacting to the meaning it has for us with particular feelings. This helps us anticipate "the consequences of a potential course of action." Even "adults can react affectively without experiencing emotion – that is, they can remain unaware of the significance of their reactions" although their tone of voice, facial expression, and behavior reveal their affect. Basch stresses (p.771) that not only emotion but also affective reactions "are part and parcel of the cognitive process" and adaptive.

3 According to Suedfeld et al. (1969), many theoretical and experimental papers in cognitive psychology have since G. Miller's paper (1956) on information processing used such a concept. Also other concepts of cybernetics and general system theory are increasingly adopted by writers in psychology and psychiatry. But there are still great differences in how these concepts are applied in describing and explaining human behavior. Tomkins, for instance, in his introduction to his two volume work (1962,1963), uses these concepts to discuss imagery, consciousness, motivation, and affect. His purpose is to develop his theory of specific discrete emotions, according to typical facial expressions. Mandler, on the other hand, states (1975:14):

The general suggestion is offered that a search for discrete emotion and a specific theory of emotion is vain and that specific investigation of important parameters that affect human experience and action are more likely to illuminate the area defined as "emotion" in the common language.

Bertalanffy, after his discussion of the value of systems theory for psychiatry, concludes (1966:716) that this means for psychotherapy that "*more important than 'digging the past'* [my italics] will be insight into present conflicts, attempts at reintegration, and orientation toward goals and the future, that is, symbolic anticipation." In contrast, Bowlby turns to the concepts of cybernetics and system theory as a theoretical basis for his presentation of attachment theory which attributes great significance to the exploration of early family ties and early separation. And Peterfreund turns to the same concepts to replace Freud's metapsychological constructs as a theoretical framework for clinical findings in psychoanalytic practice, particularly for understanding processes of learning and psychotherapeutic interaction.

4 In 1988, after completing an advanced draft of this book I found Basch's statement (1983a:107) about Darwin having established in 1872 that "an affective response has both a private and a social function."

Chapter 3

1 I use the "true self" here as the concept developed by Winnicott (1960:140).
2 This I do not only mean in the sense of the vicissitudes of the earliest developmental stage described by Erikson (1950), but also along the lines of Winnicott's concept (1971:ch. 5) of "good enough mothering," and his emphasis (1971:ch. 9) on the mother's and family's "mirror role;" Kohut's view of the "self-object" and its role in the development of the self (1977:ch. 2); Mahler's description (1975:Part II) of the successes and failures of the separation-individuation phase; Masterson's emphasis (1981:ch. 7) on the role of such failure in the developmental arrest of certain personalities; and Bowlby's concept (1980:203) of "anxious attachment" – to name some important contributions on this subject.
3 I recognize that some readers will prefer to follow the long-established convention of using either the term "affect" or the term "emotion" for a single concept: feeling states that are accessible to awareness and reflection and are accompanied by characteristic physiological patterns. I find Basch's differentiation (1976) along developmental lines, which I discussed in Chapter 2, more helpful. But the use of terms and concepts is a matter of choice. I want to make clear what I mean when I use these terms without contending that my use is necessarily better than following convention.

Chapter 5

1 Originally, when presenting his two volumes, Tomkins was planning three volumes, and apparently intended to include a new theory of depression in the third volume. This, however, was not published. But the original table of contents (1962) suggests that depression was to be presented as a strategy to cope with humiliation.
2 Each emotion is seen by Izard as having an inherently adaptive function and as having three components (1972:2): "(a) a specific innately determined neural substrate, (b) a characteristic neuromuscular-expressive pattern, and (c) a distinct, subjective or phenomenological quality."
3 Basch specifies (1976:762-3) that the behaviors prompted by the affects Tomkins calls primary, cover "those adaptive reactions necessary for survival," adding that affective responses are automatic, and appear in animals as well as humans. Thus, the infant "is equipped with a total set of adaptive patterns" long before the cognitive capacity for emotion in the adult sense develops. But, in contrast to Tomkins, Basch also discusses (1975) depression as an affect with a specific adaptive function.
4 Although Freud in the introductory paragraph of his paper specifically emphasizes (1917) that he only is speaking of a limited number and group of patients suffering from melancholia, and that one cannot generalize from this, he is referred to here as having presented a view of all depression. This misunderstanding is very common. Lindemann, on the other hand, mentions (1944) depression as a phase of pathological mourning, but not in any other sense.
5 Izard instructed (1972: ch. 10) his subjects – college students – to recall an episode of being depressed, to describe it briefly in writing, and then to answer the self-rating-scale according to that past mood. The type of descriptions by the students Izard summarizes suggests to me that some of the students might have recalled a genuine episode of being depressed, while many may have recalled some experience of frustration and unhappiness without depression. Yet, many of

the latter could in their answers have revealed a depression-prone *personality* even if what they recalled was not an episode of depression.

6 With some reservation about self-reports, Klerman concurs (1977) with Izard's view of basic (discrete) emotions; also of depression and anxiety as patterns of emotion.

7 Jacobson (1971) emphasizes conflict about aggression.

8 "In the instance of the loss of a very significant object, the total mourning process may never be completed" (Pollock 1961:354).

9 Bowlby speaks (1969:123) of "behavioural systems in a state of activation," but within the context of my discussion, Izard's term "pattern of emotion" will be more readily understood.

10 My view that pathological syndromes are not patterns of emotion in the sense that a combination of usually associated reactions appears – as in attachment behavior – is supported by the fact that DSM-III (1980) and Feighner *et al.* (1972) give a great variety of possible symptoms to be added *numerically* for a differential diagnosis, rather than a stable set of characteristic symptoms varying only in intensity.

11 This is emphasized today by an increasing number of authors. Here I shall only name a few who have sounded an alarm concerning the interplay of the depressed adult and his or her human environment: Szasz (1961), Becker (1964), Brown and Harris (1978), Lazarus and Launier (1978), and Coyne *et al.* (1981). Additional authors, in child psychiatry and child psychology, will be referred to in Part II.

12 I am thinking particularly of the diagnostic criteria in DSM-III (1980), those used by Feighner *et al.* (1972), by Spitzer *et al.* (1978), Wing *et al.* (1974), and in Beck's depression inventory (1967).

Chapter 6

1 I am thinking of the concepts presented by Buck (1984), Hall (1959,1966), Hinde (1974), Izard (1972,1977), Klerman (1977), Lazarus (1975), Tomkins (1962,1963), to name a few scholars in different fields; by Lewis (1971), Wurmser (1981), and other authors using the concepts of psychoanalytic metapsychology; and by biochemical or neurophysiological researchers.

2 Actually, emotion and cognition are two facets of the same process. "Indeed, the separation of affect and cognition, though time-honored, is an artificial one. The two are always intertwined in the human subject" (Basch (1986:270).

3 Jacobson states (1971:81): "Quite in contrast to depressive states . . ., we find in grief and in normal sadness of any kind a preoccupation with the happy experiences of the past. . . ."

4 Klerman states (1977:49):

The relation between anxiety and depression, long the subject of controversy. . ., has become the subject of renewed interest. . . .Today, the majority of depressed patients are young, ambulatory, and non-psychotic. These non-psychotic forms of depression, commonly called "reactive" or "neurotic" depression, occur in patients who also experience symptoms of anxiety, tension, insomnia, and restlessness, symptoms that also occur in the anxiety neurosis. [Also (1977:57)]. . . recent evidence demonstrated that facial patterns reliably differentiate between anxious and depressed imagery and facial poses in normal subjects.

5 Lazarus states (1975:65) that emotions such as grief and depression have

complex patterns of reaction, involving for example, anger, depression, guilt, each traditionally distinguished as a separate emotional reaction. Or they show a sequence of reactions with the predominant affect changing from one stage to another. Thus, it makes a difference whether one studies the emotion at one particular stage or at another. It may be that we will do better to separate out the various components of a complex emotion and study its cognitive appraisal determinants and the conditions that bring such appraisal about.

6 I am speaking here of the *normal affects* of being anxious or depressed. Klerman (1977) and Prusoff and Klerman (1974), on the other hand, focus on the differentiation between *syndromes* of anxiety and depression, the latter authors stating (1974:307) that "the thrust of the findings supports the view that anxiety and depressive states represent separate neurotic conditions."

7 Parkes and Weiss say (1983:157): "Indeed, it may never happen, even in a good recovery, that the widow or widower achieves an invulnerability to distress on being reminded again of how much was lost."

Chapter 7

1 In Morrison's words (1983:298),

Identity relates to conscious and unconscious strivings for continuity and synthesis of personality, maintenance of congruence with the ideals and identity of one's chosen group, and a conscious awareness of who one is.

2 I mean the construction of models of the world as described (1969) by Bowlby.

3 These features are particularly emphasized (1963) by Tomkins in his extensive discussion of shame and humiliation, and of the many behavior patterns that may develop against experiencing the pain of shame.

4 I owe this view to the formulations (1963:155) by Sandler *et al.*

5 In Piers and Singer (1953:7), Piers describes shame as "a normal concomitant of Ego development and Super-Ego formation, at least in our culture"; as a "distinctly differentiated inner tension" which "occurs when a goal (presented by the Ego-Ideal) is not being reached." In contrast, "guilt is generated whenever a boundary (set by the Super-Ego) is touched or transgressed. . ." (1953:11).

6 Lynd states (1958:64):

The characteristics that have been suggested as central in experiences of shame – the sudden exposure of unanticipated incongruity, the seemingly trivial incident that arouses overwhelming and almost unbearably painful emotion, the threat to the core of identity, the loss of trust in expectations of oneself, of other persons, of one's society, and a reluctantly recognized questioning of meaning in the world – all these things combine to make experiences of shame almost impossible to communicate. [And (67)]. . .that the anguish of the experience of shame is. . .that the experience of shame is itself isolating, alienating, incommunicable.

7 Lewis proposes (1971:23) that "identification with the threatening parent stirs an 'internalized threat' which is experienced as guilt. Identification with the beloved or admired ego-ideal stirs pride and triumphant feeling; failure to live up to this internalized admired imago stirs shame." Also (1971:84): "Shame of failure is for an involuntary event. It results from incapacity. Guilt from transgression is, by implication, guilt for a voluntary act or act of choice." She further finds (1979a,b) that pathological shame tends to lead to depression or hysteria, while pathological

guilt is more likely to result in obsessive-compulsive or paranoid patterns of behavior.

8 "The decision to fill the gap between ego-ideal and current functioning has been made alone, perhaps not consciously but quite definitely as a result of having experienced cognitive shame" (Shane 1980:350).

9 The authors referred to so far focus largely on intrapsychic aspects of shame and guilt as experienced by one person. Stierlin, on the other hand, takes the work of these authors as the point of departure for describing (1974) how shame and guilt have a homeostatic function in family relations and society as they are aroused back and forth between partners in a relationship. Then, referring to Jackson, he states that family homeostasis created by shame and guilt patterns can tie family members together in ways that become coercive, jeopardizing their growth and separation.

10 In psychoanalytic theory this is usually seen as a function of the superego in distinction from the functions of the ego-ideal or the ideal self. But the use of these concepts varies. In Piers and Singer (1953), Piers gives a clear summary of the development of these different concepts. For the concept of the ideal self see also Sandler et al. (1963).

11 If A. Miller is correct (1980,1983) in her interpretation of the role played by Hitler's childhood in the development of his personality, an individual's defenses against intolerable shame and depression, when combined with the typical defenses within a population against the humiliation of defeat and failure, can trigger off mass murder and war.

12 I owe several features of this outlook to Hinde's discussion (1974) of group structures.

13 Wurmser describes (1981) the adaptive function of shame as the protection of the inner limits of our self beyond which intrusion would damage us, and consequently as protection of privacy and creativity. In contrast, he sees the adaptive function of guilt as the intrapsychic control of our power to transgress the inner limits of others.

14 This is in keeping with Lewis's observation (1979a) that disturbed patterns of shame lead to hysteria or syndromes of depression. Also with Jacobson saying (1971:88): "The less conscious a person is of the sources from which his moods arise, the less easily can the psychic situation be mastered and the more inappropriate are the mood qualities."

15 I agree with Malerstein's position (1968:215–16) that "there are two primary, painful signal affects: *anxiety* and *depression*." But my concept of the depressed response differs in some respects from his position that "depression arises where there is recognition by the organism of its inability to achieve its goal." Consequently, I do not find that "shame and guilt may be seen as part-functions of depression."

Chapter 8

1 The damaging effect a mother's avoidance of holding and caressing has on a child's personality development is discussed and illustrated (1987) by Hopkins.

2 As Klein does (1934:197–8) in her discussion of the "manic defenses," I am thinking here of denial, hyperactivity, and heightened feelings of self-assurance (often referred to as omnipotence), but I do not share her concepts of the "paranoid" and the "depressed position" during early infancy with all their ramifications.

3 Both Arieti (Arieti and Bemporad 1978) and Basch (1980) emphasize that

physiochemical process in certain severely depressed patients may require medical therapy, but that the actual depression is always precipitated by psychological factors that require psychotherapy.

Chapter 10

1 It is tempting to take up as a further example the views on depression presented (1978) by Arieti and Bemporad. Most of their discussion I find very congenial and yet, largely because of my concept of the basic depressed response and its difference in cause and function from sadness, my views differ from some aspects of their diagnostic position. But entering this discussion in detail would take me too far afield. The same holds for the study by Brown and Harris (1978).

Chapter 11

1 The term "depressive feelings" suggests to me mainly the depressed mood, that is, the conscious psychological component of the depressed response as I define it – without the physiological depressed reactions that tend to accompany the mood or may even appear without such a mood. Izard and Schwartz, on the other hand, use (1986:55) the term "affect" in the way many others use "mood" – that is, as a conscious feeling experience that does not include physiological symptoms. Cicchetti and Schneider-Rosen, while emphasizing (1986) the role of pathological development in the appearance of "childhood depression," none the less treat the emotionally disturbed child's depressed response as pathological in itself, rather than as a normal response to a bad situation experienced by a child whose development has made him or her vulnerable.
2 Such reviews are presented in Arieti and Bemporad (1978), by Mendelson (1974), and in Rutter et al. (1986).
3 Rutter points out (1986:18) that Spitz's study and conclusions have come "under considerable methodological criticism" and that outside institutions the symptom picture Spitz describes is "a relatively rare phenomenon." On the basis of their study in an institution for infants in Beirut, Dennis and Najarian question (1957) some of Spitz's findings. On the other hand, Emde et al. state (1986:142) that subsequent observation by several authors they name "have extended this clinical picture to include depression after a marked diminution or interference with the mothering function. . .into depression at ages earlier than 6 months. . . ." They add that "Current research issues include what mothering functions are involved and how much deficit is required under what circumstances for depression to occur."
4 Izard and Schwartz discuss (1986) the development of affective responses but exclusive of any basic depressed affect. They hold that facial expressions "of most of the fundamental emotions are fully functional at 7–9 months and all are functional before the end of the second year." Fully developed facial expression would be in keeping with my concept of the social function of an affect. In the same volume (Rutter et al. 1986), other authors present recent research in this area.
5 In discussing Spitz's and Bowlby's position on "the effects of separation from mother in charitable institutions," Piaget and Inhelder state (1969:27) that it is

not necessarily the maternal element as affectively specialized. . . that plays the principal role, but the lack of stimulating interactions; but these may be associated with the mother insofar as she creates a private mode of exchange between a given adult with her character and a given child with his.

6 In recent years, on the basis of modern brain research, it is often assumed that the functions Freud attributed to primary process are largely served by the right half of the brain and those of secondary process by the left half. Gazzaniga (1985) warns against too ready generalizations of this kind.

7 The only diagnostic categories in the chapter "Disorders usually first evident in infancy, childhood, or adolescence" of DSM-III that refer (1981:35) to the ages of eight to ten as "the peak age range for referral" are "Attention Deficit Disorder with Hyperactivity" and "Attention Deficit Disorder without Hyperactivity." In children younger than eight, "more severe forms of symptoms and a greater number of symptoms are usually present," while "the opposite is true of older children" with these diagnoses. Izard and Schwartz, on the other hand, describe (1986:47–8) nine to eleven as the age when the child is "increasingly able to internalize standards of behavior," when "the conscience and ego ideal are solidifying," when there is "awareness of greater discrepancy between real and ideal self," so that a "guilt-type depression," although relatively rare in children, was "more prevalent in this 9–11-year-old group than in younger children." Yet, Rutter asks (1986:19), ". . .why does depression fall again in frequency during middle childhood only to rise once more in adolescence?"

Anthony's description (1975b) of the "depressive picture in children between 8 and 11 years" has much in common with the description given by Lagerheim.

8 Although in this literature depressed moods in adolescents are more readily accepted as normal than in adults, being depressed tends to be treated as undifferentiated from various forms of unhappiness (see Jacobson 1961:181 as an example).

Chapter 12

1 Of necessity, condensation dilutes the impact of a work of fiction on the reader, but for the reader who wants the experience of identifying with the characters facing distress and groping for solutions, the novel is available.

Chapter 13

1 To give some examples of their disagreements with these theories: none of these authors accepts libido theory and the structural theory of id, ego, and superego. They do not accept the concept of psychic energy as distinct from physical energy. They do not find the infant vulnerable to specific pathogenic developments only during a given phase of development, or as a result of fixation or regression. They do not find these metapsychological concepts borne out by infant research or observation of older children, adolescents, or adults. For the same reasons, they do not accept that disturbances seen in adult pathology correspond to normal phases of infancy; disturbances such as narcissism and omnipotence; paranoid-schizoid and depressed patterns claimed by Klein (1934) as normal infantile phases; or autism and symbiosis (Mahler *et al.* 1975). They see the human infant, within the limitations of its neurophysiological maturation and without awareness, as capable from birth of actively perceiving in various ways, of processing certain information, of learning, and of interacting socially.

2 Stern gives (1985:ch.9) a number of telling examples.

Chapter 14

1 I can no longer account for the relevant social science lectures and literature that during my university education in the USA in the 1940s oriented me, a European immigrant, to the New World. They helped me organize my thinking on the cultural differences of which I became aware. Some later influences, however, will be mentioned here: Erikson (1950,1963,1964), Fox (1967,1973), Hall (1959,1966,1976), Marris (1974), Mead (1949), and Toffler (1970).

2 Stoller states (1975:1400):

> Gender identity is a term used for one's sense of masculinity and femininity; it was introduced to contrast with the term "sex," which summarizes the biological attributes adding up to male and female .... Gender identity is the product of three kinds of forces: biological, biopsychic, and intrapsychic responses to the environment, especially the effects due to parents and societal attitudes.

3 Chodorow states (1968:211):

> Women's mothering perpetuates itself through social-structurally induced psychological mechanisms. It is not an unmediated product of physiology. Women come to mother because they have been mothered by women. By contrast, that men have been mothered by women reduces their parenting capacities.

4 This was evident in two television documentaries in the 1970s developed from unpublished psychological studies, one on life crises by Monica Kempe, the other on middle age by Margareta Cronholm and Monica Kempe, using many questionnaires and interviews. Men with advanced educational qualifications who had developed other interests or hobbies were not hit as hard by approaching retirement.

5 Torok states (1970:167):

> From a psychoanalytic viewpoint an institution is not established and does not survive unless it resolves some particular interpersonal problem. In principle, an institutional solution must have advantages for both men and women over the situation that preceded it. We should make explicit what advantages each has in the inequality of the sexes, at least in the domain accessible to psychoanalysis – that is to say, in affective life.
>
> We are right, when we suppose that this age-old inequality requires woman's complicity, in spite of her apparent protest shown by penis envy. Men and women must be exposed to specific, complementary affective conflicts to have established a *modus vivendi* which could last through many civilizations.

6 My manuscript was completed before I became acquainted with the work of Dinnerstein. Having now acquainted myself with some of her work (1976), I find her views highly pertinent and akin to mine and, despite variations in aims and avenues, her conclusions and views very similar to mine.

7 In J.B. Miller's words (1975:95):

> Depression, in general, seems to relate to feeling blocked, unable to do or get what one wants. The question is: what is it that one really wants? Here we find difficult and complicated depressions that do not seem to "make sense." On the surface it may even seem that a person has what she wants. It turns

out, however, that, instead, she has what she has been led to believe she
should want.

(J.B.Miller 1976:95)

Chapter 15

1 "...to reach a truly unique and creative solution, there must generally be a
degree of stress... an ability to avoid the simple and obvious 'solutions' which
may lessen stress and anxiety, but which may be inexact and usually involve
some loss of information" (Peterfreund 1971:197); "... truly creative activity
seems to necessitate a high degree of disordering of existing learning patterns,...
.a tolerance for new information, and a tolerance for the unknown and the
unfamiliar" (p.199).

Chapter 16

1 As Basch puts it (1980:35),

Hope, wish, and fear are names for patterns of expectation that either develop
directly through experience or are taught by example. Once established, these
anticipatory configurations are mobilized in response to situations that
resemble, or seem to resemble, the original conditions that gave rise to the
pattern. This process is called *transference.*

A pattern of expectation may change with maturation and experience, or it
may remain unaltered. Since the transference process is the basis for
goal-directed behavior, motivating one positively or negatively in any situation,
it makes a great deal of difference whether the expectation transferred to a new
situation or relationship is appropriately adapted.

2 Sandler, *et al* give (1973) a historical survey of psychoanalytical views of
transference and countertransference. Kohut has (1971,1977) presented new types
of transference characteristic of various stages of development of the self.
3 Often countertransference reactions are the result of projective identification, a
concept originally introduced by Klein (1952) in terms of the development of
the infant, modified by Bion (1967) to apply to the functioning of the adult
psyche, and now increasingly used by authors outside the strictly Kleinian
school of psychoanalysis, at times indiscriminately. Casement's discussion (1985)
of this concept, as he uses it, is very helpful. But Sandler's concept (1976) of
"role- responsiveness" gives, to my mind, the clearest description of what
happens in instances of countertransference that further the therapy.
4 Szasz's discussion (1965:48) of psychoanalysis as education and the "hierarchies
of learning" is pertinent to this on a different level of abstraction.

Chapter 17

1 Here are some of Arieti's comments on this subject (Arieti and Bemporad
1980:215–16):

When the therapist succeeds in establishing rapport and proves his genuine
desire to reach, nourish, and offer hope, he will often be accepted by the

patient, but only as a dominant third – third entity or person in addition to the patient and the dominant other (or goal). Immediate relief may be obtained because the patient sees in the therapist a new and reliable love object.

After the first stage of treatment, however, the therapeutic approach must be characterized by a therapeutic relationship in which the therapist is no longer a dominant third, but a *significant* third, a third person with a firm, sincere, and unambiguous type of personality who wants to help the patient without making threatening demands. . . .

The only demand the therapist makes is that the patient become part of a *search team*, a group of two people committed to finding the cause of the depression and to altering or making it harmless.

2 Basch states (1980:136) that it

is not the affective state that determines whether a patient is depressed, . . . the hallmark of depression is the sense or the attitude that life is meaningless – an indication that the perception of the self is no longer a unifying focus for ambitions and ideals. In the resulting condition the goals that ordinarily organize behavior seem to have been lost. . . .

The myriad symptoms of depression are an attempt to circumvent helplessness and to enlist assistance. . . . Symptom removal should not be the primary therapeutic goal in the treatment of depression, nor does the elimination of symptoms and discomfort necessarily signify the end of the illness.

The answer to the depressive's call for help lies in aiding him to regain his ability to engage in goal-directed behavior that is self-constructive and not self-destructive.

3 Hopkins gives (1987) some vivid examples of how children are damaged in their development when their mothers have an aversion to touching them. This we saw also in Margaret's case.

Chapter 18

1 Weber *et al.* (1986) and Stierlin *et al.* (1986) present helpful studies of family dynamics and family therapy in the cases of manic-depressive patients.
2 Advocating a frank approach by the therapist, whenever suicidal thoughts or impulses are suspected, Karon and Vandenbos state (1981:267): "A direct question relieves anxiety. . . .The patient feels the world is too dangerous to see clearly. The therapist knows that the more clearly you see the world, the less dangerous it becomes." Although this is said in the context of psychotherapy with schizophrenic patients, it is in my experience valid regardless of diagnosis. Basch takes (1980:129) the same position.
3 Unfortunately, I became aware of the pertinence of McDougall's work (1980,1986) to my discussion of disturbed personality and therapy too late to refer to it in the context of this and earlier chapters.

References

Aichhorn, A. (1925) *Wayward Youth,* New York: Viking Press, 1948.

Alexander, F. (1948) *Fundamentals of Psychoanalysis,* New York: W. W. Norton.

American Psychiatric Association, (1980) *Diagnostic and Statistical Manual of Mental Disorders* (DSM-III), Washington, DC: American Psychiatric Association, 3rd edn 1981.

Anthony, E.J. (1975a) "Childhood depression," in E.J. Anthony and Therese Benedek (eds) *Depression and Human Existence,* Boston: Little, Brown.

——(1975b) "Neurosis in children," in A. Freedman, H. J. Kaplan, and B. J. Sadock (eds) *Comprehensive Textbook of Psychiatry,* 2nd edn, 1976, vol.2:2142–2160, Baltimore and London: Williams & Wilkins.

Anthony, E.J. and Benedek, T. (eds) (1975) *Depression and Human Existence,* Boston: Little, Brown.

Arieti, S. and Bemporad, J. (1978) *Severe and Mild Depression: the Psychotherapeutic Approach,* New York: Basic Books; London: Tavistock Publications, 1980.

Balint, M. (1965) *Primary Love and Psycho-Analytic Technique,* London: Tavistock Publications.

——(1968) *The Basic Fault: Therapeutic Aspects of Regression,* London: Tavistock Publications.

Basch, M.F. (1975) "Toward a theory that encompasses depression: a revision of existing causal hypotheses in psychoanalysis," in E.J. Anthony and T. Benedek (eds) *Depression and Human Existence,* Boston: Little, Brown.

——(1976) "The concept of affect: a re-examination," *Journal of the American Psychoanalytic Association* 24(4):759–77.

——(1980) *Doing Psychotherapy,* New York: Basic Books.

——(1983a) "Empathic understanding: a review of the concept and some theoretical considerations," *Journal of the American Psychoanalytic Association* 31(1):101–26.

——(1983b) "The perception of reality and the disavowal of meaning," *The Annual of Psychoanalysis* xi:125–53.

——(1986) "Clinical theory and metapsychology – incompatible or complementary?" *The Psychoanalytic Review* 73(3):261–71.

Beck, A.T. (1967) *Depression: Clinical, Experimental and Theoretical Aspects,* New York: Harper & Row.

Becker, E. (1964) *Revolution in Psychiatry,* New York: Free Press; paperback edn, 1974.

Bemporad, J. (1983) "Cognitive, affective and physiologic changes in the depressive process," *The Journal of the American Academy of Psychoanalysis* ii(1):159–72.

Benedict, R. (1934) *Patterns of Culture*, Boston: Houghton.

Bernay, T. and Cantor, D.W. (eds) (1986) *The Psychology of Today's Woman: New Psychoanalytic Visions*, Hillsdale, NJ: The Analytic Press.

Bernfeld, S. (1938) "Types of adolescence," *Psychoanalytic Quarterly* vii:243–53.

Bertalanffy, L. von (1966) "General system theory and psychiatry," in Silvano Arieti (ed.) *American Handbook of Psychiatry*, vol.iii, New York: Basic Books.

Bettelheim, B. (1960) *The Informed Heart*, Los Angeles: Free Press; London: Paladin, 1970.

Bibring, E. (1953) "The mechanism of depression," in P. Greenacre (ed.) *Affective Disorders: Psychoanalytic Contributions to their Study*, New York: International Universities Press.

Bion, W.R. (1967) *Second Thoughts: Selected Papers on Psycho-Analysis*, New York: Jason Aronson.

——(1970) *Attention and Interpretation*, London: Tavistock Publications.

Bloch, D. (1978) *So the Witch Won't Eat Me: Fantasy and the Child's Fear of Infanticide*, Boston: Houghton Mifflin.

Blum, H.P. (1977) "Masochism, the ego ideal and the psychology of women," in Harold P. Blum (ed.) *Female Psychology: Contemporary Psychoanalytic Views*, New York: International Universities Press.

Bowlby, J. (1961) "Processes of mourning," *International Journal of Psycho-Analysis* 42 (4–5):317–40.

——(1969) *Attachment and Loss*, vol.1, *Attachment*, London: Hogarth Press; 2nd edn, 1982.

——(1973) *Attachment and Loss*, vol.2, *Separation: Anxiety and Anger*, London: Hogarth Press.

——(1979) "On knowing what you are not supposed to know and feeling what you are not supposed to feel," *Canadian Journal of Psychiatry* 24(5):403–8.

——(1980) *Attachment and Loss*, vol.3, *Sadness and Depression*, London: Hogarth Press.

——(1988) "Developmental psychiatry comes of age," *American Journal of Psychiatry* 145(1):1–10.

Breggin, P.R. (1979) *Electroshock: Its Brain-Disabling Effects*, New York: Springer.

Brenner, C. (1973) "The concept and phenomenology of depression, with special reference to the aged," *Journal of Geriatric Psychiatry* vii(1):6–20.

——(1974) "On the nature and development of affects: a unified theory," *Psychoanalytic Quarterly* 43(4):532–56.

——(1975) "Affects and psychic conflict," *Psychoanalytic Quarterly* 44(1):5–28.

Broverman, I., Broverman, D.M., Clarkson, F.E., Rosenkrantz, P.S., and Vogel, S.R. (1970) "Sex role stereotypes and clinical judgements of mental health," *Journal of Consulting and Clinical Psychology* 34(1):1–7.

Brown, G. (1987) "Social factors and the development and course of depressive disorders in women: a review of a research programme," *British Journal of Social Work* 17(6):615–34.

Brown, G.W. and Harris, T. (1978) *Social Origins of Depression: a Study of Psychiatric Disorder in Women*, London: Tavistock Publications.

Buck, R. (1984) *The Communication of Emotion*, New York: The Guilford Press.

Bühler, K. (1922) *Die geistige Entwicklung des Kindes*, Jena: Verlag von Gustav Fischer.

Casement, P. (1985) *On Learning from the Patient*, London: Tavistock Publications.

Cederblad, M. and Höök, B. (1986) "Vart sjätte barn har psykiska störningar," *Läkartidningen* 83(11):953–9.

References

Chasseguet-Smirgel, J. with Luquet-Parat, C.J., Grunberger, B., McDougall, J., Torok, M., and David, C. (1970) *Female Sexuality: New Psychoanalytic Views*, Ann Arbor, Mich.: University of Michigan Press.

Chodorow, N. (1968) *The Reproduction of Mothering: Psychoanalysis and the Sociology of Gender*, Berkeley, Los Angeles: University of California Press.

Cicchetti, D. and Schneider-Rosen, K. (1986) "An organizational approach to childhood depression," in M. Rutter, C. E. Izard, and P. B. Read (eds) *Depression in Young People: Developmental and Clinical Perspectives*, New York, London: The Guilford Press.

Coyne, J.C. (1976) "Depression and the response of others," *Journal of Abnormal Psychology* 85(2):186–93.

Coyne, J.C., Aldwin, C., and Lazarus, R.S. (1981) "Depression and coping in stressful episodes," *Journal of Abnormal Psychology* 90(5):439–47.

Cytryn, L. and McKnew, D.H., Jr. (1974) "Factors influencing the clinical expression of the depressive process in children," *American Journal of Psychiatry* 131(8):879–81.

Cytryn, L., McKnew, D.H., Jr., and Bunney, Wm. E., Jr. (1980) "Diagnosis of depression in children: a reassessment," *American Journal of Psychiatry* 137(1):22–5.

Davis, D.R. (1970) "Depression as adaptation to crisis," *British Journal of Medical Psychology* 43(1):109–16.

Dennis, W. and Najarian, P. (1957) "Infant development under environmental handicaps," *Psychological Monographs: General and Applied* 71(7):1–13.

Dinnerstein, D. (1976) *The Mermaid and the Minotaur: Sexual Arrangements and Human Malaise*, New York: Harper & Row.

DSM-III (1980) See American Psychiatric Association (1980).

Eaton, J.W. (1964) "Adolescence in communal society," *Mental Hygiene* 48(1):66–73.

Emde, R.N., Harmon, R.J., and Good, Wm.V. (1986) "Depressive feelings in children: a transactional model for research," in M. Rutter, C. E. Izard, and P. B. Read (eds) *Depression in Young People: Developmental and Clincal Perspectives*, New York, London: The Guilford Press.

Endler, N.S. (1982) *Holiday of Darkness*, New York, Chichester, Brisbane, Toronto, Singapore: John Wiley & Sons.

Engel, G.L. (1962) "Anxiety and depression-withdrawal: the primary affects of unpleasure," *International Journal of Psycho-Analysis* 43(1):89–97.

Engel, G.L. and Schmale, A.H. (1972) "Conservation-withdrawal: a primary regulatory process for organismic homeostasis," *Physiology, Emotion and Psychosomatic Illness*, Ciba Foundation Symposium 8 (new series), Amsterdam: Elsevier.

Erikson, E.H. (1950) *Childhood and Society*, New York: W. W. Norton; 2nd edn, 1963.

——(1964) *Insight and Responsibility: Lectures on the Ethical Implications of Psychoanalytic Insight*, New York: W. W. Norton.

Feighner, J.P., Robins, E., Guze, S.B., Woodruff, R.A., Jr., Winokur, G., and Munoz, R. (1972) "Diagnostic criteria for use in psychiatric research," *Archives of General Psychiatry* 26(1):57–63.

Fenichel, O. (1945) *The Psychoanalytic Theory of Neurosis*, New York: W.W. Norton.

Fox, R. (1967) *Kinship and Marriage: an Anthropological Perspective*, Harmondsworth, Middlesex: Penguin Books.

——(1973) *Encounter with Anthropology*, New York: Harcourt Brace Jovanovich; Harmondsworth, Middlesex: Penguin Books, 1975.

Frankl, V.E. (1963) *Man's Search for Meaning*, New York: Washington Square Press.
Freud, A. (1936) *The Ego and the Mechanisms of Defense*, New York: International Universities Press, 1946.
——(1958) "Adolescence," *The Psychoanalytic Study of the Child* xiii: 255–78.
Freud, S. (1905) "Three essays on the theory of sexuality," *Standard Edition of the Works of Sigmund Freud* 7, London: Hogarth Press.
——(1912) "The dynamics of transference," *Standard Edition of the Works of Sigmund Freud* 12, London: Hogarth Press.
——(1913) "On beginning the treatment: further recommendations on the technique of psychoanalysis," *Standard Edition of the Works of Sigmund Freud* 12, London: Hogarth Press.
——(1915) "The unconscious," *Standard Edition of the Works of Sigmund Freud* 14, London: Hogarth Press.
——(1917) "Mourning and melancholia," *Standard Edition of the Works of Sigmund Freud* 14, London: Hogarth Press.
——(1921) "Group psychology and the analysis of the ego," *Standard Edition of the Works of Sigmund Freud* 18, London: Hogarth Press.
——(1922) "Beyond the pleasure principle," *Standard Edition of the Works of Sigmund Freud* 18, London: Hogarth Press.
——(1931) "Femininity," *Standard Edition of the Works of Sigmund Freud* 21, London: Hogarth Press.
——(1932) "New introductory lectures on psychoanalysis," *Standard Edition of the Works of Sigmund Freud* 22, London: Hogarth Press.
——(1937) "An outline of psychoanalysis," *Standard Edition of the Works of Sigmund Freud* 23, London: Hogarth Press.
Fromm-Reichmann, F. (1954) "An intensive study of twelve cases of manic-depressive psychosis," in *Psychoanalysis and Psychotherapy: Selected Papers*, Chicago: University of Chicago Press, 1959.
Galenson, E. and Roiphe, H. (1977) "Some suggested revisions concerning early development," in Harold P. Blum (ed.) *Female Psychology: Contemporary Psychoanalytic Views*, New York: International Universities Press.
Gazzaniga, M.S. (1985) *The Social Brain: Discovering the Networks of the Brain*, New York: Basic Books.
Grinker, R.R. (1962) "'Mentally healthy' young males (homoclites)," *Archives of General Psychiatry* 6(6):405–53.
Guntrip, H. (1961) *Personality Structure and Human Interaction: the Developing Synthesis of Psycho-dynamic Theory*, London: Hogarth Press.
Gut, E. (1982) "Cause and function of the depressed response: a hypothesis," *International Review of Psycho-Analysis* 9(2):179–89.
——(1985) "Productive and unproductive depression: interference in the adaptive function of the basic depressed response," *British Journal of Psychotherapy* 2(2):95–113.
Haley, J. (1967) "Toward a theory of pathological systems," in G. H. Zuk and I. Boszormenyi-Nagy (eds) *Family Therapy and Disturbed Families*, Palo Alto, Cal.: Science and Behavior Books.
Hall, E.T. (1959) *The Silent Language*, New York: Doubleday; Doubleday/Anchor Books edn, 1973.
——(1966) *The Hidden Dimension*, New York: Doubleday; Doubleday/Anchor Books edn, 1969.
—— (1976) *Beyond Culture*, New York: Doubleday; Doubleday/Anchor Books edn, 1977.
Hammen, C.L. and Peters, S.D. (1977) "Differential responses to male and female

depressive reactions," *Journal of Consulting and Clinical Psychology* 45(6):994–1001.

——(1978) "Interpersonal consequences of depression: responses to men and women enacting a depressive role," *Journal of Abnormal Psychology* 87(3):322–32.

Hartmann, H. (1939) "Psychoanalysis and the concept of mental health," *Essays on Ego Psychology*, New York: International Universities Press, 1965.

Hazelton, L. (1984) *The Right to Feel Bad: Coming to Terms with Normal Depression*, New York: Doubleday.

Heimann, P. (1950) "On counter-transference," *International Journal of Psycho-Analysis* 31(1):81–4.

Hill, D. (1968) "Depression: disease, reaction, or posture?" *American Journal of Psychiatry* 125(4):445–57.

Hinde, R.A. (1974) *Biological Bases of Human Social Behavior*, New York, London: McGraw-Hill.

Högberg, G., Lagerheim, B., and Sennerstam, R. (1986) "'Nioårskrisen' speglad på habiliteringen, barnläkarmottagning och PBU," *Läkartidningen* 83(22):2038–42.

Hopkins, J. (1987) "Failure of the holding relationship: some effects of physical rejection on the child's attachment and his inner experience," *Journal of Child Psychotherapy* 13(1): 5–17.

Izard, C.E. (1972) *Patterns of Emotion*, New York and London: Academic Press.

——(1977) *Human Emotions*, New York and London: Plenum Press.

Izard, C.E. and Schwartz, G.M. (1986) "Patterns of emotion in depression," in M. Rutter, C. E. Izard, and P. B. Read (eds) *Depression in Young People: Developmental and Clinical Perspectives*, New York: The Guilford Press.

Jacobson, E. (1961) "Adolescent moods and the remodeling of psychic structures in adolescence," *The Psychoanalytic Study of the Child* xvi:164–83.

——(1971) *Depression: Comparative Studies of Normal, Neurotic, and Psychotic Conditions*, New York: International Universities Press.

Joffe, W.G. and Sandler, J. (1965) "Notes on pain, depression and individuation," *The Psychoanalytic Study of the Child* xx.

Jones, E. (1922) "Some problems of adolescence," in *Papers on Psycho-Analysis*, London: Baillière, Tindall & Cox; 5th edn, 1948.

Karon, B.P. and Vandenbos, G.R. (1981) *Psychotherapy of Schizophrenia: the Treatment of Choice*, New York: Jason Aronson.

Kendell, R.E. (1977) "The classification of depression: a review of contemporary confusion," in G.D. Burrow. (ed.) *Handbook of Studies of Depression*, Amsterdam: Excerpta Medica: 3–19.

——(1983) "The risks and adverse effects of ECT," in C.N. Stefanis (ed.) *Recent Advances in Depression*, Oxford: Pergamon Press.

Kernberg, O. (1985) *Borderline Conditions and Pathological Narcissism*, New York: Jason Aronson.

Klein, M. (1934) "A contribution to the psychogenesis of manic-depressive states," in *Contributions to Psychoanalysis 1921–1945*, London: Hogarth Press, 1973.

——(1952) "Some theoretical conclusions regarding the emotional life of the infant," in Joan Riviere (ed.) *Developments in Psycho-Analysis*, London: Hogarth Press.

Klerman, G.L. (1973) "Pharmacological aspects of depression," in John Paul Scott and Edward Senay (eds) *Separation and Depression: Clinical and Research Aspects*, Washington, DC: Publication No.94 of the American Association for the Advancement of Science.

——(1974) "Depression and adaptation," in J.R. Friedman and M.M. Katz (eds) *The Psychology of Depression: Contemporary Theory and Research*, New York, Toronto, London, Sydney: John Wiley & Sons.

——(1975) "Overview of depression," in A.M. Freedman, H.J. Kaplan, and B.J. Sadock (eds) *Comprehensive Textbook of Psychiatry*, 2nd edn, 1976, vol.1:1003–12, Baltimore and London: Williams & Wilkins.

——(1977) "Anxiety and depression," in G.D. Burrows (ed.) *Handbook of Studies on Depression*, Amsterdam: Excerpta Medica.

Klerman, G.L., Weissman, M. M., Rounsaville, B.J., and Chevron, E.S. (1984) *Interpersonal Psychotherapy of Depression*, New York: Basic Books.

Kohut, H. (1971) *The Analysis of the Self: a Systematic Approach to the Psychoanalytic Treatment of Narcissistic Personality Disorders*, London: Hogarth Press.

—— (1977) *The Restoration of the Self*, Madison, Conn.: International Universities Press.

——(1984) *How Does Analysis Cure?*, Chicago and London: University of Chicago Press.

Lagerheim, B. (1983) "Why me?" in Å. Gyllensvärd and K. Laurén (eds) *Psychosomatic Diseases in Children*, Stockholm: Sven-Jerring Foundation.

——(1986) "Preparing disabled children for coping with adolescent stress," *International Journal for Adolescent Medicine and Health* 2(4):309–16.

Lamers, Wm.M., Jr. (1982) "Grief and bereavement," in L. Feigenberg (ed.) *Death, Dying and Bereavement*, Stockholm: The Swedish Cancer Society.

Langs, R. (1978) *The Listening Process*, New York: Jason Aronson.

Lazarus, R.S. (1975) "Self-regulation of emotion," in L. Levi (ed.) *Emotions: Their Parameters and Measurements*, New York: Raven Press.

——(1977) "Cognitive and coping processes in emotions," in A. Monat and R.S. Lazarus (eds) *Stress and Coping, an Anthology*, New York: Columbia University Press.

——(1984) "On the primacy of cognition," *American Psychologist* 39(2):124–9.

Lazarus, R.S. and Launier, R. (1978) "Stress-related transactions between person and environment," in L.A. Pervin and M. Lewis (eds) *Perspectives in Interactional Psychology*, New York and London: Plenum Press.

Leff, M.J., Roatch, J.F., and Bunney, W.E., Jr. (1970) "Environmental factors preceding the onset of severe depression," *Psychiatry* 33(3):293–311.

Lerner, H.E. (1977) "Parental mislabeling of female genitalia as a determinant of penis envy and learning inhibitions in women," in H.P. Blum (ed.) *Female Psychology: Contemporary Psychoanalytic Views*, New York: International Universities Press.

Lewis, H.B. (1971) *Shame and Guilt in Neurosis*, New York: International Universities Press.

——(1979a) "Shame in depression and hysteria," in C.E. Izard (ed.) *Emotions in Personality and Psychopathology*, New York and London: Plenum Press.

—— (1979b) "Guilt in obsession and paranoia," in Carroll E. Izard (ed.) *Emotions in Personality and Psychopathology*, New York and London: Plenum Press.

Lindemann, E. (1944) "Symptomatology of acute grief," in H.J. Parad (ed.) *Crisis Intervention: Selected Readings*, New York: Family Service Association of America, 1965.

Little, M. (1951) "Counter-transference and the patient's response to it," *International Journal of Psycho-Analysis* 32(1):32–40.

Lynd, H.M. (1958) *On Shame and the Search for Identity*, London: Routledge & Kegan Paul.

McDougall, J. (1980) *Plea for a Measure of Abnormality*, New York: International Universities Press.

References

——(1986) *Theatres of the Mind: Illusion and Truth on the Psychoanalytic Stage*, London: Free Association Books.

McRae, M. (1986) *A State of Depression*, London: Macmillan Education.

Mahler, M.S., Pine, F., and Bergmann, A. (1975) *The Psychological Birth of the Infant: Symbiosis and Individuation*, London: Hutchinson.

Malerstein, A.J. (1968) "Depression as a pivotal affect," *American Journal of Psychotherapy* 22(2):202–17.

Mandler, G. (1975) "The search for emotion," in Lennart Levi (ed.) *Emotions: Their Parameters and Measurements*, New York: Raven Press.

Marris, P. (1974) *Loss and Change*, London: Routledge & Kegan Paul.

Masterson, J.F. (1981) *The Narcissistic and Borderline Disorders: an Integrated Developmental Approach*, New York: Brunner/Mazel.

Matthis, I. (1981) "On shame, women and social conventions," *The Scandinavian Psychoanalytic Review* 4(1):45–58.

Mead, M. (1949) *Male and Female*, New York: William Morrow.

Mendelson, M. (1974) *Psychoanalytic Concepts of Depression*, 2nd edn, New York, Toronto, London, Sydney: John Wiley & Sons.

Miller, A. (1980) *Prisoners of Childhood*, New York: Basic Books.

——(1983) *For Your Own Good*, New York: Farrar, Strauss & Giroux.

Miller, G. (1956) "The magical number seven, plus or minus two: some limits on our capacity for processing information," *The Psychological Review* 63(2):181–97.

Miller, J.B. (ed.) (1973) *Psychoanalysis and Women*, Harmondsworth, Middlesex; Baltimore, Md.: Penguin Books.

——(1976) *Toward a New Psychology of Women*, Boston: Beacon Press; London: Penguin Books.

Money-Kyrle, R. (1956) "Normal counter-transference and some of its deviations," *International Journal of Psycho-Analysis* 37(3):360–6.

Morrison, A.P. (1983) "Shame, the ideal self, and narcissism," *Contemporary Psychoanalysis* 19(2):295–318.

Offer, D. (1969) *The Psychological World of the Teenager: a Study of Normal Adolescent Boys*, New York: Basic Books.

Parkes, C.M. (1972) *Bereavement: Studies of Grief in Adult Life*, London: Tavistock Publications.

Parkes, C.M. and Weiss, R.S. (1983) *Recovery from Bereavement*, New York: Basic Books.

Peterfreund, E. (1971) "Information, systems, and psychoanalysis," *Psychological Issues: an Evolutionary Biological Approach to Psychoanalytic Theory*, Monograph 25/26, New York: International Universities Press.

——(1978) "Some critical comments on psychoanalytic conceptualization of infancy," *International Journal of Psycho-Analysis*, 59(4):427–41.

——(1983) *The Process of Psychoanalytic Therapy: Models and Strategies*, Hillsdale, NJ: The Analytic Press.

Piaget, J. and Inhelder, B. (1969) *The Psychology of the Child*, New York: Basic Books.

Piers, G. and Singer, M.B. (1953) *Shame and Guilt: a Psychoanalytic and Cultural Study*, Springfield, Ill.: Charles C. Thomas.

Pollock, G.H. (1961) "Mourning and adaptation," *International Journal of Psycho-Analysis* 42(4–5):341–61.

——(1975)"On anniversary suicide and mourning," in E.J. Anthony and T. Benedek (eds) *Depression and Human Existence*, Boston: Little, Brown.

——(1978) "Process and affect: mourning and grief," *International Journal of Psycho-Analysis* 59(2–3): 255–76.

Poston, C. and Lison, K. (1989) *Reclaiming Our Lives: Hope for Adult Survivors of Incest*, Boston: Little, Brown.

Potok, C. (1972) *My Name Is Asher Lev*, New York: Knopf; London: William Heinemann Ltd; Penguin Books, 1973.

Poznanski, E., Krahenbuhl, V., and Zrull, J.P. (1976) "Childhood depression: a longitudinal perspective," *Journal of the American Academy of Child Psychiatry* 15(3):491–501.

Prusoff, B. and Klerman, G.D. (1974) "Differentiating depressed from anxious neurotic outpatients," *Archives of General Psychiatry* 30 (March):302–9.

Rutter, M. (1986) "The developmental psychopathology of depression: issues and perspectives," in M. Rutter, C.E. Izard, and P.B. Read (eds) *Depression in Young People: Developmental and Clinical Studies*, New York, London: The Guilford Press.

Rutter, M., Izard, C.E., and Read, P.B. (eds) (1986) *Depression in Young People: Developmental and Clinical Studies*, New York, London: The Guilford Press.

Salzman, L. (1970) "Depression: a clinical review," in J.H. Massermann (ed.) *Depressions: Theories and Therapies*, New York, London: Grune & Stratton.

Sandler, J. (1976) "Countertransference and role-responsiveness," *International Review of Psycho-Analysis* 3(1):43–7.

Sandler, J., Dare, C., and Holder, A. (1973) *The Patient and the Analyst: the Basis of the Psychoanalytic Process*, London: Allen & Unwin; reprinted, London: H. Karnac (Books) Ltd, 1979.

Sandler, J., Holder, A., and Meers, D. (1963) "The ego ideal and the ideal self," *The Psychoanalytic Study of the Child* xviii:139–58.

Sandler, J. and Joffe, W.G. (1965) "Notes on childhood depression," *International Journal of Psycho-Analysis* 46(1):88–96.

Schmale, A.H. and Engel, G. (1973) "Adaptive role of depression in health and disease," in J.P. Scott and E.C. Senay (eds) *Separation and Depression: Clinical and Research Aspects*, Washington, DC: Publication No. 94 of the American Association for the Advancement of Science.

——(1975) "The role of conservation-withdrawal in depressive reactions," in E. J. Anthony and T. Benedek (eds) *Depression and Human Existence*, Boston: Little, Brown.

Schur, M. (1969) "Affects and cognition," *International Journal of Psycho-Analysis* 50(4):647–53.

Searles, H. (1975) "The patient as therapist to his analyst," in P.L. Giovacchini (ed.) *Tactics and Techniques in Psychoanalytic Therapy*, vol. II, *Countertransference*, New York: Jason Aronson.

Seligman, M.E.P. (1975) *Helplessness: On Depression, Development and Death*, San Francisco: W.H. Freeman.

Shane, P. (1980) "Shame and learning," *American Journal of Orthopsychiatry* 50(2):348–55.

Singer, K. (1975) "Depressive disorders from a transcultural perspective," *Social Science and Medicine* 9(6): 289–301.

Solnit, A.J. (1966) "Some adaptive functions of aggressive behavior," in R.M. Loewenstein, L.M. Newman, M. Schur, and A.J. Solnit (eds) *Psychoanalysis – a General Psychology*, New York: International Universities Press.

Spitz, R.A. (1945) "Hospitalism," *The Psychoanalytic Study of the Child* 1:53–74.

——(1946) "Anaclitic depression," *The Psychoanalytic Study of the Child* 2:313–42.

Spitzer, R.L., Endicott, J., and Robins, E. (1978) "Research diagnostic criteria," *Archives of General Psychiatry* 35 (June): 773–82.

Stern, D.N. (1985) *The Interpersonal World of the Infant: a View from Psychoanalysis and Developmental Psychology*, New York: Basic Books.

Stierlin, H. (1974) "Shame and guilt in family relations: theoretical and clinical aspects," *Archives of General Psychiatry* 30 (March): 381–9.

Stierlin, H., Weber, G., Schmidt, G., and Simon, F.B. (1986) "Features of families with major affective disorders," *Family Process* 25(3):325–36.

Stoller, R.J. (1975) "Gender identity," in A.M. Freedman, H.J. Kaplan, and B.J. Sadock, (eds) *Comprehensive Textbook of Psychiatry*; 2nd edn 1976, vol.2:1400, Baltimore: Williams & Wilkins.

Suedfeld, P., Tomkins, S.S., and Tucker, W.H. (1969) "On relations among perceptual and cognitive measures in information processing," *Perception and Psychophysics* 6(1):45–6.

Szasz, T.S. (1961) *The Myth of Mental Illness: Foundations of a Theory of Personal Conduct*, New York: Harper & Row reprinted, London: Paladin, 1972.

——(1965) *The Ethics of Psychoanalysis: the Theory and Method of Autonomous Psychotherapy*, New York: Basic Books.

Toffler, A. (1970) *Future Shock*, New York: Random House; Bantam Books edn, 1971.

Tomkins, S.S. (1962) *Affect, Imagery, Consciousness*, vol.I, *The Positive Affects*, New York: Springer.

——(1963) *Affect, Imagery, Consciousness*, vol. II, *The Negative Affects*, New York: Springer.

Torok, M. (1970) "The significance of penis envy in women," in Janine Chasseguet-Smirgel *et al.* (eds) *Female Sexuality: New Psychoanalytic Views*, Ann Arbor, Mich.: The University of Michigan Press.

Weber, G., Simon, F.B., Stierlin, H., and Schmidt, G. (1988) "Therapy to families manifesting manic-depressive behavior," *Family Process* 27(1):33–49.

Weiss, R.S. (1973) *Loneliness: the Experience of Social and Emotional Isolation*, Cambridge, Mass., and London: MIT Press.

——(1975) *Marital Separation: Coping with the End of a Marriage and the Transition to Being Single Again*, New York: Basic Books.

——(1982) "Issues in the study of loneliness," in L.A. Peplau and D. Perlman (eds) *Loneliness: a Sourcebook of Current Theory, Research and Therapy*, New York: Wiley-Interscience.

Wing, J.K., Cooper, J.E., and Sartorius, N. (1974) *Measurement and Classification of Psychiatric Symptoms: an Instruction Manual for the PSE and Catego Programs*, London: Cambridge University Press.

Winnicott, D.W. (1960) "Ego distortion in terms of true and false self," in *The Maturational Process and the Facilitating Environment: Studies in the Theory of Emotional Development*, London: Hogarth Press, 1965.

——(1964) "The value of depression," *British Journal of Psychiatric Social Work* 7(3):123–7.

——(1965) *The Maturational Process and the Facilitating Environment: Studies in the Theory of Emotional Development*, London: Hogarth Press.

——(1971) *Playing and Reality*, London: Tavistock Publications; Pelican Books, 1974.

Wurmser, L. (1981) *The Mask of Shame*, Baltimore and London: Johns Hopkins University Press.

Zajonc, R.B. (1984) "On the primacy of affect," *American Psychologist* 39(2):117–23.

Name index

Subject index